Collins
German
Grammar

HarperCollins Publishers
Westerhill Road
Bishopbriggs
Glasgow
G64 2QT
Great Britain

Third Edition 2011

Reprint 10 9 8 7 6 5 4 3 2 1 0

© HarperCollins Publishers 2005, 2007, 2011

ISBN 978-0-00-736781-8

Collins® is a registered trademark of HarperCollins Publishers Limited

www.collinslanguage.com

A catalogue record for this book is available from the British Library

Typeset by Davidson Publishing Solutions, Glasgow

Printed in India by Gopsons Papers Ltd

This book is set in Collins Fedra, a typeface specially created for Collins dictionaries by Peter Bil'ak

SERIES EDITOR
Rob Scriven

MANAGING EDITOR
Gaëlle Amiot-Cadey

PROJECT CO-ORDINATOR
Susanne Reichert

CONTRIBUTOR
Horst Kopleck

We would like to give special thanks to Simone Conboy, Foreign Languages Consultant, for all her advice on teaching practice in today's classroom. Her contribution has been invaluable in the writing of this book.

Acknowledgements
We would like to thank those authors and publishers who kindly gave permission for copyright material to be used in the Collins Word Web. We would also like to thank Times Newspapers Ltd for providing valuable data.

CONTENTS

Note on trademarks

FOREWORD FOR LANGUAGE TEACHERS

The *Easy Learning German Grammar* is designed to be used with both young and adult learners, as a group reference book to complement your course book during classes, or as a recommended text for self-study and homework/coursework.

The text specifically targets learners from *ab initio* to intermediate or GCSE level, and therefore its structural content and vocabulary have been matched to the relevant specifications up to and including Higher GCSE.

The approach aims to develop knowledge and understanding of grammar and to improve the ability of learners to apply it by:

- defining parts of speech at the start of each major section, with examples in English to clarify concepts
- minimizing the use of grammar terminology and providing clear explanations of terms both within the text and in the **Glossary**
- illustrating all points with examples (and their translations) based on topics and contexts which are relevant to beginner and intermediate course content

The text helps you develop positive attitudes to grammar learning in your classes by:

- giving clear, easy-to-follow explanations
- prioritizing content according to relevant specifications for the levels
- sequencing points to reflect course content, e.g. verb tenses
- highlighting useful **Tips** to deal with common difficulties
- summarizing **Key points** at the end of sections to consolidate learning

In addition to fostering success and building a thorough foundation in German grammar, the optional **Grammar Extra** sections will encourage and challenge your learners to further their studies to higher and advanced levels.

INTRODUCTION FOR STUDENTS

Whether you are starting to learn German for the very first time, brushing up on topics you have studied in class, or revising for your GCSE exams, the *Easy Learning German Grammar* is here to help. This easy-to-use guide takes you through all the basics you will need to speak and understand modern, everyday German.

Newcomers can sometimes struggle with the technical terms they come across when they start to explore the grammar of a new language. The *Easy Learning German Grammar* explains how to get to grips with all the parts of speech you will need to know, using simple language and cutting out jargon.

The text is divided into sections, each dealing with a particular area of grammar. Each section can be studied individually, as numerous cross-references in the text point you to relevant points in other sections of the book for further information.

Every major section begins with an explanation of the area of grammar covered on the following pages. For quick reference, these definitions are also collected together on pages x–xiv in a glossary of essential grammar terms.

What is a verb?
A **verb** is a 'doing' word which describes what someone or something does, what someone or something is, or what happens to them, for example, *be*, *sing*, *live*.

Each grammar point in the text is followed by simple examples of real German, complete with English translations, helping you understand the rules. Underlining has been used in examples throughout the text to highlight the grammatical point being explained.

➤ If you are talking about a part of your body, you usually use a word like *my* or *his* in English, but in German you usually use the definite article.

| Er hat sich <u>das</u> Bein gebrochen. | He's broken his leg. |
| Sie hat sich <u>die</u> Hände schon gewaschen. | She's already washed her hands. |

In German, as with any foreign language, there are certain pitfalls which have to be avoided. Tips and Information notes throughout the text are useful reminders of the things that often trip learners up.

Key points sum up all the important facts about a particular area of grammar, to save you time when you are revising and help you focus on the main grammatical points.

Key points

✔ With masculine singular nouns in the nominative → use **ein**.

✔ With feminine singular nouns in the nominative → use **eine**.

✔ With plural nouns → use **die**, **der** or **den**, depending on the case.

✔ The indefinite article is not usually used when you say what jobs people do.

If you think you would like to continue with your German studies to a higher level, check out the **Grammar Extra** sections. These are intended for advanced students who are interested in knowing a little more about the structures they will come across beyond GCSE.

Grammar Extra!

Some German adjectives are used as feminine nouns. They have feminine adjective endings which change according to the article which comes before them.

eine Deutsche	a German woman
die Abgeordnete	the female MP

➪ For more information on **Adjectives which can be used as nouns** and for **Feminine adjective endings**, see pages 50 and 42.

Finally, the supplement at the end of the book contains **Verb Tables**, where 97 important German verbs are conjugated in full. Examples show you how to use these verbs in your own work. If you are unsure of how a verb conjugates in German, you can look up the **Verb Index** on pages 99–103 to find either the conjugation of the verb itself, or a cross-reference to a model verb, which will show you the pattern that verb follows.

We hope that you will enjoy using the *Easy Learning German Grammar* and find it useful in the course of your studies.

GLOSSARY OF GRAMMAR TERMS

ABSTRACT NOUN a word used to refer to a quality, idea, feeling or experience, rather than a physical object, for example, *size, reason, happiness*.

ACCUSATIVE CASE the form of nouns, adjectives, pronouns and articles used in German to show the direct object of a verb and after certain prepositions. Compare with **direct object**.

ACTIVE in an active sentence, the subject of the verb is the person or thing that carries out the action described by the verb.

ADJECTIVE a 'describing' word that tells you more about a person or thing, such as their appearance, colour, size or other qualities, for example, *pretty, blue, big*.

ADVERB a word usually used with verbs, adjectives or other adverbs that gives more information about when, where, how or in what circumstances something happens, for example, *quickly, happily, now*.

AGREE (to) to change word endings according to whether you are referring to masculine, feminine, neuter, singular or plural people and things.

AGREEMENT see **agree (to)**.

APOSTROPHE S an ending ('s) added to a noun to show who or what someone or something belongs to, for example, *Danielle's dog, the doctor's husband, the book's cover*.

ARTICLE a word like *the, a* and *an*, which is used in front of a noun. Compare with **definite article** and **indefinite article**.

AUXILIARY VERB a verb such as *be, have* and *do* when used with a main verb to form some tenses and questions.

BASE FORM the form of the verb without any endings added to it, for example, *walk, have, be, go*. Compare with **infinitive**.

CASE the grammatical function of a noun, adjective, pronoun or article in a sentence.

CLAUSE a group of words containing a verb.

COMPARATIVE an adjective or adverb with *-er* on the end of it or *more* or *less* in front of it that is used to compare people, things or actions, for example, *slower, less important, more carefully*.

COMPOUND NOUN a word for a living being, thing or idea, which is made up of two or more words, for example, *tin-opener, railway station*.

CONDITIONAL a verb form used to talk about things that would happen or would be true under certain conditions, for example, *I would help you if I could*. It is also used to say what you would like or need, for example, *Could you give me the bill?*

CONJUGATE (to) to give a verb different endings according to whether you are referring to *I, you, they* and so on, and according to whether you are referring to past, present or future, for example, *I have, she had, they will have*.

CONJUGATION a group of verbs which have the same endings or change according to the same pattern.

CONJUNCTION a word such as *and, because* or *but* that links two words or phrases of a similar type or two parts of a sentence, for example, *Diane and I have been friends for years; I left because I was bored*. Compare with **coordinating conjunction** and **subordinating conjunction**.

COORDINATING CONJUNCTION a word such as *and*, *but* or *however* that links two words, phrases or clauses.

CONSONANT a letter of the alphabet which is not a vowel, for example, *b*, *f*, *m*, *s*, *v*. Compare with **vowel**.

CONSTRUCTION an arrangement of words together in a phrase or sentence.

DATIVE CASE the form of nouns, adjectives, pronouns and articles used in German to show the indirect object of a verb and after certain verbs and prepositions.

DECLENSION German nouns change according to their gender, case and number. This is called declension.

DEFINITE ARTICLE the word *the*. Compare with **indefinite article**.

DEMONSTRATIVE ADJECTIVE one of the words *this*, *that*, *these* and *those* used with a noun to point out a particular person or thing, for example, <u>*this*</u> *woman*, <u>*that*</u> *dog*.

DEMONSTRATIVE PRONOUN one of the words *this*, *that*, *these* and *those* used instead of a noun to point out people or things, for example, <u>*That*</u> *looks fun*.

DIRECT OBJECT a noun referring to the person or thing affected by the action described by a verb, for example, *She wrote* <u>*her name*</u>; *I shut* <u>*the window*</u>. Compare with **indirect object**.

DIRECT OBJECT PRONOUN a word such as *me*, *him*, *us* and *them* which is used instead of a noun to stand in for the person or thing directly affected by the action described by the verb. Compare with **indirect object pronoun**.

ENDING a form added to a verb stem, for example, *geh* → *geht*, and to adjectives, nouns and pronouns depending on whether they refer to masculine, feminine, neuter, singular or plural things or persons.

FEMININE one of three classifications for the gender of German nouns which determines the form of articles, pronouns and adjectives used with the noun and to refer to it. The other two classifications are **masculine** and **neuter**.

FUTURE a verb tense used to talk about something that will happen or will be true.

GENDER whether a noun, article, pronoun or adjective is feminine, masculine or neuter.

GENITIVE CASE the form of nouns, adjectives, pronouns and articles used in German to show that something belongs to someone and after certain prepositions and verbs.

IMPERATIVE the form of a verb used when giving orders and instructions, for example, *Shut the door!*; *Sit down!*; *Don't go!*

IMPERFECT one of the verb tenses used to talk about the past, especially in descriptions, and to say what was happening, for example, *It was sunny at the weekend* or what used to happen, for example, *I used to walk to school*. Compare with **perfect**.

IMPERSONAL VERB one which does not refer to a real person or thing and where the subject is represented by *it*, for example, *It's going to rain*; *It's 10 o'clock*.

INDEFINITE ADJECTIVE one of a small group of adjectives used to talk about people or things in a general way, without saying exactly who or what they are, for example, *several*, *all*, *every*.

INDEFINITE ARTICLE the words *a* and *an*. Compare with **definite article**.

INDEFINITE PRONOUN a small group of pronouns such as *everything*, *nobody* and *something*, which are used to refer to people or things in a general way, without saying exactly who or what they are.

INDIRECT OBJECT a noun or pronoun typically used in English with verbs that take two objects. For example, in *I gave the carrot to the rabbit*, *the rabbit* is the indirect object and *carrot* is the direct object. With some German verbs, what is the direct object in English is treated as an indirect object in, for example, **Ich helfe ihr** → *I'm helping her*. Compare with **direct object**.

INDIRECT OBJECT PRONOUN when a verb has two objects (a direct one and an indirect one), the indirect object pronoun is used instead of a noun to show the person or the thing the action is intended to benefit or harm, for example, *me* in *He gave me a book* and *Can you get me a towel?* Compare with **direct object pronoun**.

INDIRECT SPEECH the words you use *to* report what someone has said when you aren't using their actual words, for example, *He said that he was going out*.

INFINITIVE the form of the verb with *to* in front of it and without any endings added, for example, *to walk, to have, to be, to go*. Compare with **base form**.

INTERROGATIVE ADJECTIVE a question word used with a noun to ask *who?, what?* or *which?*, for example, *What instruments do you play?; Which shoes do you like?*

INTERROGATIVE PRONOUN one of the words *who, whose, whom, what* and *which* when they are used instead of a noun to ask questions, for example, *What's happening?; Who's coming?*

MASCULINE one of three classifications for the gender of German nouns which determines the form of articles, pronouns and adjectives used with the noun and to refer to it. The other two classifications are **feminine** and **neuter**.

MIXED VERB a German verb whose stem changes its vowel to form the imperfect tense and the past participle, like strong verbs. Its past participle is formed by adding *–t* to the verb stem, like weak verbs. Compare with **strong verb** and **weak verb**.

MODAL VERBS are used to modify or change other verbs to show such things as *ability, permission* or *necessity*. For example, *he can swim, may I come?* and *he ought to go*.

NEGATIVE a question or statement which contains a word such as *not, never* or *nothing*, and is used to say that something is not happening or is not true, for example, *I never eat meat; Don't you love me?*

NEUTER one of three classifications for the gender of German nouns which determines the form of articles, pronouns and adjectives used with the noun and to refer to it. The other two classifications are **masculine** and **feminine**.

NOMINATIVE CASE the basic form of nouns, pronouns, adjectives and articles used in German and the one you find in the dictionary. It is used for the subject of the sentence. Compare with **subject**.

NOUN a 'naming' word for a living being, thing or idea, for example, *woman, desk, happiness, Andrew*.

OBJECT a noun or pronoun which refers to a person or thing that is affected by the action described by the verb. Compare with **direct object**, **indirect object** and **subject**.

OBJECT PRONOUN one of the set of pronouns including *me, him* and *them*, which are used instead of the noun as the object of a verb or preposition. Compare with **subject pronoun**.

ORDINAL NUMBER a number used to indicate where something comes in an order or sequence, for example, *first, fifth, sixteenth*.

PART OF SPEECH one of the categories to which all words are assigned and which describe their forms and how they are used in sentences, for example, *noun, verb, adjective, preposition, pronoun*.

PASSIVE a form of the verb that is used when the subject of the verb is the person or thing that is affected by the action, for example, *we were told*.

PAST PARTICIPLE a verb form, for example, *watched, swum*, which is used with an auxiliary verb to form perfect and pluperfect tenses and passives. Some past participles are also used as adjectives, for example, *a broken watch*

PERFECT one of the verb tenses used to talk about the past, especially about actions that took place and were completed in the past. Compare with **imperfect**.

PERSONAL PRONOUN one of the group of words including *I, you* and *they* which are used to refer to yourself, the people you are talking to, or the people or things you are talking about.

PLUPERFECT one of the verb tenses used to describe something that *had* happened or had been true at a point in the past, for example, *I had forgotten to finish my homework*.

PLURAL the form of a word which is used to refer to more than one person or thing. Compare with **singular**.

POSSESSIVE ADJECTIVE one of the words *my, your, his, her, its, our* or *their*, used with a noun to show that one person or thing belongs to another.

POSSESSIVE PRONOUN one of the words *mine, yours, hers, his, ours* or *theirs*, used instead of a noun to show that one person or thing belongs to another.

PREPOSITION a word such as *at, for, with, into* or *from*, which is usually followed by a noun, pronoun or, in English, a word ending in *-ing*. Prepositions show how people and things relate to the rest of the sentence, for example, *She's at home; a tool for cutting grass; It's from David*.

PRESENT a verb form used to talk about what is true at the moment, what happens regularly, and what is happening now, for example, *I'm a student; I travel to college by train; I'm studying languages*.

PRESENT PARTICIPLE a verb form ending in *-ing* which is used in English to form verb tenses, and which may be used as an adjective or a noun, for example, *What are you doing?; the setting sun; Swimming is easy!*

PRONOUN a word which you use instead of a noun, when you do not need or want to name someone or something directly, for example, *it, you, none*.

PROPER NOUN the name of a person, place, organization or thing. Proper nouns are always written with a capital letter, for example, *Kevin, Glasgow, Europe, London Eye*.

QUESTION WORD a word such as *why, where, who, which* or *how* which is used to ask a question.

REFLEXIVE PRONOUN a word ending in *-self* or *-selves*, such as *myself* or *themselves*, which refers back to the subject, for example, *He hurt himself; Take care of yourself*.

REFLEXIVE VERB a verb where the subject and object are the same, and where the action 'reflects back' on the subject. A reflexive verb is used with a reflexive pronoun such as *myself, yourself, herself*, for example, *I washed myself; He shaved himself*.

RELATIVE CLAUSE part of the sentence in which the relative pronoun appears.

RELATIVE PRONOUN a word such as *that, who* or *which*, when it is used to link two parts of a sentence together.

SENTENCE a group of words which usually has a verb and a subject. In writing, a sentence has a capital letter at the beginning and a full stop, question mark or exclamation mark at the end.

SINGULAR the form of a word which is used to refer to one person or thing. Compare with **plural**.

STEM the main part of a verb to which endings are added.

STRONG VERB a German verb whose stem changes its vowel to form the imperfect tense and the past participle. Its past participle is not formed by adding –t to the verb stem. Also known as irregular verbs. Compare with **weak verb**.

SUBJECT the noun or pronoun used to refer to the person which does the action described by the verb, for example, *My cat doesn't drink milk*. Compare with **object**.

SUBJECT PRONOUN a word such as *I, he, she* and *they* which carries out the action described by the verb. Pronouns stand in for nouns when it is clear who is being talked about, for example, *My brother isn't here at the moment. He'll be back in an hour.* Compare with **object pronoun**.

SUBJUNCTIVE a verb form used in certain circumstances to express some sort of feeling, or to show doubt about whether something will happen or whether something is true. It is only used occasionally in modern English, for example, *If I were you, I wouldn't bother.; So be it.*

SUBORDINATE CLAUSE a clause which begins with a subordinating conjunction such as *because* or *while* and which must be used with a main clause. In German, the verb always goes to the end of the subordinate clause.

SUBORDINATING CONJUNCTION a word such as *when, because* or *while* that links the subordinate clause and the main clause in a sentence. Compare with **subordinate clause**.

SUPERLATIVE an adjective or adverb with *-est* on the end of it or *most* or *least* in front of it that is used to compare people, things or actions, for example, *thinnest, most quickly, least interesting*.

SYLLABLE consonant+vowel units that make up the sounds of a word, for example, ca-the-dral (3 syllables), im-po-ssi-ble (4 syllables).

TENSE the form of a verb which shows whether you are referring to the past, present or future.

VERB a 'doing' word which describes what someone or something does, what someone or something is, or what happens to them, for example, *be, sing, live*.

VOWEL one of the letters *a, e, i, o* or *u*. Compare with **consonant**.

WEAK VERB a German verb whose stem does not change its vowel to form the imperfect tense and the past participle. Its past participle is formed by adding –t to the verb stem. Also known as regular verbs. Compare with **strong verbs**.

NOUNS

What is a noun?
A **noun** is a 'naming' word for a living being, thing or idea, for example, *woman*, *happiness*, *Andrew*. German nouns change, according to their gender, case and number. This is called declension.

Using nouns

➤ In German, all nouns are either masculine, feminine or neuter. This is called their gender. In English, we call all things – for example, *table*, *car*, *book*, *apple* – 'it', but in German, even words for things have a gender. It is important to know that the gender of German nouns rarely relates to the sex of the person or thing it refers to. For example, in German, the word for 'man' is masculine, but the word for 'girl' is neuter and the word for 'person' is feminine.

der Mann	man
das Mädchen	girl
die Person	person

> *Tip*
>
> German nouns are <u>always</u> written with a capital letter.

➤ Whenever you are using a noun, you need to know whether it is masculine, feminine or neuter as this affects the form of other words used with it, such as:

- adjectives that describe it
- articles (such as **der** or **ein**) that go before it
- pronouns (such as **er** or **sie**) that replace it

➪ *For more information on **Adjectives**, **Articles** or **Pronouns**, see pages 40, 25 and 69.*

➤ You can find information about gender by looking the word up in a dictionary – in the *Easy Learning German Dictionary*, for example, you will find the definite article (the word for *the*) in front of the word. When you come across a new noun, always learn the word for *the* that goes with it to help you remember its gender.

- **der** before a noun tells you it is masculine
- **die** before a noun tells you it is feminine
- **das** before a noun tells you it is neuter

➪ *For more information on the **Definite article**, see page 25.*

2 NOUNS

➤ We refer to something as <u>singular</u> when we are talking about just one, and as <u>plural</u> when we are talking about more than one. The singular is the form of the noun you will usually find when you look a noun up in the dictionary. As in English, nouns in German change their form in the <u>plural</u>.

    die Katze cat → **die Katzen** cats

➤ Adjectives, articles and pronouns are also affected by whether a noun is singular or plural.

> *Tip*
>
> Remember that you have to use the right word for *the*, *a* and so on according to the gender and case of the German noun.

For further explanation of grammatical terms, please see pages x-xiv.

Gender

➤ In German a noun can be masculine, feminine or neuter. Gender is quite unpredictable – the best thing is simply to learn each noun with its definite article, that is the word for *the* (**der**, **die** or **das**) which goes with it:

der Teppich	carpet
die Zeit	time
das Bild	picture

However, there are some clues which can help you work out or remember the gender of a noun, as explained below.

1 Masculine nouns

➤ Nouns referring to male people and animals are <u>masculine</u>.

der Mann	man
der Löwe	(male) lion

➤ Seasons, months, days of the week, and points of the compass are <u>masculine</u>.

der Sommer	summer
der August	August
der Freitag	Friday
der Norden	north

➤ Most nouns referring to things that perform an action are also <u>masculine</u>.

der Wecker	alarm clock
der Computer	computer

Grammar Extra!

German nouns taken from other languages and ending in **-ant**, **-ast**, **-ismus**, and **-or** are <u>masculine</u>:

der Trabant	satellite
der Ballast	ballast
der Kapitalismus	capitalism
der Tresor	safe

➤ Nouns with the following endings are <u>masculine</u>.

Masculine Ending	Example	Meaning
-ich	**der** Teppich	carpet
-ig	**der** Essig	vinegar
-ling	**der** Frühling	spring

> **Key points**
> ✔ Nouns referring to male people and animals are masculine.
> ✔ Seasons, months, days of the week, weather and points of the compass are masculine.

2 Feminine nouns

➤ Most nouns ending in **-e** are <u>feminine</u>.

die Falte	crease, wrinkle
die Brücke	bridge

🛈 Note that male people or animals ending in **-e** are masculine, and, nouns beginning with **Ge-** and ending in **-e** are normally neuter.

der Löwe	the lion
das Getreide	crop

➤ Nouns with the following endings are <u>feminine</u>.

Feminine Ending	Example	Meaning
-heit	**die** Schönheit	beauty
-keit	**die** Sehenswürdigkeit	sight
-schaft	**die** Gewerkschaft	trade union
-ung	**die** Zeitung	newspaper
-ei	**die** Bäckerei	bakery

Grammar Extra!

German nouns, some taken from other languages and ending in **-anz, -enz, -ie, -ik, -ion, -tät, -ur** are <u>feminine</u>, with some exceptions.

die Distanz	distance	BUT:	**der Kranz**	wreath
die Konkurrenz	competition			
die Theorie	theory	BUT:	**das Knie**	knee
die Panik	panic	BUT:	**der Pazifik**	Pacific
die Union	union	BUT:	**der Spion**	spy
die Elektrizität	electricity			
die Temperatur	temperature	BUT:	**das Abitur**	A levels

➤ Numbers used in counting, for example *one*, *three*, *fifty* are <u>feminine</u>.

> **Er hat <u>eine</u> Drei gekriegt.**   He got a three.

➤ In German, there are sometimes very different words for male and female, just as in English.

<u>der</u> Mann	man
<u>die</u> Frau	woman
<u>der</u> Vater	father
<u>die</u> Mutter	mother
<u>der</u> Bulle	bull
<u>die</u> Kuh	cow

➤ Many masculine German nouns can be made feminine by adding **-in** in the singular and **-innen** in the plural.

der Lehrer	(male) teacher
die Lehrerin	(female) teacher
Lehrer und Lehrer<u>innen</u>	(male and female) teachers
der Leser	(male) reader
die Leserin	(female) reader
unsere Leser und Leser<u>innen</u>	our readers (male and female)

Grammar Extra!

Some German adjectives are used as feminine nouns. They have feminine adjective endings which change according to the article which comes before them.

eine Deutsche	a German woman
die Abgeordnete	the woman MP

⇨ For more information on **Adjectives used as nouns** and for **Feminine adjective endings**, see pages 50 and 42.

Key points

✔ Most nouns ending in **-e** are feminine.

✔ Many feminine nouns end in: **-heit**, **-keit**, **-schaft**, **-ung**, **-ei**.

✔ Masculine German words referring to people can be made feminine by adding **-in** in the singular and **-innen** in the plural.

✔ Numbers used in counting are feminine.

3 | Neuter nouns

➤ Most nouns beginning with **Ge-** are <u>neuter</u>.

das Geschirr	crockery, dishes
das Geschöpf	creature
das Getreide	crop

➤ Nouns ending in **-lein** or **-chen** are also neuter. These are called the <u>diminutive form</u> and refer to small persons or objects.

Endings to form the diminutive	Example	Meaning
-lein	**das** Kind<u>lein</u>	little child
-chen	**das** Häus<u>chen</u>	little house

i Note that if these words have one of the vowels **a**, **o** or **u**, an umlaut should be added above the vowel. The final **-e** should also be dropped before these endings.

der Bach → B<u>ä</u>ch → **das** B<u>ä</u>chlein	(small) stream
die Katze → K<u>ä</u>tz → **das** K<u>ä</u>tzchen	kitten

➤ Fractions are also <u>neuter</u>.

ein Drittel davon	a third of it

➤ Nouns which refer to young humans and animals are <u>neuter</u>.

das Baby	baby
das Kind	child
das Kalb	calf
das Lamm	lamb

i Note that the animals themselves can be any gender.

der Hund	dog
die Schlange	snake
das Vieh	cattle

➤ Infinitives (the 'to' form of verbs) used as nouns are <u>neuter</u>.

das Schwimmen	swimming
das Spielen	playing
das Radfahren	cycling

⇨ *For more information on **Infinitives**, see page 134.*

➤ Most nouns with the following endings are <u>neuter</u>.

Neuter Ending	Example	Meaning
-nis	das Ereignis	event
-tum	das Eigentum	property

Grammar Extra!

German nouns taken from other languages and ending in -at, -ett, -fon, -ma, -ment, -um are <u>neuter</u>.

das Reservat	reservation			
das Tablett	tray			
das Telefon	phone			
das Thema	subject, topic			
das Medikament	drug			
das Ultimatum	ultimatum	BUT:	der Reichtum	wealth
das Studium	studies			

Key points
✔ Most nouns beginning with **Ge-** are neuter.
✔ The diminutive form of nouns is neuter.
✔ Nouns referring to young humans and animals are neuter.
✔ Infinitives used as nouns are neuter.
✔ Nouns ending in **-nis** or **-tum** are neuter.

4 Compound nouns

What is a compound noun?
A **compound noun** is a noun made up of two or more words, for example, *tin-opener* and *railway station*.

➤ In German, these words nearly always take their gender from the <u>LAST</u> noun of the compound word.

<u>die</u> Armbanduhr (Armband + <u>die</u> Uhr)	wristwatch
<u>der</u> Tomatensalat (Tomaten + <u>der</u> Salat)	tomato salad
<u>der</u> Fußballspieler (Fußball + <u>der</u> Spieler)	footballer

Grammar Extra!

Some German nouns have more than one gender. A few nouns have two genders and sometimes one of them can only be used in certain regions.

der/das Marzipan	marzipan	(*der Marzipan* is used mostly in Austria)
der/das Keks	biscuit	(*das Keks* is used mostly in Austria)
der/das Kaugummi	chewing gum	

Other nouns have two genders and the meaning of the word changes depending on which gender it has.

der Band	volume, book
das Band	ribbon, band, tape; bond
der See	lake
die See	sea
der Leiter	leader, manager
die Leiter	ladder

➤ In German, abbreviations have the same gender as the word they come from.

die BRD	the Federal Republic of Germany (from die Bundesrepublik Deutschland)
die DB	the German Railways (from die Deutsche Bahn)
das ZDF	German TV channel (from das Zweite Deutsche Fernsehen)

Key points

✔ Compound nouns are nouns made up of two or more words and usually take their gender from the last part of the compound word.

✔ Some German nouns have more than one gender and this can affect their meaning.

✔ German abbreviations have the same gender as the words they come from.

For further explanation of grammatical terms, please see pages x-xiv.

The Cases

➤ In German, there are four grammatical cases – nominative, accusative, genitive and dative. The case you should use depends on the grammatical function of the noun in the sentence.

1 The nominative case

➤ The nominative case is the basic form of the noun and is the one you find in the dictionary.

Case	Masculine	Feminine	Neuter
Nominative	der Wagen	die Dose	das Lied
	ein Wagen	eine Dose	ein Lied

⇨ *For more information on* **Articles**, *see page 25.*

➤ The nominative case is used for:

- the subject of the sentence, that is the person, animal or thing 'doing' the action

Das Mädchen singt.	The girl is singing.
Die Katze schläft.	The cat is sleeping.

- after the verbs **sein** (meaning *to be*) and **werden** (meaning *to be, to become*)

Er ist ein guter Lehrer.	He is a good teacher.
Das wird ein Pullover.	It's going to be a jumper.

2 The accusative case

➤ The article for feminine and neuter nouns in the accusative case has the same form as in the nominative. **Der** for masculine nouns changes to **den** and **ein** to **einen**.

Case	Masculine	Feminine	Neuter
Nominative	der Wagen	die Dose	das Lied
	ein Wagen	eine Dose	ein Lied
Accusative	den Wagen	die Dose	das Lied
	einen Wagen	eine Dose	ein Lied

⇨ *For more information on* **Articles**, *see page 25.*

➤ The accusative case is used:

- to show the direct object of a verb. This is the person, animal or thing affected by the action of the verb.

He gave me a book. → *What did he give me?* → a book (*=direct object*)

Can you get me a towel? → *What can you get me?* → a towel (*=direct object*)

Ich sehe <u>den Hund</u>. → *What do I see?* → <u>den Hund</u> (*=direct object*)

Er hat <u>ein Lied</u> gesungen. → *What did he sing?* → <u>ein Lied</u> (*=direct object*)

- after certain prepositions (words in English such as *at, for, with, into* or *from*) which are always used with the accusative.

Es ist <u>für</u> seine Freundin.	It's for his girlfriend.
Es ist schwierig <u>ohne</u> einen Wagen.	It's difficult without a car.
<u>durch</u> das Rauchen wurde ich krank.	Smoking made me ill.

⇨ For more information on **Prepositions followed by the accusative case**, see page 156.

- after certain prepositions of place when movement is involved:

an	on, to, at
auf	on, in, to, at
hinter	behind
in	in, into, to
neben	next to, beside
über	over, across, above
unter	under, among
vor	in front of, before
zwischen	between

Stell dein Rad <u>neben</u> mein Auto.	Put your bike next to my car.
Sie legten ein Brett <u>über das</u> Loch.	They put a board over the hole.

[i] Note that when there is no movement involved after these prepositions, the <u>dative case</u> is used.

Sie geht <u>in die</u> Stadt. (*accusative*)	She's going into town.
Er war <u>in der</u> Stadt. (*dative*)	He was in town.

⇨ For more information on **Prepositions followed by the accusative or the dative case**, see page 158.

- in many expressions of time and place which do not have a preposition

Das macht sie <u>jeden</u> Donnerstag.	She does that every Thursday.
Die Schule ist <u>einen</u> Kilometer entfernt.	The school is a kilometre away.

- in some set expressions

Guten Abend!	Good evening!
Vielen Dank!	Thank you very much!

3 The genitive case

➤ Der for masculine nouns and das for neuter nouns change to des. Ein changes to eines. The endings of <u>masculine</u> and <u>neuter singular</u> nouns also change in the genitive case.

➤ -s is added to masculine and neuter nouns ending in -en, -el, -er.

der Wagen car → des Wagens
das Rauchen smoking → des Rauchens
der Esel donkey → des Esels
der Computer computer → des Computers

Ich mag die Farbe des Wagens.	I like the colour of the car.
Die Größe des Computers ist nicht wichtig.	The size of the computer isn't important.

➤ -es is added to most masculine and neuter nouns of one syllable ending in a consonant.

der Freund friend → des Freundes
der Mann man → des Mannes
der Sitz seat → des Sitzes
der Arzt doctor → des Arztes
der Tisch table → des Tisches
das Schloss castle → des Schlosses

Die Schwester des Arztes hilft manchmal in der Sprechstunde.	The doctor's sister helps him in the surgery sometimes.
Das Museum befindet sich in der Nähe des Schlosses.	The museum is near the castle.

➤ Die changes to der and eine to einer in the genitive. The endings of <u>feminine singular</u> nouns in the genitive case are the same as in the nominative.

die Ärztin (female) doctor → der Ärztin

Case	Masculine	Feminine	Neuter
Nominative	der Wagen	die Dose	das Lied
	ein Wagen	eine Dose	ein Lied
Accusative	den Wagen	die Dose	das Lied
	einen Wagen	eine Dose	ein Lied
Genitive	des Wagens	der Dose	des Lieds
	eines Wagens	einer Dose	eines Lieds

⟹ For more information on Articles, see page 25.

➤ The genitive case is used:

- to show that something belongs to someone

  Das Auto der Frau war rot.   The woman's car was red.
  Der Hund meiner Mutter ist ganz   My mother's dog is really small.
  klein.

- after certain prepositions which always take the genitive

  Wegen des schlechten Wetters   We'll have to go home because
  müssen wir nach Hause gehen.   of the bad weather.
  Trotz ihrer Krankheit geht sie   She goes for a walk every day,
  jeden Tag spazieren.   despite her illness.

- in some expressions of time

  eines Tages   one day

4 The dative case

➤ Der changes to dem and ein to einem in the dative. Singular nouns in the dative
have the same form as in the nominative.

  dem Auto   to the car
  dem Mädchen   to the girl

➤ Die changes to der and eine to einer in the dative. Singular nouns in the dative
have the same form as in the nominative.

Case	Masculine	Feminine	Neuter
Nominative	der Wagen	die Dose	das Lied
	ein Wagen	eine Dose	ein Lied
Accusative	den Wagen	die Dose	das Lied
	einen Wagen	eine Dose	ein Lied
Genitive	des Wagens	der Dose	des Lieds
	eines Wagens	einer Dose	eines Lieds
Dative	dem Wagen	der Dose	dem Lied
	einem Wagen	einer Dose	einem Lied

⇨ For more information on **Articles**, see page 25.

➤ -e is added to some nouns in certain set phrases.

  Wir gehen nach Hause.   We're going home.
  Er hat sich zu Tode gearbeitet.   He worked himself to death.

Grammar Extra!

-e may also be added to the dative singular of masculine and neuter nouns to make the phrase easier to pronounce.

zu welchem Zwecke?   to what purpose?

➤ The dative case is used:

- to show the indirect object of a verb – an indirect object answers the question *who to/for?* or *to/for what?*

  He gave the man the book. → *Who did he give the book to?* → the man
  (= *noun indirect object*)

  Er gab dem Mann das Buch.   He gave the man the book.

- after certain verbs

  Er hilft seiner Mutter im Haushalt.   He helps his mother with the housework.

➪ For more information on **Verbs followed by the dative case**, see page 148.

- after certain prepositions which always take the dative

  Nach dem Essen gingen wir spazieren.   After eating we went for a walk.

  Er kam mit einer Freundin.   He came with a friend.

➪ For more information on **Prepositions followed by the dative case**, see page 153.

- after certain prepositions to show position

an	on, to, at
auf	on, in, to, at
hinter	behind
in	in, into, to
neben	next to, beside
über	over, across, above
unter	under, among
vor	in front of, before
zwischen	between

  Ich sitze neben dem Fenster.   I'm sitting next to the window.

  Die Katze lag unter dem Tisch.   The cat lay under the table.

i Note that when there is some movement involved after these prepositions, the <u>accusative case</u> is used.

Er war <u>in der</u> Stadt. (*dative*)	He was in town.
Sie geht <u>in die</u> Stadt. (*accusative*)	She's going into town.

⇨ *For more information on* **Prepositions followed by the accusative or the dative case**, *see page 158.*

- in certain expressions

<u>Mir</u> ist kalt.	I'm cold.

- instead of the possessive adjective (*my, your, his, her, its, our* or *their*) to refer to parts of the body and items of clothing

Ich habe <u>mir die</u> Haare gewaschen.	I washed my hair.
Zieh <u>dir die</u> Jacke aus.	Take your jacket off.

⇨ *For more information on* **Possessive adjectives**, *see page 37.*

➤ Changes to the definite and indefinite articles der, die or das and ein, eine or ein for each case are summarized in the table below, to help make it easier for you to remember them.

Case	Masculine Singular	Feminine Singular	Neuter Singular
Nominative	der	die	das
	ein	eine	ein
Accusative	den	die	das
	einen	eine	ein
Genitive	des	der	des
	eines	einer	eines
Dative	dem	der	dem
	einem	einer	einem

⇨ *For more information on* **Articles**, *see page 25.*

Key points

✔ In German, there are four grammatical cases – nominative, accusative, genitive and dative.

✔ The case you use depends on the grammatical function of the noun in the sentence.

✔ The nominative case is used to show the subject of a sentence and after the verbs **sein** and **werden**.

✔ The accusative case is used to show the direct object of a sentence, and after certain prepositions.

✔ The genitive case is used to show that something belongs to somebody, and after certain prepositions.

✔ The dative case is used to show the indirect object of a sentence, and after certain prepositions and verbs.

Forming plurals

➤ In English we usually make nouns plural by adding an -s to the end (*garden* → *gardens*; *house* → *houses*), although we do have some nouns which are <u>irregular</u> and do not follow this pattern (*mouse* → *mice*; *child* → *children*).

➤ In German, there are several different ways of making nouns plural.

➤ The definite article changes in the plural, as shown in the table below.

Case	Masculine Singular	Feminine Singular	Neuter Singular	All Genders Plural
Nominative	der	die	das	die
Accusative	den	die	das	die
Genitive	des	der	des	der
Dative	dem	der	dem	den

⇨ For more information on **Articles**, see page 25.

Tip

Nouns in the dative plural <u>ALWAYS</u> end in -n, except those nouns which come from other languages. Most of their plural forms end in -s. For example:

Mit <u>den</u> Autos hatte sie ständig Probleme.

The cars caused her constant problems.

---

1 Feminine plural nouns ending in -n, -en, -nen

➤ Most German <u>feminine nouns</u> form their plural by adding -n, -en or -nen to their singular form.

Case	Singular	Plural
Nominative	die Blume (flower)	die Blumen
	die Frau (woman)	die Frauen
	die Lehrerin (teacher)	die Lehrerinnen
Accusative	die Blume	die Blumen
	die Frau	die Frauen
	die Lehrerin	die Lehrerinnen
Genitive	der Blume	der Blumen
	der Frau	der Frauen
	der Lehrerin	der Lehrerinnen
Dative	der Blume	den Blumen
	der Frau	den Frauen
	der Lehrerin	den Lehrerinnen

Die Blumen waren nicht teuer.	The flowers weren't expensive.
Die Lehrerinnen sind ziemlich jung.	The (female) teachers are quite young.
Das Leben der Frauen in vielen Ländern ist schwierig.	In many countries, women's lives are difficult.
Wo gehst du mit den Blumen hin?	Where are you going with the flowers?

2 | Nouns with no ending in the plural

➤ Many nouns have no plural ending – these are mostly masculine or neuter nouns ending in -en, -er or -el.

Case	Singular	Plural
Nominative	der Kuchen (cake) der Lehrer (teacher) der Onkel (uncle)	die Kuchen die Lehrer die Onkel
Accusative	den Kuchen den Lehrer den Onkel	die Kuchen die Lehrer die Onkel
Genitive	des Kuchens des Lehrers des Onkels	der Kuchen der Lehrer der Onkel
Dative	dem Kuchen dem Lehrer dem Onkel	den Kuchen den Lehrern den Onkeln

Die Kuchen sehen lecker aus.	The cakes look delicious.
Die Onkel kommen morgen an.	The uncles are coming tomorrow.
Das war die Schuld der Lehrer.	That was the teachers' fault.
Es gibt ein kleines Problem mit den Kuchen.	There's a slight problem with the cakes.

➤ Some of these nouns also have an umlaut added to the first vowel a, o or u in the plural.

Case	Singular	Plural
Nominative	der Apfel (apple) der Garten (garden)	die Äpfel die Gärten
Accusative	den Apfel den Garten	die Äpfel die Gärten
Genitive	des Apfels des Gartens	der Äpfel der Gärten
Dative	dem Apfel dem Garten	den Äpfeln den Gärten

Die Äpfel sind nicht reif genug.	The apples aren't ripe enough.
Die Gärten waren wunderschön.	The gardens were beautiful.
Schau mal die Größe der Äpfel an!	Look at the size of the apples!
Den Äpfeln fehlt ein bisschen Sonne.	The apples need a bit of sun.

3 Plural nouns ending in ̈e

➤ Some masculine nouns add an umlaut above the first vowel a, o or u and an -e ending to form the plural. A few feminine nouns with a in the stem also follow this pattern. Nouns in this group often have one syllable only.

Case	Singular	Plural
Nominative	der Stuhl (chair) die Angst (fear)	die Stühle die Ängste
Accusative	den Stuhl die Angst	die Stühle die Ängste
Genitive	des Stuhl(e)s der Angst	der Stühle der Ängste
Dative	dem Stuhl der Angst	den Stühlen den Ängsten

Die Stühle sind neu.	The chairs are new.
Die Regierung muss die Ängste der Bevölkerung ernst nehmen.	The government has to take the population's fears seriously.
Die Farbe der Stühle.	The colour of the chairs.
Der Tischler macht den Stühlen neue Beine.	The carpenter is making new legs for the chairs.

4 Masculine and neuter plural nouns ending in -e, -er or ̈er

➤ Masculine or neuter nouns often add -e or -er to form the plural.

Case	Singular	Plural
Nominative	das Geschenk (present) der Tisch (table) das Kind (child)	die Geschenke die Tische die Kinder
Accusative	das Geschenk den Tisch das Kind	die Geschenke die Tische die Kinder
Genitive	des Geschenks des Tisches des Kindes	der Geschenke der Tische der Kinder
Dative	dem Geschenk dem Tisch dem Kind	den Geschenken den Tischen den Kindern

Die Geschenke sind auf dem Tisch.	The presents are on the table.
Ich muss die Kinder abholen.	I have to pick up the children.
Die Auswahl der Tische im Laden war groß.	The shop had a large selection of tables.
Sie geht mit den Kindern spazieren.	She's going for a walk with the children.

➤ Some masculine and neuter nouns add an umlaut above the first vowel a, o or u and an -er ending in the plural.

Case	Singular	Plural
Nominative	das Dach (roof) der Mann (man)	die Dächer die Männer
Accusative	das Dach den Mann	die Dächer die Männer
Genitive	des Dach(e)s des Mannes	der Dächer der Männer
Dative	dem Dach dem Mann	den Dächern den Männern

Die Dächer werden repariert.	The roofs are being repaired.
Man hatte die Männer völlig vergessen.	The men had been completely forgotten.
Was ist die Rolle der Männer in unserer Gesellschaft?	What is the role of men in our society?
Die Frauen sollten den Männern nicht immer recht geben.	Women should not always agree with men.

5 Some unusual plurals

➤ There is another group of German nouns which don't follow any of the rules for forming plurals – you just have to remember them! Here are some of the most common ones. As you will see, many of them are words from other languages, and it is common for such words to form their plural by adding -s.

Singular	Meaning	Plural
das Auto	car	die Autos
das Hotel	hotel	die Hotels
das Restaurant	restaurant	die Restaurants
das Baby	baby	die Babys
das Thema	theme, topic, subject	die Themen
das Drama	drama	die Dramen
das Risiko	risk	die Risiken
der Park	park	die Parks
der Chef	boss, chief, head	die Chefs
die Firma	firm	die Firmen

Die Hotels in der Stadt sind ziemlich teuer.	The hotels in town are quite expensive.
Die Risiken sind sehr hoch.	The risks are very high.
Die Kinder finden die Babys ganz niedlich.	The children think the babies are really cute.
Was hältst du von den Preisen der Autos?	What do you think of the prices of the cars?
Das ist die Stadt mit den vielen Parks.	That's the town with all the parks.

6 Plural versus singular

➤ Some nouns are always plural in English, but singular in German.

eine Brille	glasses, spectacles
eine Schere	scissors
eine Hose	trousers

➤ These nouns are only used in the plural in German to mean more than one pair.

zwei Hosen	two pairs of trousers

7 Nouns of measurement and quantity

➤ These nouns, used to describe the quantity or size of something, usually remain singular in German, even if preceded by a plural number.

Möchten Sie zwei Stück?	Would you like two?
Ich wiege fünfzig Kilo.	I weigh fifty kilos.

➤ The substance which they measure follows in the same case as the noun of quantity, and NOT in the genitive case as in English.

Sie hat drei Tassen Kaffee getrunken.	She drank three cups of coffee.
Er wollte zwei Kilo Kartoffeln.	He wanted two kilos of potatoes.
Drei Glas Weißwein, bitte!	Three glasses of white wine, please.

Key points

✔ Most German feminine nouns form their plural by adding -n, -en or -nen to their singular form.

✔ Many nouns have no plural ending – these are mostly masculine or neuter singular nouns ending in -en, -er or -el. Some of these nouns also have an umlaut added to the vowel in the plural.

✔ Some masculine nouns add an umlaut above the first vowel a, o or u and an -e ending to form the plural. A few feminine nouns with a in the stem also follow this pattern.

✔ Masculine and neuter nouns often add -e or -er in the plural, and can sometimes add an umlaut above the first vowel a, o or u.

✔ There are some unusual plural nouns in German which don't follow any pattern.

✔ Some nouns are always plural in English, but singular in German.

✔ Nouns of measurement and quantity usually remain singular even if preceded by a plural number.

✔ The substance which they measure follows in the same case as the noun of quantity.

Weak nouns

➤ As we have seen, German nouns may change, according to their <u>gender</u>, <u>case</u> and <u>number</u>. This is called <u>declension</u>.

➤ Some masculine nouns have a <u>weak declension</u> – this means that they end in -en or, if the word ends in a vowel, in -n, in every case <u>EXCEPT</u> in the nominative singular case.

➤ Weak masculine nouns follow the pattern shown.

Case	Singular	Plural
Nominative	der Junge	die Jungen
Accusative	den Jungen	die Jungen
Genitive	des Jungen	der Jungen
Dative	dem Jungen	den Jungen

➤ Weak masculine nouns include:

- those ending in -og(e) referring to men

der Psychologe	the psychologist
Der Psychologe half ihm in seiner Krise.	The psychologist helped him through his crisis.

- those ending in -aph (or -af) or -oph

der Paragraf	the paragraph
der Philosoph	the philosopher
Der Paragraf umfasste 350 Wörter.	The paragraph was 350 words long.

- those ending in -ant

der Elefant	the elephant
der Diamant	the diamond
Der Diamant war sehr viel Geld wert.	The diamond was worth a lot of money.

- those ending in -t referring to men

der Astronaut	the astronaut
der Komponist	the composer
der Architekt	the architect
Um Astronaut zu werden, muss man jahrelang trainieren.	You have to train for years to become an astronaut.

For further explanation of grammatical terms, please see pages x-xiv.

● some other common masculine nouns

der Chirurg	surgeon
der Franzose	Frenchman
der Kollege	colleague
der Mensch	human being
der Ochse	ox
der Spatz	sparrow

Der junge Franzose wollte Schottland besuchen.	The young French guy wanted to visit Scotland.
Ich habe den Franzosen seit einer Woche nicht mehr gesehen.	I haven't seen the French guy for a week.

Grammar Extra!

The noun der Name follows the same pattern as der Junge, except in the genitive singular, where it adds -ns instead of just -n. Der Buchstabe (meaning *letter (of the alphabet)*), der Funke (meaning *spark*) and der Gedanke (meaning *thought*) also follow this pattern.

Case	Singular	Plural
Nominative	der Name	die Namen
Accusative	den Namen	die Namen
Genitive	des Namens	der Namen
Dative	dem Namen	den Namen

Das hängt von der Wichtigkeit des Namens ab.	That depends on how important the name is.

Proper nouns

> **What is a proper noun?**
> A **proper noun** is the name of a person, place, organization or thing. Proper nouns
> are always written with a capital letter, for example, *Kevin, Glasgow, Europe,
> London Eye.*

➤ In German, names of people and places only change in the <u>genitive singular</u>
   when they add **-s**, unless they are preceded by the definite article or a
   demonstrative adjective (in English, *this, that, these* and *those*).

Annas Buch	Anna's book
Klaras Mantel	Klara's coat
die Werke Goethes	Goethe's works
BUT	
der Untergang <u>der</u> Titanic	the sinking of <u>the</u> Titanic

⇨ *For more information on **Articles** and demonstrative adjectives, see pages 25 and 31.*

Grammar Extra!

Where proper names end in **-s**, **-sch**, **-ss**, **-ß**, **-x**, **-z**, or **-tz**, adding an extra **-s** for the genitive
makes them very difficult to pronounce. This is best avoided by using **von** + the dative case.

das Buch von Hans	Hans's book
die Werke von Marx	the works of Marx
die Freundin von Klaus	Klaus's girlfriend

➤ **Herr** (meaning *Mr*) is always declined when it is part of a proper name.

an Herr<u>n</u> Schmidt	to Mr Schmidt
Sehr geehrte Herr<u>en</u>	Dear Sirs

➤ Surnames usually form their plurals by adding **-s**, unless they end in **-s**, **-sch**, **-ss**,
   -ß, **-x**, **-z**, or **-tz**, in which case they add **-ens**. They are often preceded by the
   definite article.

Die Schmidt<u>s</u> haben uns zum Abendessen eingeladen.	The Schmidts have invited us to dinner.
Die Schultz<u>ens</u> waren nicht zu Hause.	The Schultzes weren't at home.

⇨ *For more information on **Articles**, see page 25.*

For further explanation of grammatical terms, please see pages x-xiv.

ARTICLES

What is an article?
In English, an **article** is one of the words *the*, *a* and *an* which is used in front of a noun.

1 Different types of articles

➤ There are two types of article.

- the **definite** article: *the* in English. This is used to identify a particular thing or person.

  I'm going to <u>the</u> supermarket.
  That's <u>the</u> woman I was talking to.

- the <u>indefinite</u> article: *a* or *an* in English, *some* or *any* (or no word at all) in the plural. This is used to refer to something unspecific, or something that you do not really know about.

  Is there <u>a</u> supermarket near here?
  I need <u>a</u> day off.

2 The definite article

➤ In English the definite article *the* always keeps the same form.

  the book
  the books
  with *the* books

➤ In German, however, the definite article has many forms. All German nouns are either <u>masculine</u>, <u>feminine</u> or <u>neuter</u> and, just as in English, they can be either <u>singular</u> or <u>plural</u>. The word you choose for *the* depends on whether the noun it is used with is masculine, feminine or neuter, singular or plural AND it also depends on the case of the noun. This may sound complicated, but it is not too difficult.

<u>Die</u> Frau ging spazieren.	The woman went for a walk.
<u>Der</u> Mann ist geschieden.	The man is divorced.
Sie fährt mit <u>dem</u> Auto in die Stadt.	She travels into town by car.
<u>Die</u> Farbe <u>der</u> Jacke gefällt mir nicht.	I don't like the colour of the jacket.
Ich muss <u>die</u> Kinder abholen.	I have to pick up the children.
Das will ich mit <u>den</u> Behörden besprechen.	I want to discuss that with the authorities.

⇨ *For more information on **Nouns**, see page 1.*

➤ The definite article changes for <u>masculine</u>, <u>feminine</u> and <u>neuter singular</u> nouns.

	Definite Article +Singular Noun	Meaning
Masculine	<u>der</u> Mann	the man
Feminine	<u>die</u> Frau	the woman
Neuter	<u>das</u> Mädchen	the girl

➤ The <u>plural</u> forms of the definite article are the same for all genders.

	Definite Article + Plural Noun	Meaning
Masculine	<u>die</u> Männer	the men
Feminine	<u>die</u> Frauen	the women
Neuter	<u>die</u> Mädchen	the girls

Tip

It is a good idea to learn the <u>article</u> or the <u>gender</u> with the noun when you come across a word for the first time, so that you know whether it is masculine, feminine or neuter. A good dictionary will also give you this information.

➤ The definite article also changes according to the case of the noun in the sentence – nominative, accusative, genitive or dative.

➪ *For more information on **Cases**, see page 9.*

➤ The forms of the definite article in each case are as follows:

Case	Masculine Singular	Feminine Singular	Neuter Singular	All Genders Plural
Nominative	der	die	das	die
Accusative	den	die	das	die
Genitive	des	der	des	der
Dative	dem	der	dem	den

Der Mann ging ins Haus.	The man went into the house.
Die Frau geht jeden Abend schwimmen.	The woman goes swimming every night.
Sie wollen **das** Mädchen adoptieren.	They want to adopt the girl.
Die zwei Frauen nebenan wollen ihr Haus renovieren.	The two women next door want to renovate their house.
Der Mann mit **der** reichen Frau.	The man with the rich wife.
Die Mädchen gehen morgen ins Kino.	The girls are going to the cinema tomorrow.
Ich will nicht nur mit **den** Männern arbeiten.	I don't just want to work with the men.

Key points

✔ The definite article changes for masculine, feminine and neuter singular nouns.

✔ The plural forms of the definite article are the same for all genders.

✔ The form of the definite article also changes depending on the case of the noun in the sentence.

---

3 Using the definite article

➤ The definite article in German (**der**, **die** or **das**) is used in more or less the same way as we use *the* in English, but it is also used in German in a few places where you might not expect it.

➤ The definite article is used with words like *prices*, *life* and *time* that describe qualities, ideas or experiences (called <u>abstract nouns</u>) rather than something that you can touch with your hand. Usually, *the* is missed out in English with this type of word.

Die Preise sind wirklich hoch.	Prices are really high.
Das Leben ist schön.	Life is wonderful.
Die Zeit vergeht schnell.	Time passes quickly.

i Note that these nouns are sometimes used <u>WITHOUT</u> the article.

Es braucht <u>Mut</u>.	It needs (some) courage.
Gibt es dort <u>Leben</u>?	Is there (any) life there?

➤ You also use the definite article with the genitive case to show that something belongs to someone.

die Jacke **der** Frau	the woman's jacket

i Note that you do not usually use the definite article with the genitive case if the noun is a proper name or is being used as a proper name. A proper name is the name of a person, place, organization or thing.

Jans Auto	Jan's car
Muttis Auto	Mummy's car

Occasionally, the definite article IS used with proper names:

- to make the sex of the person or the case clearer

  Er hat es <u>dem</u> Kekilli gegeben.　　He gave it to Kekilli.

- where an adjective is used before the proper name

  Die <u>alte</u> Frau Schnorr ist gestorben.　　Old Frau Schnorr has died.

- in certain informal situations or to emphasize something

  Ich habe heute <u>den</u> Kevin gesehen.　　I saw Kevin today.

➤ In German, you have to use the definite article in front of <u>masculine</u> and <u>feminine</u> countries and districts, but you don't need it for neuter ones.

<u>Die</u> Schweiz ist auch schön.	Switzerland is also beautiful.
Deutschland ist sehr schön.	Germany is very beautiful.

Grammar Extra!

You also use the definite article when geographical names are preceded by an adjective.

<u>das</u> heutige Deutschland　　today's Germany

➤ The definite article is used with names of seasons.

<u>Der</u> Winter kommt bald.　　Soon it will be winter.

➤ You often use the definite article with meals.

Im Hotel wird <u>das</u> Abendessen ab acht Uhr serviert.　　Dinner is served from eight o'clock in the hotel.

i Note that there are certain expressions with meals when you don't use the definite article.

Um acht Uhr ist Frühstück.　　Breakfast is at eight o'clock.

➤ You also use the definite article with the names of roads.

Sie wohnt jetzt in <u>der</u> Geisener Straße.	She lives in Geisener Road now.

➤ The definite article is used with months of the year, except after the prepositions seit, nach and vor.

Der Dezember war ziemlich kalt.	The December was quite cold.
Wir sind seit September hier.	We have been here since September.

⇨ For more information on **Prepositions**, see page 153.

➤ If you're talking about prices and want to say each, per or a, you use the definite article.

Die kosten fünf Euro <u>das</u> Pfund.	They cost five euros a pound.
Ich habe sechs Euro <u>das</u> Stück bezahlt.	I paid six euros each.

➤ In certain common expressions the definite article is used.

in <u>die</u> Stadt fahren	to go into town
mit <u>der</u> Post	by post
mit <u>dem</u> Zug/Bus/Auto	by train/bus/car

Grammar Extra!

In German, the definite article can be used instead of a demonstrative adjective.

Du willst <u>das</u> Buch lesen!	You want to read <u>that</u> book!

⇨ For more information on demonstrative adjectives, see page 31.

➤ In German, the definite article is left out in certain set expressions.

von Beruf	by profession
Nachrichten hören	to listen to the news

4 Shortened forms of the definite article

➤ After certain prepositions, the definite article can be shortened, though it is best to avoid using some of these forms in writing.

- **für das→ fürs**

  Es ist <u>fürs</u> Baby.   It's for the baby.

- **vor dem→ vorm**

  Es liegt vorm Haus.   It's lying in front of the house.

- **um das→ ums**

  Es geht ums Geld.   It's a question of money.

➤ The following shortened forms can be used in writing.

- **an dem→ am**

  Am 1. Mai fahren wir in die   We go on holiday on the
  Ferien.   1st of May.

- **in dem→ im**

  Das Buch liegt im Haus.   The book's in the house.

- **zu dem→ zum**

  Ich muss zum Bahnhof gehen.   I have to go to the station.

- **zu der→ zur**

  Sie geht jeden Tag zur Schule.   She goes to school every day.

⇨ *For more information on **Shortened forms of prepositions**, see page 165.*

Key points

✔ The definite article is used in German with:

- abstract nouns
- the genitive case to show possession
- proper names, in certain exceptional cases
- masculine and feminine countries and districts
- names of seasons and with months of the year, except after the prepositions **seit**, **nach** and **vor**
- names of roads
- meals and prices
- certain set expressions

✔ When combined with certain prepositions, the definite article can be shortened.

---

5 | Words declined like the definite article

➤ These words follow the same patterns as the definite article:

	Nominative	Accusative	Genitive	Dative
Plural only	alle	alle	aller	allen
Singular	beides	beides	beides	beiden
Plural	beide	beide	beider	beiden
Singular	dieser, diese, dieses	diesen, diese, dieses	dieses/diesen, dieser, dieses/diesen	diesem, dieser, diesem
Plural	diese	diese	dieser	diesen
Singular	einiger, einige, einiges	einigen, einige, einiges	einiges/einigen, einiger, einiges/einigen	einigem, einiger, einigem
Plural	einige	einige	einiger	einigen
Singular	jeder, jede, jedes	jeden, jede, jedes	jedes/jeden, jeder, jedes/jeden	jedem, jeder, jedem
Plural	jede	jede	jeder	jeden
Singular	jener, jene, jenes	jenen, jene, jenes	jenes/jenen, jener, jenes/jenen	jenem, jener, jenem
Plural	jene	jene	jener	jenen
Singular	mancher, manche, manches	manchen, manche, manches	manches/manchen, mancher, manches/manchen	manchem, mancher, manchem
Plural	manche	manche	mancher	manchen
Singular	solcher, solche, solches	solchen, solche, solches	solches/solchen, solcher, solches/solchen	solchem, solcher, solchem
Plural	solche	solche	solcher	solchen
Singular	welcher, welche, welches	welchen, welche, welches	welches/welchen, welcher, welches/welchen	welchem, welcher, welchem
Plural	welche	welche	welcher	welchen

i Note that **dieser** or **jener** are used to translate the English demonstrative adjectives *this, that, these* and *those*.

- **alle, aller, allen** (*plural* only) — all, all of them
  Wir haben <u>alle</u> gesehen. — We saw all of them.
  Die Eltern fuhren mit <u>allen</u> Kindern weg. — The parents went off with all their children.

- beide (*plural* only)   both
  Ich habe <u>beide</u> Bücher gelesen.   I've read both books.

- dieser, diese, dieses   this, this one, these
  <u>Dieser</u> junge Mann ist begabt.   This young man is talented.
  <u>Dieses</u> alte Haus ist wirklich schön.   This old house is really beautiful.

- einiger, einige, einiges   some, a few, a little
  <u>Einige</u> von uns gingen spazieren.   Some of us went for a walk.
  Wir haben <u>einiges</u> gesehen.   We saw quite a lot of things.

- jeder, jede, jedes   each, each one, every
  <u>Jeder</u> Schüler bekommt ein Zeugnis.   Every pupil receives a report.
  Sie kommt <u>jedes</u> Mal zu spät.   She arrives late every time.

- jener, jene, jenes   that, that one, those
  <u>Jener</u> Junge hatte seine Brieftasche   That boy had lost his wallet.
  verloren.

- mancher, manche, manches   many a, some
  <u>Mancher</u> Mann bleibt gern mit den   Some men like staying at home
  Kindern zu Hause.   with the children.
  <u>Manches</u> Auto fährt schneller als   Some cars can go faster than
  220 km/h.   220 km/h.

- solcher, solche, solches   such, such a
  Ein <u>solches</u> Mountainbike hätte ich   I'd really like to have a mountain
  auch gern.   bike like that too.

- welcher, welche, welches   which, which one
  <u>Welche</u> Frau hat die Stelle bekommen?   Which woman got the job?

Grammar Extra!

sämtliche and irgendwelcher also follow the same pattern as the definite article:

- sämtliche   all, entire (*usually plural*)
  Sie besitzt Tolkiens <u>sämtliche</u> Werke.   She owns the complete works of Tolkien.

- irgendwelcher, -e, -es   some or other
  Sind noch <u>irgendwelche</u> Reste da?   Are there any leftovers?

➤ The words listed above can be used as:

- articles
  <u>Dieser</u> Mann kommt aus Südamerika.   This man comes from South America.
  Sie geht <u>jeden</u> Tag ins Büro.   She goes to the office every day.

For further explanation of grammatical terms, please see pages x-xiv.

- pronouns – a pronoun is a word you use instead of a noun, when you do not need or want to name someone or something directly, for example, *it, you, none.*

Willst du <u>diesen</u>?	Do you want this one?
Man kann ja nicht <u>alles</u> wissen.	You can't know everything.
Es gibt <u>manche</u>, die keinen Alkohol mögen.	There are some people who don't like alcohol.

⇨ *For more information on* **Pronouns**, *see page 69.*

Grammar Extra!

einiger and **irgendwelcher** end in -en in the genitive before masculine or neuter nouns ending in -s.

Er musste wegziehen wegen irgendwelch<u>en</u> Geredes.	He had to move away because of some gossip.

jeder, welcher, mancher and **solcher** can also do this or can have the usual -es ending.

Das Kind solch<u>er</u> Eltern wird Probleme haben.	The child of such parents will have problems.
Trotz jed<u>en</u> Versuchs scheiterten die Verhandlungen.	Despite all attempts, the negotiations failed.

➤ **solcher, beide** and **sämtliche** can be used after another article or possessive adjective (in English, one of the words *my, your, his, her, its, our* or *their*).

Ein <u>solches</u> Rad habe ich früher auch gehabt.	I used to have a bike like that too.
Diese <u>beiden</u> Männer haben es gesehen.	Both of these men have seen it.

➤ Although **beide** generally has plural forms only, there is one singular form, **beides**. While **beide** is more common and can refer to both people and things, **beides** refers only to things. **Beide** is used for two examples of the same thing or person, while **beides** is used for two different examples.

Es gab zwei Bleistifte und er hat <u>beide</u> genommen.	There were two pencils and he took both.

BUT

Es gab einen Bleistift und ein Bild und er hat <u>beides</u> genommen.	There was one pencil and one picture and he took both.

ⓘ Note that **beides** is singular in German, whereas *both* is plural in English.

Beides <u>ist</u> richtig.	Both <u>are</u> correct.

➤ **dies** often replaces the nominative and accusative **dieses** and **diese** when it is used as a pronoun.

| Hast du <u>dies</u> schon gelesen? | Have you already read this? |
| **Dies** sind meine neuen Sachen. | These are my new things. |

⇨ *For more information on **Pronouns**, see page 69.*

➤ **alle** also has a fixed form, **all**, which is used together with other articles or possessive pronouns.

| <u>All</u> sein Mut war verschwunden. | All his courage had disappeared. |
| Was machst du mit <u>all</u> diesem Geld? | What are you doing with all this money? |

➤ **ganz** can be used to replace both **alle** and **all** and is declined like an adjective.

| Sie ist mit dem ganzen Geld verschwunden. | She disappeared with all the money. |

⇨ *For more information on **Adjectives**, see page 40.*

➤ **ganz** must be used:

- in time phrases

| Es hat den <u>ganzen</u> Tag geschneit. | It snowed all day. |

- when talking about geography

| Im <u>ganzen</u> Land gab es keinen besseren Wein. | There wasn't a better wine in the whole country. |

- with nouns referring to a collection of people or animals (*collective* nouns)

| Die <u>ganze</u> Gesellschaft war auf der Versammlung vertreten. | The entire company was represented at the meeting. |

Grammar Extra!

derjenige/diejenige/dasjenige (*the one, those*) is declined in the same way as the definite article **der** + a weak adjective.

⇨ *For more information on **Weak adjectives**, see page 42.*

Case	Masculine	Feminine	Neuter
Nominative	<u>derjenige</u> Mann	<u>diejenige</u> Frau	<u>dasjenige</u> Kind
Accusative	<u>denjenigen</u> Mann	<u>diejenige</u> Frau	<u>dasjenige</u> Kind
Genitive	<u>desjenigen</u> Mann(e)s	<u>derjenigen</u> Frau	<u>desjenigen</u> Kind(e)s
Dative	<u>demjenigen</u> Mann	<u>derjenigen</u> Frau	<u>demjenigen</u> Kind

derselbe/dieselbe/dasselbe (*the same, the same one*) is declined in the same way as **derjenige**. However, after prepositions, the shortened forms of the definite article are used for the appropriate parts of **derselbe**.

| zur selben (=zu derselben) Zeit | at the same time |
| im selben (=in demselben) Zimmer | in the same room |

⇨ *For more information on **Shortened forms of prepositions**, see page 165.*

For further explanation of grammatical terms, please see pages x-xiv.

> **Key points**
>
> ✔ There is a group of words which are declined like the definite article **der**.
>
> ✔ These words can be used as articles or pronouns.
>
> ✔ **solcher**, **beide** and **sämtliche** can be used after another article or possessive adjective.
>
> ✔ **beide** generally has plural forms only, but there is one singular form, **beides**.
>
> ✔ When it is used as a pronoun **dies** often replaces the nominative and accusative **dieses** and **diese**.
>
> ✔ **alle** also has a fixed form, **all**.
>
> ✔ **ganz** must be used instead of **alle** in certain situations.

6 The indefinite article

➤ In English we have the indefinite article *a*, which changes to *an* in front of a word that starts with a vowel. In the plural we say either *some*, *any* or nothing at all.

➤ In German the word you choose for *a* depends on whether the noun it is used with is masculine, feminine or neuter, singular or plural AND it also depends on the case of the noun.

Da ist <u>ein</u> Auto.	There's a car.
Sie hat <u>eine</u> Wohnung.	She has a flat.
Er gab es <u>einem</u> Kind.	He gave it to a child.

➤ It has no plural forms.

Computer sind in letzter Zeit teurer geworden.	Computers have become more expensive recently.

➤ The indefinite article is formed as follows.

Case	Masculine	Feminine	Neuter
Nominative	ein	eine	ein
Accusative	einen	eine	ein
Genitive	eines	einer	eines
Dative	einem	einer	einem

7 Using the indefinite article

➤ The indefinite article is used very much as in English.

Da ist <u>ein</u> Bus.	There's <u>a</u> bus.
Sie hat eine neue Jacke.	She has a new jacket.
Sie gab es <u>einer</u> alten Dame.	She gave it to <u>an</u> old lady.

➤ In certain situations, you do not use the indefinite article:

● when talking about the job someone does

| Sie ist Ärztin. | She's a doctor. |

● when talking about someone's nationality or religion

| Sie ist Deutsche. | She's (a) German. |
| Er ist Moslem. | He's (a) Muslim. |

i Note that the indefinite article IS used when an adjective comes before the noun.

| Sie ist **eine** sehr begabte Journalistin. | She's a very talented journalist. |

● in certain fixed expressions

| Es ist Geschmacksache. | It's a question of taste. |
| Tatsache ist ... | It's a fact ... |

● after **als** (meaning *as a*)

| Als Lehrerin verdiene ich nicht gut. | I don't earn very much as a teacher. |
| Als Großmutter darf ich meine Enkel verwöhnen. | As a grandmother, I'm allowed to spoil my grandchildren. |

8 The indefinite article in negative sentences

➤ In English we use words like *not* and *never* to indicate that something is not happening or is not true. The sentences that these words are used in are called negative sentences.

I don't know him.

I never do my homework on time.

➤ In German, you use a separate negative form of the indefinite article, which is formed exactly like **ein** in the singular, and also has plural forms. It means *no/not a/not one/not any*.

Case	Masculine Singular	Feminine Singular	Neuter Singular	All Genders Plural
Nominative	kein	keine	kein	keine
Accusative	keinen	keine	kein	keine
Genitive	keines	keiner	keines	keiner
Dative	keinem	keiner	keinem	keinen

Er hatte <u>keine</u> Geschwister.	He had no brothers or sisters.
Ich sehe <u>keinen</u> Unterschied.	I don't see any difference.
Das ist <u>keine</u> richtige Antwort.	That's not a correct answer.
<u>Kein</u> Mensch hat es gesehen.	Not one person has seen it.

Tip

This negative form of the indefinite article is even used when the *positive* form of the phrase has no article.

Er hatte Angst davor.	He was afraid of it.
Er hatte <u>keine</u> Angst davor.	He wasn't afraid of it.

Grammar Extra!

The negative form of the indefinite article is also used in many informal expressions.

Sie hatte <u>kein</u> Geld mehr.	All her money was gone.
Es waren <u>keine</u> drei Monate vergangen, als ...	It was less than three months later that ...
Es hat mich <u>keine</u> zehn Euro gekostet.	It cost me less than ten euros.

If you want to emphasize the **ein** in the sentence, **nicht ein** can be used instead of **kein**.

<u>Nicht ein</u> Kind hat es singen können.	Not *one* child could sing it.

➪ For more information on **Negatives**, see page 179.

Key points

✔ The indefinite article is used in German:
  - to translate the English *a* and *any* in the singular
  - in negative sentences in its separate negative form, **kein**, to translate *no*

✔ The indefinite article in German is NOT used when:
  - talking about someone's job, nationality or religion, unless an adjective is used before the noun
  - in certain set expressions or after **als** meaning *as a*

9 | Words declined like the indefinite article

➤ The following words are <u>possessive adjectives</u>, one of the words *my, your, his, her, its, our* or *their* used with a noun to show that one person or thing belongs to another. They follow the same pattern as the indefinite articles **ein** and **kein**.

mein	my
dein	your (*singular familiar*)
sein	his/its
ihr	her/its
unser	our
euer	your (*plural familiar*)
ihr	their
Ihr	your (*polite singular and plural*)

➤ Possessive adjectives are formed in the following way.

	Nominative	Accusative	Genitive	Dative
Singular	mein, meine, mein	meinen, meine, mein	meines, meiner, meines	meinem, meiner, meinem
Plural	meine	meine	meiner	meinen
Singular	dein, deine, dein	deinen, deine, dein	deines, deiner, deines	deinem, deiner, deinem
Plural	deine	deine	deiner	deinen
Singular	sein, seine, sein	seinen, seine, sein	seines, seiner, seines	seinem, seiner, seinem
Plural	seine	seine	seiner	seinen
Singular	ihr, ihre, ihr	ihren, ihre, ihr	ihres, ihrer, ihres	ihrem, ihrer, ihrem
Plural	ihre	ihre	ihrer	ihren
Singular	unser, unsere, unser	unseren, unsere, unser	unseres, unserer, unseres	unserem, unserer, unserem
Plural	unsere	unsere	unserer	unseren
Singular	euer, eu(e)re, eu(e)res	eu(e)ren, eu(e)re, eu(e)res	eu(e)res, eu(e)rer, eu(e)res	eu(e)rem, eu(e)rer, eu(e)rem
Plural	eu(e)re	eu(e)re	eu(e)rer	eu(e)ren
Singular	ihr, ihre, ihr	ihren, ihre, ihr	ihres, ihrer, ihres	ihrem, ihrer, ihrem
Plural	ihre	ihre	ihrer	ihren
Singular	Ihr, Ihre, Ihr	Ihren, Ihre, Ihr	Ihres, Ihrer, Ihres	Ihrem, Ihrer, Ihrem
Plural	Ihre	Ihre	Ihrer	Ihren

For further explanation of grammatical terms, please see pages x-xiv.

Mein kleiner Bruder will auch mitkommen.	My little brother wants to come too.
Wo steht dein altes Auto?	Where is your old car?
Er spielt Fußball mit seiner Tante.	He is playing football with his aunt.
Was ist mit ihrem Computer los?	What is wrong with her computer?
Ihre Kinder sind wirklich verwöhnt.	Their children are really spoiled.
Wie geht es Ihrer Schwester?	How is your sister?
Ich will meine Kinder regelmäßig sehen.	I want to see my children regularly.

Grammar Extra!

Possessive adjectives are often followed by other adjectives in German sentences. These adjectives then have the same endings as the indefinite article.

Er liebt sein altes Auto.	He loves his old car.
Sie hat ihren neuen Computer verkauft.	She sold her new computer.
Wo ist deine rote Jacke?	Where is your red jacket?

irgendein (meaning some ... or other) and its plural form irgendwelche also take these endings.

Er ist irgendein bekannter Schauspieler.	He's some famous actor or other.
Sie ist nur irgendeine alte Frau.	She's just some old woman or other.
Sie hat irgendein neues Buch gekauft.	She bought some new book or other.
Ich muss irgendwelche blöden Touristen herumführen.	I have to show some stupid tourists or other round.

Key point

✔ Possessive adjectives, one of the words my, your, his, her, its, our or their, are declined like the indefinite articles ein and kein.

ADJECTIVES

> **What is an adjective?**
> An **adjective** is a 'describing' word that tells you more about a person or thing, such as their appearance, colour, size or other qualities, for example, *pretty, blue, big*.

Using adjectives

➤ Adjectives are words like *clever*, *expensive* and *silly* that tell you more about a noun (a living being, thing or idea). They can also tell you more about a pronoun, such as *he* or *they*. Adjectives are sometimes called 'describing words'. They can be used right next to a noun they are describing, or can be separated from the noun by a verb like *be*, *look*, *feel* and so on.

> a <u>clever</u> girl
> an <u>expensive</u> coat
> a <u>silly</u> idea
> He's just being <u>silly</u>.

➪ For more information on **Nouns** and **Pronouns**, see pages 1 and 69.

➤ In English, the only time an adjective changes its form is when you are making a comparison.

> She's <u>cleverer</u> than her brother.
> That's the <u>silliest</u> idea I ever heard!

➤ In German, however, adjectives usually <u>agree</u> with what they are describing. This means that their endings change depending on whether the person or thing you are referring to is masculine, feminine or neuter, and singular or plural. It also depends on the case of the person or thing you are describing and whether it is preceded by the definite or indefinite article.

> **Das neue Buch ist da.**   The new book has arrived.
>
> **Ich wollte es der alten Frau geben.**   I wanted to give it to the old woman.
>
> **Sie erzählte mir eine langweilige Geschichte.**   She told me a boring story.
>
> **Die deutschen Traditionen**   German traditions

➪ For more information on **Cases** and **Articles**, see pages 9 and 25.

For further explanation of grammatical terms, please see pages x-xiv.

➤ As in English, German adjectives come <u>BEFORE</u> the noun they describe, but <u>AFTER</u> the verb in the sentence. The only time the adjective does not agree with the word it describes is when it comes <u>AFTER</u> the verb.

eine <u>schwarze</u> Katze	a <u>black</u> cat
Das Buch ist <u>neu</u>.	The book is <u>new</u>.

Key points

✔ Most German adjectives change their form according to the case of the noun they are describing and whether the noun is masculine, feminine or neuter, singular or plural.

✔ In German, the only time the adjective does not agree with the word it describes is when it comes <u>AFTER</u> the verb.

Making adjectives agree

1 The basic rules

➤ In dictionaries, only the basic form of German adjectives is shown. You need to know how to change it to make it agree with the noun or pronoun the adjective describes.

➤ To make an adjective agree with the noun or pronoun it describes, you simply add one of three sets of different endings:

2 The Weak Declension

➤ The endings used after the definite articles der, die and das and other words declined like them are shown below.

Case	Masculine Singular	Feminine Singular	Neuter Singular	All Genders Plural
Nominative	-e	-e	-e	-en
Accusative	-en	-e	-e	-en
Genitive	-en	-en	-en	-en
Dative	-en	-en	-en	-en

➤ The following table shows you how these different endings are added to the adjective alt, meaning *old*, when it is used with the definite article.

Case	Masculine Singular	Feminine Singular	Neuter Singular
Nominative	der alte Mann	die alte Frau	das alte Haus
Accusative	den alten Mann	die alte Frau	das alte Haus
Genitive	des alten Mann(e)s	der alten Frau	des alten Hauses
Dative	dem alten Mann	der alten Frau	dem alten Haus

Nominative:
> **Der alte Mann wohnt nebenan.** | The old man lives next door.

Accusative:
> **Ich habe die alte Frau in der Bibliothek gesehen.** | I saw the old woman in the library.

Genitive:
> **Die Besitzerin des alten Hauses ist ganz reich.** | The owner of the old house is very rich.

Dative:
> **Er hilft dem alten Mann beim Einkaufen.** | He helps the old man to do his shopping.

For further explanation of grammatical terms, please see pages x-xiv.

➤ These are the plural endings of adjectives in the weak declension.

Plural	All Genders
Nominative	die alten Männer/Frauen/Häuser
Accusative	die alten Männer/Frauen/Häuser
Genitive	der alten Männer/Frauen/Häuser
Dative	den alten Männern/Frauen/Häusern

3 The Mixed Declension

➤ The endings used after **ein, kein, irgendein** and the possessive adjectives are shown below.

i Note that this declension differs from the weak declension only in the three forms underlined below.

Case	Masculine Singular	Feminine Singular	Neuter Singular	All Genders Plural
Nominative	-er	-e	-es	-en
Accusative	-en	-e	-es	-en
Genitive	-en	-en	-en	-en
Dative	-en	-en	-en	-en

➪ For more information on the **Possessive adjectives**, see page 37.

➤ The following table shows you how these different endings are added to the adjective **lang**, meaning *long*.

Case	Masculine Singular	Feminine Singular	Neuter Singular
Nominative	ein langer Weg	eine lange Reise	ein langes Spiel
Accusative	einen langen Weg	eine lange Reise	ein langes Spiel
Genitive	eines langen Weg(e)s	einer langen Reise	eines langen Spiel(e)s
Dative	einem langen Weg	einer langen Reise	einem langen Spiel

Nominative:

Eine lange Reise muss geplant werden.   You have to plan a long trip.

Accusative:

Ich habe einen langen Weg nach Hause.   It takes me a long time to get home.

Genitive:

Die vielen Nachteile einer langen Reise ...   The many disadvantages of a long journey ...

Dative:

Bei einem langen Spiel kann man sich langweilen.   You can get bored with a long game.

➤ These are the plural endings of adjectives when they have a mixed declension.

Plural	All Genders
Nominative	ihre langen Wege/Reisen/Spiele
Accusative	ihre langen Wege/Reisen/Spiele
Genitive	ihrer langen Wege/Reisen/Spiele
Dative	ihren langen Wegen/Reisen/Spielen

4 The Strong Declension

➤ The endings used when there is no article before the noun are shown below.

Case	Masculine Singular	Feminine Singular	Neuter Singular	All Genders Plural
Nominative	-er	-e	-es	-e
Accusative	-en	-e	-es	-e
Genitive	-en	-er	-en	-er
Dative	-em	-er	-em	-en

➤ The following table shows you how these different endings are added to the adjective **gut**, meaning *good*.

Case	Masculine Singular	Feminine Singular	Neuter Singular
Nominative	guter Käse	gute Marmelade	gutes Bier
Accusative	guten Käse	gute Marmelade	gutes Bier
Genitive	guten Käses	guter Marmelade	guten Bier(e)s
Dative	gutem Käse	guter Marmelade	gutem Bier

For further explanation of grammatical terms, please see pages x-xiv.

Nominative:

Gutes Bier ist sehr wichtig auf
einer Party.

Good beer is very important at
a party.

Accusative:

Wo finde ich guten Käse?

Where will I get good cheese?

Genitive:

Das ist ein Zeichen guter Marmelade.

That is a sign of good jam.

Dative:

Zu gutem Käse braucht man auch
Oliven.

You need olives to go with good
cheese.

➤ These are the plural endings of adjectives when they have a strong declension.

ℹ️ Note that the plural form of Käse is normally Käsesorten.

Plural	All Genders
Nominative	gute Käsesorten/Marmeladen/Biere
Accusative	gute Käsesorten/Marmeladen/Biere
Genitive	guter Käsesorten/Marmeladen/Biere
Dative	guten Käsesorten/Marmeladen/Bieren

ℹ️ Note that these endings allow the adjective to do the work of the missing article by showing the case of the noun and whether it is singular or plural, masculine, feminine or neuter.

➤ The article is omitted more often in German than in English, especially where you have *preposition + adjective + noun* combinations.

Nach kurzer Fahrt kamen wir in
Glasgow an.

After a short journey we arrived
in Glasgow.

Mit gleichem Gehalt wie du würde
ich mir einen Urlaub leisten können.

I'd be able to afford a holiday on the
same salary as you.

➤ These strong declension endings are also used after any of the following words when the noun they refer to is not preceded by an article.

Word	Meaning
ein bisschen	a little, a bit of
ein wenig	a little
ein paar	a few, a couple
weniger	fewer, less
einige (*plural forms only*)	some
etwas	some, any (*singular*)
mehr	more
lauter	nothing but, sheer, pure
solch	such
was für	what, what kind of
viel	much, many, a lot of
welch ...!	what ...! what a ...!
manch	many a
wenig	little, few, not much
zwei, drei *etc*	two, three *etc*

Morgen hätte ich ein wenig freie Zeit für dich.	I could spare you some time tomorrow.
Sie hat mir ein paar gute Tipps gegeben.	She gave me a few good tips.
Er isst weniger frisches Obst als ich.	He eats less fresh fruit than me.
Heutzutage wollen mehr junge Frauen Ingenieurin werden.	Nowadays, more young women want to be engineers.
Solche leckere Schokolade habe ich schon lange nicht mehr gegessen.	I haven't had such good chocolate for a long time.
Wir haben viel kostbare Zeit verschwendet.	We have wasted a lot of valuable time.
Welch herrliches Wetter!	What wonderful weather!

➤ With **wenig** and numbers from **zwei** onwards, adjectives behave as follows:

- Strong, when there is no article:

Es gab damals nur wenig frisch<u>es</u> Obst.	There was little fresh fruit at that time.
Zwei klein<u>e</u> Jungen kamen die Straße entlang.	Two small boys came along the street.

- Weak, when the definite article comes first:

<u>Das</u> **wenige frisch<u>e</u> Obst, das es damals gab, war teuer.**	The little fresh fruit that was available then, was expensive.
<u>Die</u> **zwei klein<u>en</u> Jungen, die die Straße entlangkamen.**	The two small boys who came along the street.

- Mixed, when a possessive adjective comes first:

<u>Meine</u> **zwei klein<u>en</u> Jungen sind manchmal frech.**	My two small sons are cheeky sometimes.

➤ These strong declension endings also need to be used after possessives where no other word shows the case of the following noun and whether it's masculine, feminine or neuter, singular or plural.

Sebastians alt<u>es</u> Buch lag auf dem Tisch.	Sebastian's old book was lying on the table.
Mutters neu<u>er</u> Computer sieht toll aus.	Mother's new computer looks great.

Tip

When these various endings are added to adjectives, you have to watch out for some spelling changes.

When endings are added to the adjective **hoch**, meaning *high*, the simple form changes to **hoh**.

Das Gebäude ist hoch.	The building is high.
Das ist ein hohes Gebäude.	That is a high building.

Adjectives ending in **-el** lose the **-e** when endings are added.

Das Zimmer ist dunkel.	The room is dark.
Man sieht nichts in dem dunklen Zimmer.	You can't see anything in the dark room.

Adjectives ending in **-er** often lose the **-e** when endings are added.

Das Auto war teuer.	The car was expensive.
Sie kaufte ein teures Auto.	She bought an expensive car.

> **Key points**
>
> ✔ To make an adjective agree with the noun it is describing, you simply add one of three sets of endings: weak, mixed or strong.
>
> ✔ Strong endings are also used after particular words when not preceded by an article, for example, **ein bisschen**, **ein paar**, **wenig**, and after possessive adjectives.

5 Participles as adjectives

➤ In English, the present participle is a verb form ending in *-ing*, which may be used as an adjective or a noun. In German, you simply add **-d** to the infinitive of the verb to form the present participle, which may then be used as an adjective with all the usual endings.

Auf dem Tisch stand ein Foto von einem <u>lachenden</u> Kind.	There was a photo of a laughing child on the table.

ⓘ Note that the present participles of **sein** and **haben** cannot be used like this.

➤ The past participle of a verb can also be used as an adjective.

Meine Mutter hat meine <u>verlorenen</u> Sachen gefunden.	My mother found my lost things.

⇨ *For more information on **Past participles**, see page 113.*

6 Adjectives preceded by the dative case

➤ With many adjectives you use the dative case, for example:

- **ähnlich**   similar to
  Er ist seinem Vater sehr ähnlich.   He's very like his father.

- **bekannt**   familiar to
  Sie kommt mir bekannt vor.   She seems familiar to me.

- **dankbar**   grateful to
  Ich bin dir sehr dankbar.   I'm very grateful to you.

- **fremd**   strange, alien to
  Das ist mir fremd.   That's alien to me.

- **gleich**   all the same to/like
  Es ist mir gleich.   It's all the same to me.

- leicht   easy for
  Du machst es dir wirklich zu leicht.   You really make things too easy for yourself.

- nah(e)   close to
  Unser Haus ist nahe der Universität.   Our house is near the university.

- peinlich   embarrassing for
  Das war ihr aber peinlich.   She was really embarrassed.

- unbekannt   unknown to
  Das war mir unbekannt.   I didn't know that.

Key points

✔ In German, both present and past participles can also be used as adjectives.

✔ With many German adjectives you use the dative case.

Adjectives used as nouns

➤ All adjectives in German, and participles used as adjectives, can also be used as nouns. These are often called <u>adjectival nouns</u>.

➤ Adjectives and participles used as nouns have:

- a capital letter like other nouns

Der neue Angestellte ist früh angekommen.	The new employee arrived early.

- weak, strong or mixed endings, depending on which article, if any, comes before them

Sie ist die neue Angestellte.	She is the new employee.
Das Gute daran ist, dass ich mehr verdiene.	The good thing about it is that I'm earning more.
Es bleibt beim Alten.	Things remain as they were.

Key points

✔ Adjectives in German, and participles used as adjectives, can also be used as nouns. These are often called <u>adjectival nouns</u>.

✔ <u>Adjectival nouns</u> begin with a capital letter and take the same endings as normal adjectives.

Some other points about adjectives

1 Adjectives describing nationality

➤ These are not spelt with a capital letter in German except in public or official names.

Die deutsche Sprache ist schön.	The German language is beautiful.
Das französische Volk war entsetzt.	The people of France were horrified.

BUT:

Die Deutsche Bahn hat Erfolg.	The German railways are successful.

➤ However, when these adjectives are used as nouns to refer to a language, a capital letter is used.

Sie sprechen kein Englisch.	They don't speak English.

➤ In German, for expressions like *he is English/he is German etc* a noun or adjectival noun is used instead of an adjective.

Er ist Deutscher.	He is German.
Sie ist Deutsche.	She is German.

2 Adjectives taken from place names

➤ These are formed by adding -er to names of towns. They never change by adding endings to show case.

Kölner, Frankfurter, Berliner *etc*	from Cologne, Frankfurt, Berlin *etc*
Der Kölner Dom ist wirklich beeindruckend.	Cologne cathedral is really impressive.
Ich möchte ein Frankfurter Würstchen.	I'd like a frankfurter sausage.

➤ Adjectives from die Schweiz, meaning Switzerland, and some other regions can also be formed in this way.

Schweizer Käse mag ich gern.	I really like Swiss cheese.

➤ Adjectives like these can be used as nouns denoting the inhabitants of a town, in which case they take the same endings as normal nouns.

Die Sprache des Kölners heißt Kölsch.	People from Cologne speak Kölsch.
Die Entscheidung wurde von den Frankfurtern begrüsst.	People from Frankfurt welcomed the decision.

📖 Note that the feminine form of such nouns is formed by adding -in in the singular and -innen in the plural.

Christine, die Londonerin war, wollte nach Glasgow ziehen.	Christine, who was from London, wanted to move to Glasgow.

Key points

✔ Adjectives describing nationality are not spelt with a capital letter in German except in public or official names, BUT when they are used as nouns to refer to a language, they do have a capital letter.

✔ Adjectives taken from place names are formed by adding -er to the name of the town and never change by adding endings to show case.

✔ They can also be used as nouns denoting the inhabitants of a place.

Comparatives of adjectives

What is a comparative adjective?

A **comparative adjective** in English is one with -er added to it or more or less in front of it, that is used to compare people or things, for example, *slower, more beautiful*.

➤ In German, to say that something is *easier, more expensive* and so on, you add **-er** to the simple form of most adjectives.

> einfach → einfach<u>er</u>
> Das war viel einfacher für dich.   That was much easier for you.

[i] Note that adjectives whose simple form ends in **-en** or **-er** may drop the final **-e** to form the comparative, as in **teurer**.

> teuer → teurer
> Diese Jacke ist teur<u>er</u>.   This jacket is more expensive.

➤ To introduce the person or thing you are making the comparison with, use **als** (meaning *than*).

> Er ist kleiner <u>als</u> seine Schwester.   He is smaller than his sister.
> Diese Frage ist einfacher <u>als</u> die   This question is easier than the
> erste.   first one.

➤ To say that something or someone is *as … as* something or someone else, you use **so … wie** or **genauso … wie**, if you want to make it more emphatic. To say *not as … as*, you use **nicht so … wie**.

> Sie ist <u>so</u> gut <u>wie</u> ihr Bruder.   She is as good as her brother.
> Er war <u>genauso</u> glücklich <u>wie</u> ich.   He was just as happy as I was.
> Sie ist <u>nicht so</u> alt <u>wie</u> du.   She is not as old as you.

➤ Here are some examples of commonly used adjectives which have a vowel change in the comparative form:

Adjective	Meaning	Comparative	Meaning
alt	old	älter	older
stark	strong	stärker	stronger
schwach	weak	schwächer	weaker
scharf	sharp	schärfer	sharper
lang	long	länger	longer
kurz	short	kürzer	shorter
warm	warm	wärmer	warmer
kalt	cold	kälter	colder
hart	hard	härter	harder
groß	big	größer	bigger

➤ Adjectives whose simple form ends in **-el** lose the **-e** before adding the comparative ending **-er**.

eitel → eitler		vain → vainer
Er ist eitl<u>er</u> als ich.		He is vainer than me.
dunkel → dunkler		dark → darker
Deine Haare sind dunkl<u>er</u> als ihre.		Your hair is darker than hers.

➤ When used before the noun, comparative forms of adjectives take the same weak, strong or mixed endings as their simple forms.

Die jünger<u>e</u> Schwester ist größer als die ältere.	The younger sister is bigger than the older one.
Mein jünger<u>er</u> Bruder geht jetzt zur Schule.	My younger brother goes to school now.

⇨ For more information on **Making adjectives agree**, see pages 42-48.

Grammar Extra!

➤ With a few adjectives, comparative forms may also be used to translate the idea of -ish or rather.

Comparative	Meaning
älter	elderly
dünner	thinnish
dicker	fattish
größer	largish
jünger	youngish
kleiner	smallish
kürzer	shortish
neuer	newish

Eine ältere Frau kam die Straße entlang.	An elderly woman was coming along the street.
Er war von jüngerem Aussehen.	He was of youngish appearance.

Key points

✔ In German, to form the comparative you add -er to the simple form of most adjectives.

✔ To compare people or things in German, you use so ... wie, genauso ... wie, if you want to make it more emphatic, or nicht so ... wie.

✔ *Than* in comparatives corresponds to als.

✔ There is a change in the vowel in many of the simple forms of German adjectives when forming their comparatives.

✔ Adjectives whose simple form ends in -el, such as dunkel, lose the -e before adding the comparative ending -er.

For further explanation of grammatical terms, please see pages x-xiv.

Superlatives of adjectives

What is a superlative adjective?
A **superlative adjective** in English is one with -est on the end of it or *most* or *least* in front of it, that is used to compare people or things, for example, *thinnest, most beautiful*.

➤ In German, to say that something or someone is *easiest, youngest, most expensive* and so on, you add -st to the simple form of the adjective. As with comparative forms, the vowel in the simple form can change. Superlative forms are generally used with the definite article and take the same weak endings as their simple forms.

Deine Hausaufgaben waren die einfachsten.	Your homework was easiest.
Sie ist die Jüngste in der Familie.	She is the youngest in the family.
Ich wollte die teuerste Jacke im Laden kaufen.	I wanted to buy the most expensive jacket in the shop.

➤ Adjectives ending in -t, -tz, -z, -sch, -ss or -ß form the superlative by adding -est instead of -st.

der/die/das schlechteste	the worst
Das war der schlechteste Film seit Jahren.	That was the worst film in years.
der/die/das schmerzhafteste	the most painful
Das war ihre schmerzhafteste Verletzung.	That was her most painful injury.
der/die/das süßeste	the sweetest
Ich möchte den süßesten Nachtisch.	I would like the sweetest dessert.
der/die/das stolzeste	the proudest
Sie war die stolzeste Mutter in der Gegend.	She was the proudest mother in the area.
der/die/das frischeste	the freshest
Für dieses Rezept braucht man das frischeste Obst.	You need the freshest fruit for this recipe.

➤ Adjectives ending in -eu and -au also add -est to form the superlative.

der/die/das neueste	the newest, the latest
Ich brauche die neueste Ausgabe des Wörterbuchs.	I need the latest edition of the dictionary.
der/die/das schlaueste	the cleverest
Sie ist die schlaueste Schülerin in der Klasse.	She is the cleverest student in the class.

➤ The English superlative *most*, meaning *very*, can be expressed in German by any of the following words.

Superlative	Meaning
äußerst	extremely
sehr	very
besonders	especially
außerordentlich	exceptionally
höchst	extremely (*not used with words of one syllable*)
furchtbar	terribly (*used only in conversation*)
richtig	really/most (*used only in conversation*)

Sie ist ein äußerst begabter Mensch.	She is a most gifted person.
Das Essen war besonders schlecht.	The food was really dreadful.
Der Wein war furchtbar teuer.	The wine was terribly expensive.
Das sieht richtig komisch aus.	That looks really funny.

Tip

Just as English has some irregular comparative and superlative forms – *better* instead of '*more good*', and *worst* instead of '*most bad*' – German also has a few irregular forms.

Adjective	Meaning	Comparative	Meaning	Superlative	Meaning
gut	good	besser	better	der beste	the best
hoch	high	höher	higher	der höchste	the highest
viel	much/a lot	mehr	more	der meiste	the most
nah	near	näher	nearer	der nächste	the nearest

Ich habe eine bessere Idee.	I have a better idea.
Wo liegt der nächste Bahnhof?	Where is the nearest station?

Key points

✔ Most German superlatives are formed by adding **-st** to the simple form of the adjective.

✔ Adjectives ending in **-t, -tz, -z, -sch, -ss, -ß, -eu** or **-au** form the superlative by adding **-est** instead of **-st**.

✔ **Gut, hoch, viel** and **nah** have irregular comparative and superlative forms: **gut/besser/der beste, hoch/höher/der höchste, viel/mehr/ der meiste, nah/näher/der nächste**.

For further explanation of grammatical terms, please see pages x–xiv.

(ADVERBS)

> **What is an adverb?**
> An **adverb** is a word usually used with verbs, adjectives or other adverbs that
> gives more information about when, how, where or in what circumstances
> something happens: *quickly, happily, now* are all adverbs.

How adverbs are used

➤ In general, adverbs are used together with:

- verbs (*act quickly, speak strangely, smile cheerfully*)
- adjectives (*rather ill, a lot better, deeply sorry*)
- other adverbs (*really fast, too quickly, very well*)

➤ Adverbs can also relate to the whole sentence; they often tell you what the
speaker is thinking or feeling.

> Fortunately, Jan had already left.
> Actually, I don't think I'll come.

How adverbs are formed

The basic rules

➤ Many English adverbs end in -ly, which is added to the end of the adjective (*quick*
→ *quickly*; *sad* → *sadly*; *frequent* → *frequently*).

➤ In contrast, most German adverbs used to comment on verbs are simply
adjectives used as adverbs. And the good news is that unlike adjectives, they do
not change by adding different endings.

> **Habe ich das richtig gehört?**   Did I hear that correctly?
> **Er war schick angezogen.**   He was stylishly dressed.

➤ A small number of German adverbs which do not directly comment on the verb
are formed by adding **-weise** or **-sweise** to a noun.

Noun	Meaning	Adverb	Meaning
das Beispiel	example	beispielsweise	for example
die Beziehung	relation, connection	beziehungsweise	or/or rather/ that is to say
der Schritt	step	schrittweise	step by step
die Zeit	time	zeitweise	at times
der Zwang	compulsion	zwangsweise	compulsorily

Grammar Extra!

Some German adverbs are also formed by adding -erweise to an uninflected adjective. These adverbs are mainly used by the person speaking to express an opinion.

Adjective	Meaning	Adverb	Meaning
erstaunlich	astonishing	erstaunlicherweise	astonishingly enough
glücklich	happy, fortunate	glücklicherweise	fortunately
komisch	strange, funny	komischerweise	strangely enough

➤ There is another important group of adverbs which are NOT formed from adjectives or nouns, for example, words like unten, oben and leider.

> Das beste Buch lag <u>unten</u> auf dem Stapel.
> The best book was at the bottom of the pile.
>
> Die Schlafzimmer sind <u>oben</u>.
> The bedrooms are upstairs.
>
> Ich kann <u>leider</u> nicht kommen.
> Unfortunately I can't come.

➤ Adverbs of time fit into this category and the following are some common ones.

Adverb of time	Meaning
endlich	finally
heute	today
immer	always
morgen	tomorrow
morgens	in the mornings
sofort	at once

> Sie kann erst <u>morgen</u> kommen.
> She can't come till tomorrow.
>
> Priska hat <u>immer</u> Hunger.
> Priska is always hungry.
>
> Ja, ich mache das <u>sofort</u>.
> Yes, I'll do it at once.

For further explanation of grammatical terms, please see pages x-xiv.

➤ Adverbs often express the idea of 'to what extent', for example, words in English like *extremely* and *especially*. These are sometimes called adverbs of degree. Some common adverbs of this type in German are:

Adverb of degree	Meaning
äußerst	extremely
besonders	especially
beträchtlich	considerably
fast	almost
kaum	hardly, scarcely
ziemlich	fairly

Es hat mir nicht <u>besonders</u> gefallen.	I didn't particularly like it.
Ich bin <u>fast</u> fertig.	I'm almost finished.
Er war <u>ziemlich</u> sauer.	He was quite angry.

Adverbs of place

➤ Adverbs of place are words such as *where?*, *there*, *up*, *nowhere*. German adverbs of place behave very differently from their English counterparts.

- where there is no movement involved and the adverb is simply referring to a location, you use the form of the adverb you find in the dictionary.

<u>Wo</u> ist sie?	Where is she?
Sie sind nicht <u>da</u>.	They're not there.
<u>Hier</u> darf man nicht parken.	You can't park here.

- to show some movement AWAY from the person speaking, you use the adverb **hin**.

Oliver und Andrea geben heute eine Party. Gehen wir <u>hin</u>?	Oliver and Andrea are having a party today. Shall we go?

In German, **hin** is often added to another adverb to create what are called compound adverbs, which show there is some movement involved. In English, we would just use adverbs in this case.

Compound adverb	Meaning
dahin	(to) there
dorthin	there
hierhin	here
irgendwohin	(to) somewhere or other
überallhin	everywhere
wohin?	where (to)?

<u>Wohin</u> fährst du?	Where are you going?
Sie liefen <u>überallhin</u>.	They ran everywhere.

- To show some movement TOWARDS the person speaking, you use the adverb **her**. As with **hin**, this is often added to another adverb.

Compound adverb	Meaning
daher	from there
hierher	here
irgendwoher	from somewhere or other
überallher	from all over
woher?	where from?

<u>Woher</u> kommst du?	Where do you come from?
<u>Woher</u> hast du das?	Where did you get that from?
Das habe ich <u>irgendwoher</u> gekriegt.	I got that from somewhere or other.

For further explanation of grammatical terms, please see pages x-xiv.

Key points

✔ Many German adverbs are simply adjectives used as adverbs, but they are not declined, unlike adjectives.

✔ In German, some adverbs are formed by adding **-weise** or **-sweise** to a noun.

✔ Compound adverbs formed by adding **hin** or **her** are often used to show movement away from or towards the person speaking (or writing).

Comparatives and superlatives of adverbs

1 Comparative adverbs

> **What is a comparative adverb?**
> A **comparative adverb** is one which, in English, has -er on the end of it or *more* or *less* in front of it, for example, *earlier, later, sooner, more/less frequently.*

➤ Adverbs can be used to make comparisons in German, just as they can in English. The comparative of adverbs is formed in exactly the same way as that of adjectives, that is by adding **-er** to the basic form. **Als** is used for *than*.

Sie läuft schnell<u>er</u> als ihr Bruder.	She runs faster than her brother.
Ich sehe ihn selten<u>er</u> als früher.	I see him less often than before.

➤ To make *as ... as* or *not as ... as* comparisons with adverbs, you use the same phrases as with adjectives.

- **so ... wie**   as ... as

  Er läuft <u>so</u> schnell <u>wie</u> sein Bruder.   He runs as fast as his brother.

- **nicht so ... wie**   not as ... as

  Sie kann <u>nicht so</u> gut schwimmen <u>wie</u> du.   She can't swim as well as you.

➤ The idea of *more and more ...* is expressed in German by using **immer** and the comparative form.

Die Männer sprachen <u>immer</u> lauter.	The men were talking louder and louder.

➤ *the more ... the more ...* is expressed in German by **je ... desto ...** or **je ... umso ...**

<u>Je</u> eher, <u>desto</u> besser.	The sooner the better.
<u>Je</u> schneller sie fährt, <u>umso</u> mehr Angst habe ich!	The faster she drives, the more frightened I am!

⇨ For more information on **Comparatives of adjectives**, see page 53.

2 | Superlative adverbs

> **What is a superlative adverb?**
> A **superlative adverb** is one which, in English, has -est on the end of it or most or least in front of it, for example, soonest, fastest, most/least frequently.

➤ The superlative of adverbs in German is formed in the following way and, unlike adjectives, is not declined:

am + adverb + -sten	
Wer von ihnen arbeitet **am schnellsten?**	Which of them works fastest?
Er hat es **am langsamsten** gemacht.	He did it slowest.

➤ Adverbs ending in -d, -t, -tz, -z, -sch, -ss, or -ß form the superlative by adding -esten. This makes pronunciation easier.

Das Erdbeereis war bei den Kindern **am beliebtesten.**	The strawberry ice cream was the most popular one with the kids.
Am heißesten war es in Südspanien.	It was hottest in southern Spain.

⟶ For more information on **Superlatives of adjectives**, see page 55.

i Note that some superlative adverbs are used to show the extent of a quality rather than a comparison. The following adverbs are used in this way:

Adverb	Meaning
bestens	very well
höchstens	at the most/at best
meistens	mostly/most often
spätestens	at the latest
wenigstens	at least

Die Geschäfte gehen **bestens.**	Business is going very well.
Er kommt **meistens** zu spät an.	He usually arrives late.
Wenigstens bekomme ich mehr Geld dafür.	At least I'm getting more money for it.

3 Adverbs with irregular comparatives and superlatives

➤ A few German adverbs have irregular comparative and superlative forms.

Adverb	Meaning	Comparative	Meaning	Superlative	Meaning
gern	well	**lieber**	better	**am liebsten**	best
bald	soon	**eher**	sooner	**am ehesten**	soonest
viel	much, a lot	**mehr**	more	**am meisten**	most

Am liebsten lese ich Kriminalromane.   I like detective stories best.
Sie hat <u>am meisten</u> gewonnen.   She won the most.

Key points

✔ Comparatives of adverbs are formed in the same way as comparatives of adjectives, adding **-er** to the basic form.

✔ To compare people or things, you use **so ... wie**, **ebenso ... wie** or **nicht so ... wie**.

✔ *Than* in comparatives of adverbs corresponds to **als**.

✔ Superlatives of adverbs are formed by using the formula **am** + *adverb* + **-sten/-esten**.

✔ Unlike adjectives, adverbs do not change their form to agree with the verb, adjective or other adverb they relate to.

Word order with adverbs

➤ In English, adverbs can come in different places in a sentence.

I'm <u>never</u> coming back.

See you <u>soon</u>!

<u>Suddenly</u> the phone rang.

I'd <u>really</u> like to come.

➤ This is also true of adverbs in German, but as a general rule they are placed close to the word to which they refer.

● Adverbs of <u>time</u> often come first in the sentence, but this is not fixed.

<u>Morgen</u> gehen wir ins Theater OR	
Wir gehen <u>morgen</u> ins Theater.	We're going to the theatre tomorrow.

● Adverbs of <u>place</u> can be put at the beginning of a sentence to provide emphasis.

<u>Dort</u> haben sie Fußball gespielt OR	
Sie haben <u>dort</u> Fußball gespielt	They played football there.

● Adverbs of <u>manner</u> are adverbs which comment on verbs. These are likely to come <u>after</u> the verb to which they refer, but in tenses which are made up of **haben** or **sein** + the past participle of the main verb, they come immediately <u>before</u> the past participle.

Sie spielen <u>gut</u>.	They play well.
Sie haben heute <u>gut</u> gespielt.	They played well today.
Du benimmst dich immer <u>schlecht</u>.	You always behave badly.
Du hast dich <u>schlecht</u> benommen.	You have behaved badly.

⇨ For more information on **Forming the past participle**, see page 114.

➤ Where there is more than one adverb in a sentence, it's useful to remember the following rule:

'time, manner, place'

Wir haben <u>gestern gut dorthin</u> gefunden.	We found our way there all right yesterday.

gestern = adverb of time

gut = adverb of manner

dorthin = adverb of place

➤ Where there is a pronoun object (a word like *her, it, me* or *them*) in a sentence, it comes before all adverbs.

> **Sie haben <u>es gestern sehr billig</u> gekauft.**
>
> They bought it very cheaply yesterday.
>
> **es** = pronoun object
> **gestern** = adverb of time
> **billig** = adverb of manner

⇨ *For more information on **using direct object pronouns**, see page 74.*

Key points

✔ In German, the position of adverbs in a sentence is not fixed, but they generally come close to the words they refer to.

✔ Where there is more than one adverb in a sentence, it is useful to remember the rule: time, manner, place.

✔ Where there is a pronoun object in a sentence, it comes before all adverbs.

Emphasizers

What is an emphasizer?
An **emphasizer** is a type of word commonly used in both German and English, especially in the spoken language, to emphasize or change the meaning of a sentence.

➤ The following words are the most common emphasizers.

- **aber** is used to add emphasis to a statement

Das ist <u>aber</u> schön!	Oh, that's pretty!
Diese Jacke ist <u>aber</u> teuer!	This jacket is really expensive!

- **denn** is also used as a conjunction, but here it is used as an adverb to emphasize the meaning.

Was ist <u>denn</u> hier los?	What's going on here then?
Wo <u>denn</u>?	Where?

Tip

You can't always translate emphasizers directly, especially **denn** and **aber**.

⇨ *For more information on **Conjunctions**, see page 168.*

- **doch** is used in one of three ways

As a positive reply to a negative statement or question:

Hat es dir nicht gefallen? – <u>Doch</u>!	Didn't you like it? – Oh yes, I did!

To strengthen an imperative, that is the form of a verb used when giving instructions:

Lass ihn <u>doch</u>!	Just leave him.

To make a question out of a statement:

Das schaffst du <u>doch</u>?	You'll manage it, won't you?

⇨ *For more information on **Imperatives**, see page 105.*

- **mal** can be used in one of two ways

With imperatives:

Komm <u>mal</u> her!	Come here!
Moment <u>mal</u>, bitte!	Just a minute!

In informal language:

Mal sehen.	We'll see.
Hören Sie mal ...	Look here now ...
Er soll es nur mal versuchen!	Just let him try it!

- **ja** can also be used in one of two ways

To strengthen a statement:

Er sieht ja wie seine Mutter aus.	He looks like his mother.
Das kann ja sein.	That may well be.

In informal language:

Ja und?	So what?/What then?
Das ist ja lächerlich.	That's ridiculous.
Das ist es ja.	That's just it.

- **schon** also has more than one use

It is used informally with an imperative:

Mach schon!	Get on with it!

It is also used in other informal statements:

Da kommt sie schon wieder!	Here she comes again!
Schon gut. Ich habe verstanden.	Okay, I get the message.

Key points

✔ There are lots of little adverbs used in both English and German to emphasize the meaning of a sentence in some way.

✔ The most common of these are **aber**, **denn**, **doch**, **mal**, **ja** and **schon**.

PRONOUNS

What is a pronoun?
A **pronoun** is a word you use instead of a noun, when you do not need or want to name someone or something directly, for example, *it, you, none.*

➤ There are several different types of pronoun:

- <u>personal pronouns</u> such as *I, you, he, her* and *they*, which are used to refer to yourself, the person you are talking to, or other people and things. They can be either <u>subject pronouns</u> (*I, you, he* and so on) or <u>object pronouns</u> (*him, her, them* and so on).

- <u>possessive pronouns</u> like *mine* and *yours*, which show who someone or something belongs to.

- <u>indefinite pronouns</u> like *someone* or *nothing*, which refer to people or things in a general way without saying exactly who or what they are.

- <u>relative pronouns</u> like *who, which* or *that*, which link two parts of a sentence together.

- <u>demonstrative pronouns</u> like *this* or *those*, which point things or people out.

- <u>reflexive pronouns</u> – a type of object pronoun that forms part of German reflexive verbs like **sich setzen** (meaning *to sit down*) or **sich waschen** (meaning *to wash*).

➡️ *For more information on* **Reflexive verbs***, see page 102.*

- the pronouns **wer?** (meaning *who?*) and **was?** (meaning *what?*) and their different forms, which are used to ask questions.

➤ Pronouns often stand in for a noun to save repeating it.

> I finished my homework and gave <u>it</u> to my teacher.
> Do you remember Jack? I saw <u>him</u> at the weekend.

➤ Word order with personal pronouns is usually different in German and English.

Personal pronouns: subject

> **What is a subject pronoun?**
> A **subject pronoun** is a word such as *I*, *he*, *she* and *they*. It refers to the person or thing which performs the action expressed by the verb. Pronouns stand in for nouns when it is clear who is being talked about, for example: *My brother isn't here at the moment. He'll be back in an hour.*

1 Using subject pronouns

➤ Here are the German subject pronouns or personal pronouns in the nominative case:

Subject Pronoun (Nominative Case)	Meaning
ich	I
du	you *(familiar)*
er	he/it
sie	she/it
es	it/he/she
man	one
wir	we
ihr	you *(plural)*
sie	they
Sie	you *(polite)*

<u>Ich</u> fahre nächste Woche nach Italien.	I'm going to Italy next week.
<u>Wir</u> wohnen in Frankfurt.	We live in Frankfurt.

➪ *For more information on the **Nominative case**, see page 9.*

2 du, ihr or Sie?

➤ In English we have only <u>one</u> way of saying *you*. In German, there are <u>three</u> words: **du**, **ihr** and **Sie**. The word you use depends on:
- whether you are talking to one person or more than one person
- whether you are talking to a friend or family member, or someone else

➤ Use the familiar **du** if talking to one person <u>you know well</u>, such as a friend, someone younger than you or a relative

Kommst <u>du</u> mit ins Kino?	Are you coming to the cinema?

For further explanation of grammatical terms, please see pages x-xiv.

➤ Use the formal or polite **Sie** if talking to one person <u>you do not know so well</u>, such as your teacher, your boss or a stranger.

Was haben <u>Sie</u> gesagt?   What did you say?

Tip

If you are in doubt as to which form of *you* to use, it is safest to use **Sie** and you will not offend anybody. However, once a colleague or acquaintance has suggested you call each other **du**, starting to use **Sie** again may be considered insulting.

➤ Use the familiar **ihr** if talking to <u>more than one person you know well</u> or relatives.

Also, was wollt <u>ihr</u> heute Abend essen?   So, what do you want to eat tonight?

➤ Use **Sie** if talking to <u>more than one person you do not know so well</u>.

Wo fahren <u>Sie</u> hin?   Where are you going to?

Tip

Use **Sie** in more formal situations for both the singular and plural *you*.

Tip

All of the subject pronouns only have a capital letter when they begin a sentence, except for the polite form of *you*, **Sie**, which always has a capital letter.

<u>Ich</u> gebe dir das Buch zurück, wenn <u>ich</u> es zu Ende gelesen habe.   I'll give you the book back when I've finished reading it.

<u>Du</u> kannst mich morgen besuchen, wenn <u>du</u> Zeit hast.   You can come and visit me tomorrow, if you have time.

Wir wären Ihnen sehr dankbar, wenn <u>Sie</u> uns telefonisch benachrichtigen würden.   We'd be very grateful if you could phone and let us know.

3 Er/sie/es

➤ In English we generally refer to things (such as *table*, *book*, *car*) only as *it*. In German, er (meaning *he*), sie (meaning *she*) and es (meaning *it*) are used to talk about a thing, as well as about a person or an animal. You use er for <u>masculine nouns</u>, sie for <u>feminine nouns</u> and es for <u>neuter nouns</u>.

Der Tisch ist groß.	→	**Er** ist groß.
The table is large.	→	It is large.
Die Jacke ist blau.	→	**Sie** ist blau.
The jacket is blue.	→	It is blue.
Das Kind stand auf.	→	**Es** stand auf.
The child stood up.	→	He/she stood up.

i Note that English speakers often make the mistake of calling all objects es.

➤ The subject pronoun sie (meaning *they*) is used in the plural to talk about things, as well as people or animals. Use sie for <u>masculine</u>, <u>feminine</u> and <u>neuter nouns</u>.

„Wo sind Michael und Sebastian?" –	"Where are Michael and Sebastian?" –
„**Sie** sind im Garten."	"They're in the garden."
„Hast du die Karten gekauft?" –	"Did you buy the tickets?" –
„Nein, <u>sie</u> waren ausverkauft."	"No, they were sold out."

4 Man

➤ This is often used in German in the same way as we use *you* in English to mean people in general.

Wie schreibt <u>man</u> das?	How do you spell that?
Man kann nie wissen.	You never know.

➤ Man can also mean *they* used in a vague way.

Man sagt, dass das Wetter immer schlecht ist.	They say the weather is always bad.

> *Tip*
>
> **Man** is often used to avoid a passive construction in German.
>
> | | |
> |---|---|
> | <u>Man</u> hat das schon oft im Fernsehen gezeigt. | It's already been shown a lot on TV. |
>
> ⇨ *For more information on the **Passive**, see page 150.*
>
> The form of the verb you use with **man** is the same as the **er/sie/es** form.
>
> ⇨ *For more information on **Verbs**, see page 91.*

Key points

- ✔ The German subject pronouns are: **ich, du, er, sie, es, Sie** and **man** in the singular, and **wir, ihr, sie** and **Sie** in the plural.

- ✔ To say *you* in German, use **du** if you are talking to one person you know well or to a child; use **ihr** if you are talking to more than one person you know well and use **Sie** if you are talking to one or more people you do not know well.

- ✔ **Er/sie/es** (masculine/feminine/neuter singular) and **sie** (masculine or feminine or neuter plural) are used to refer to things, as well as to people or animals.

- ✔ **Man** can mean *you*, *they* or people in general. It is often used instead of a passive construction.

Personal pronouns: direct object

> **What is a direct object pronoun?**
> A **direct object pronoun** is a word such as *me, him, us* and *them* which is used
> instead of the noun to stand in for the person or thing most directly affected by
> the action expressed by the verb.

1 Using direct object pronouns

➤ Direct object pronouns stand in for nouns when it is clear who or what is being
talked about, and save having to repeat the noun.

  I've lost my glasses. Have you seen <u>them</u>?

  "Have you met Jo?"– "Yes, I really like <u>her</u>!"

➤ Here are the German direct object pronouns in the accusative case:

Direct Object Pronoun (Accusative Case)	Meaning
mich	me
dich	you (*familiar*)
ihn	him/it
sie	her/it
es	it/him/her
einen	one
uns	us
euch	you (*plural*)
sie	them
Sie	you (*polite*)

  Ich lade <u>dich</u> zum Essen ein.   I'll invite you for a meal.

  Sie hat <u>ihn</u> letztes Jahr kennengelernt.   She met him last year.

2 Word order with direct object pronouns

➤ In tenses consisting of one verb part only, for example the present and the simple
past, the direct object pronoun usually comes directly <u>AFTER</u> the verb.

  Sie bringen <u>ihn</u> nach Hause.   They'll take him home.

➤ In tenses such as the perfect that are formed with **haben** or **sein** and the past
participle, the direct object pronoun comes <u>AFTER</u> the part of the verb that comes
from **haben** or **sein** and <u>BEFORE</u> the past participle.

  Er hat <u>mich</u> durchs Fenster gesehen.   He saw me through the window.

➤ When a modal verb like **wollen** (meaning *to want*) or **können** (meaning *to be able to, can*) is followed by another verb in the infinitive (the *to* form of the verb), the direct object pronoun comes directly <u>AFTER</u> the modal verb.

    Wir wollen <u>Sie</u> nicht mehr sehen.   We don't want to see you anymore.

➩ *For more information on **Modal verbs**, see page 136.*

*For more information on **Modal verbs**, see page 136.*

> ### Key points
>
> ✔ The German direct object pronouns are: **mich**, **dich**, **ihn**, **sie**, **es**, **Sie** and **einen** in the singular, and **uns**, **euch**, **sie** and **Sie** in the plural.
>
> ✔ The direct object pronoun usually comes directly after the verb, but in tenses like the perfect it comes after the part of the verb that comes from **haben** or **sein** and before the past participle.
>
> ✔ When a modal verb such as **wollen** is followed by the infinitive of another verb, the direct object pronoun comes directly after the modal verb.

Personal pronouns: indirect object

> **What is an indirect object pronoun?**
> When a verb has two objects (a <u>direct</u> one and an <u>indirect</u> one), the **indirect object pronoun** is used instead of a noun to show the person or thing the action is intended to benefit or harm, for example, *me* in *He gave me a book; Can you get me a towel?*

1 Using indirect object pronouns

➤ It is important to understand the difference between direct and indirect object pronouns, as they have different forms in German:

- an <u>indirect object</u> answers the question *who to?* or *who for?* and *to what?* or *for what?*

    He gave me a book. → *Who did he give the book to?* → me (=*indirect object pronoun*)
    Can you get me a towel? → *Who can you get a towel for?* → me (=*indirect object pronoun*)

- if something answers the question *what?* or *who?*, then it is the <u>direct object</u> and <u>NOT</u> the indirect object

    He gave me a book → *What did he give me?* → a book (=*direct object*)
    Can you get me a towel? → *What can you get me?* → a towel (=*direct object*)

➤ Here are the German indirect object pronouns in the dative case:

Indirect Object Pronoun (Dative Case)	Meaning
mir	to/for me
dir	to/for you (*familiar*)
ihm	to/for him/it
ihr	to/for her/it
ihm	to/for it/him/her
einem	to/for one
uns	to/for us
euch	to/for you (*plural*)
ihnen	to/for them
Ihnen	to/for you (*polite*)

Er hat <u>mir</u> das geschenkt.	He gave me that as a present.
Sie haben <u>ihnen</u> eine tolle Geschichte erzählt.	They told them a great story.

2 | Word order with indirect object pronouns

➤ Word order for indirect object pronouns is the same as for direct object pronouns. The pronoun usually comes directly after the verb, except with tenses like the perfect and modal verbs such as **wollen**.

Sie bringt <u>mir</u> **das Schwimmen bei.**	She's teaching me how to swim.
Sie hat es <u>ihm</u> **gegeben.**	She gave it to him.
Ich will <u>dir</u> **etwas sagen.**	I want to tell you something.

➤ When you have both a direct object pronoun AND an indirect object pronoun in the same sentence, the direct object pronoun or personal pronoun in the accusative <u>always</u> comes first. A good way of remembering this is to think of the following:

PAD = Pronoun Accusative Dative

Sie haben <u>es</u> <u>ihm</u> **verziehen.**	They forgave him for it.
Ich bringe <u>es</u> <u>dir</u> **schon bei.**	I'll teach you.

Key points

✔ The German indirect object pronouns are: **mir, dir, ihm, ihr, ihm, Ihnen** and **einem** in the singular, and **uns, euch, Ihnen** and **Ihnen** in the plural.

✔ The indirect object pronoun comes after the verb, except with tenses like the perfect and when used with modal verbs such as **wollen**.

✔ The indirect object pronoun always comes after the direct object pronoun.

Personal pronouns: after prepositions

➤ When a personal pronoun is used after a preposition and refers to a person, the personal pronoun is in the case required by the preposition. For example, the preposition **mit** is always followed by the dative case.

> **Ich bin <u>mit ihm</u> spazieren gegangen.**   I went for a walk with him.

➤ When a thing rather than a person is referred to, **da-** is added at the beginning of the preposition:

> **Manuela hatte ein Messer geholt und wollte <u>damit</u> den Kuchen schneiden.**   Manuela had brought a knife and was about to cut the cake with it.

[*i*] Note that before a preposition beginning with a vowel, the form **dar-** + preposition is used.

> **Lege es bitte <u>darauf</u>.**   Put it there please.

➤ The following prepositions are affected in this way:

Preposition	Preposition + da or dar
an	<u>da</u>ran
auf	<u>da</u>rauf
aus	<u>da</u>raus
bei	<u>da</u>bei
durch	<u>da</u>durch
für	<u>da</u>für
in	<u>da</u>rin
mit	<u>da</u>mit
nach	<u>da</u>nach
neben	<u>da</u>neben
über	<u>da</u>rüber
unter	<u>da</u>runter
zwischen	<u>da</u>zwischen

⇨ *For more information on **Prepositions**, see page 153.*

[*i*] Note that these combined forms are also used after verbs followed by prepositions.

> **sich erinnern an** + accusative case =   to remember
> **Ich erinnere mich nicht <u>daran</u>.**   I don't remember (it).

Grammar Extra!

After certain prepositions used to express movement, that is **aus** (meaning *out* or *from*), **auf** (meaning *on*) and **in** (meaning *in* or *into*), combined forms with **hin** and **her** are used to give more emphasis to the action being carried out.

Preposition	hin or her + Preposition
aus	hinaus/heraus
auf	hinauf/herauf
in	hinein/herein

Er ging die Treppe leise <u>hinauf</u>.	He went up the stairs quietly.
Endlich fand sie unser Zelt und kam <u>herein</u>.	She finally found our tent and came inside.
Sie öffnete die Reisetasche und legte die Hose <u>hinein</u>.	She opened the bag and put in her trousers.

Key points

✔ When a personal pronoun referring to a person is used after a preposition, the personal pronoun is in the case required by the preposition.

✔ When a personal pronoun referring to a thing is used after a preposition, the construction **da(r)-** + preposition is used.

Possessive pronouns

> **What is a possessive pronoun?**
> In English you can say *This is my car* or *This car is mine*. In the first sentence *my* is
> a possessive adjective. In the second, *mine* is a possessive pronoun.
>
> A **possessive pronoun** is one of the words *mine, yours, hers, his, ours* or *theirs*,
> which are used instead of a noun to show that one thing or person belongs to
> another, for example, *Ask Carol if this pen is hers*.

➤ German possessive pronouns are the same words as the possessive adjectives
mein, dein, sein, ihr, unser, euer, ihr, Ihr, with the same endings, EXCEPT in the
masculine nominative singular, the neuter nominative singular and the neuter
accusative singular, as shown below.

	Possessive Adjective	Meaning	Possessive Pronoun	Meaning
Masculine Nominative Singular	Das ist <u>mein</u> Wagen	That is my car	Dieser Wagen ist <u>meiner</u>	That car is mine
Neuter Nominative Singular	Das ist <u>mein</u> Buch	That is my book	Dieses Buch ist <u>meins</u>	That book is mine
Neuter Accusative Singular	Sie hat <u>mein</u> Buch genommen	She has taken my book	Sie hat <u>meins</u> genommen	She has taken mine

➤ Here is the German possessive pronoun **meiner**, meaning *mine*, in all its forms:

Case	Masculine Singular	Feminine Singular	Neuter Singular	All Genders Plural
Nominative	mein<u>er</u>	mein<u>e</u>	mein(e)s	mein<u>e</u>
Accusative	mein<u>en</u>	mein<u>e</u>	mein(e)s	mein<u>e</u>
Genitive	mein<u>es</u>	mein<u>er</u>	mein<u>es</u>	mein<u>er</u>
Dative	mein<u>em</u>	mein<u>er</u>	mein<u>em</u>	mein<u>en</u>

ℹ️ Note that the nominative and accusative neuter forms only of all the possessive
pronouns are often pronounced without the last **-e**, for example **meins** instead
of **meines**.

Der Wagen da drüben ist <u>meiner</u>.	The car over there is mine.
Er ist kleiner als <u>deiner</u>.	It is smaller than yours.
Das ist besser als <u>meins</u>!	That's better than mine!
Das Haus nebenan ist schöner als <u>seins</u>.	The house next door is nicer than his.
Meine Jacke war teurer als <u>ihre</u>.	My jacket was more expensive than hers.

For further explanation of grammatical terms, please see pages x-xiv.

i Note that **deiner**, meaning *yours (familiar)*, **seiner**, meaning *his/its*, **ihrer**, meaning *hers/its/theirs*, **Ihrer**, meaning *yours (polite)*, **unserer**, meaning *ours* and **euerer**, meaning *yours (plural familiar)* have the same endings as **meiner**.

Tip

Unserer, meaning *ours* is often pronounced **unsrer** and **euerer**, meaning *yours (plural familiar)* is often pronounced **eurer**. This pronunciation is occasionally reflected in writing.

Case	Masculine Singular	Feminine Singular	Neuter Singular	All Genders Plural
Nominative	uns(e)rer	uns(e)re	uns(e)res	uns(e)re
Accusative	uns(e)ren	uns(e)re	uns(e)res	uns(e)re
Genitive	uns(e)res	uns(e)rer	uns(e)res	uns(e)rer
Dative	uns(e)rem	uns(e)rer	uns(e)rem	uns(e)ren

Case	Masculine Singular	Feminine Singular	Neuter Singular	All Genders Plural
Nominative	eu(e)rer	eu(e)re	eu(e)res	eu(e)re
Accusative	eu(e)ren	eu(e)re	eu(e)res	eu(e)re
Genitive	eu(e)res	eu(e)rer	eu(e)res	eu(e)rer
Dative	eu(e)rem	eu(e)rer	eu(e)rem	eu(e)ren

War euer Urlaub billiger als unsrer?	Was your holiday cheaper than ours?

i Note the translation of *of mine*, *of yours* etc, where the personal pronoun in the dative is used:

Er ist ein Freund von mir.	He is a friend of mine.
Ich habe eine CD von dir bei mir zu Hause.	I have a CD of yours at home.

Key points

✔ German possessive pronouns have the same form and endings as the possessive adjectives **mein**, **dein**, **sein**, **ihr**, **unser**, **euer**, **ihr**, **Ihr**, except in the masculine nominative singular, the neuter nominative singular and the neuter accusative singular.

✔ The nominative and accusative neuter forms of all the possessive pronouns are often pronounced without the last **-e**, for example **meins** instead of **meines**.

✔ **Unserer**, meaning *ours* is often pronounced **unsrer** and **euerer**, meaning *yours (plural familiar)* is often pronounced **eurer**. This pronunciation is occasionally reflected in writing.

Indefinite pronouns

> **What is an indefinite pronoun?**
> An **indefinite pronoun** is one of a small group of pronouns such as *everything*, *nobody* and *something* which are used to refer to people or things in a general way without saying exactly who or what they are.

➤ In German, the indefinite pronouns **jemand** (meaning *someone, somebody*) and **niemand** (meaning *no-one, nobody*) are often used in speech without any endings. In written German, the endings are added.

Case	Indefinite Pronoun
Nominative	jemand/niemand
Accusative	jemanden/niemanden
Genitive	jemand(e)s/niemand(e)s
Dative	jemandem/niemandem

Ich habe es jemandem gegeben.	I gave it to someone.
Jemand hat es genommen.	Someone has taken it.
Sie hat niemanden gesehen.	She didn't see anyone.
Ich bin unterwegs niemandem begegnet.	I didn't meet anyone on the way.

Tip

If you want to express the sense of *somebody or other*, use **irgendjemand** which is declined like **jemand**.

Ich habe es irgendjemandem gegeben.   I gave it to somebody or other.

➤ The indefinite pronoun **keiner** has the same endings as the article **kein, keine, kein** except in the nominative masculine and nominative and accusative neuter forms, and can be used to refer to people or things. When referring to people it means *nobody*, *not … anybody* or *none* and when referring to things, it means *not … any* or *none*.

Case	Masculine Singular	Feminine Singular	Neuter Singular	All Genders Plural
Nominative	keiner	keine	keins	keine
Accusative	keinen	keine	keins	keine
Genitive	keines	keiner	keines	keiner
Dative	keinem	keiner	keinem	keinen

For further explanation of grammatical terms, please see pages x–xiv.

Ich kenne hier keinen.	I don't know anybody here.
Keiner weiß Bescheid über ihn.	Nobody knows about him.
Das trifft auf keinen zu.	That does not apply to anybody.
Er wollte ein Stück Schokolade, aber ich hatte keine.	He wanted a piece of chocolate, but I didn't have any.
„Hast du Geld?" – „Nein, gar keins."	"Have you got any money?" – "No, none at all."

➤ The indefinite pronoun **einer** (meaning *one*) only has a singular form and can also be used to refer to people or things.

Case	Masculine Singular	Feminine Singular	Neuter Singular
Nominative	einer	eine	ein(e)s
Accusative	einen	eine	ein(e)s
Genitive	eines	einer	eines
Dative	einem	einer	einem

Sie trifft sich mit einem ihrer alten Studienfreunde.	She's meeting one of her old friends from university.

Ich brauche nur einen (e.g. einen Wagen, einen Pullover etc) OR
Ich brauche nur eine (e.g. eine Blume, eine Tasche etc) OR
Ich brauche nur eins (e.g. ein Buch, ein Notizbuch etc) I only need one.

Key points

✔ **Jemand** and **niemand** can be used without endings in spoken German but have endings added in written German.

✔ **Keiner** has the same endings as the article **kein, keine, kein** except in the nominative masculine and nominative and accusative neuter forms, and refers to people or things.

✔ **Einer** only has a singular form and refers to people or things.

Reflexive pronouns

What is a reflexive pronoun?
A **reflexive pronoun** is an object pronoun such as *myself, yourself, himself, herself* and *ourselves* that forms part of German reflexive verbs like **sich waschen** (meaning *to wash*) or **sich setzen** (meaning *to sit down*). A reflexive verb is a verb whose subject and object are the same and whose action is 'reflected back' to its subject.

➤ German reflexive pronouns have two forms: accusative (for the direct object pronoun) and dative (for the indirect object pronoun), as follows:

Accusative Form	Dative Form	Meaning
mich	mir	myself
dich	dir	yourself (*familiar*)
sich	sich	himself/herself/itself
uns	uns	ourselves
euch	euch	yourselves (*plural*)
sich	sich	themselves
sich	sich	yourself/yourselves (*polite*)

Er hat <u>sich</u> rasiert.	He had a shave.
Du hast <u>dich</u> gebadet.	You had a bath.
Ich will es <u>mir</u> zuerst überlegen.	I'll have to think about it first.

[*i*] Note that unlike personal pronouns and possessives, the polite forms have no capital letter.

Setzen Sie <u>sich</u> bitte.	Please take a seat.
Nehmen Sie <u>sich</u> ruhig etwas Zeit.	Take your time.

➤ The reflexive pronoun usually follows the first verb in the sentence, with certain exceptions:

Sie wird <u>sich</u> darüber freuen.	She'll be pleased about that.

• If the subject and verb are swapped round in the sentence, and the subject is a personal pronoun, then the reflexive pronoun must come AFTER the personal pronoun.

Darüber wird sie <u>sich</u> freuen.	She'll be pleased about that.

• If the sentence is made of up two parts or clauses, then the reflexive pronoun comes AFTER the subject in the second clause.

Ich frage mich, ob sie <u>sich</u> darüber freuen wird.	I wonder if she'll be pleased about that.

⇨ For more information on **Word order**, see page 175.
⇨ For more information on **Reflexive verbs**, see page 102.

For further explanation of grammatical terms, please see pages x–xiv.

➤ Unlike English, reflexive pronouns are also used after prepositions when the pronoun 'reflects back' to the subject of the sentence.

Er hatte nicht genug Geld bei <u>sich</u>.	He didn't have enough money on him.
Hatten Sie nicht genug Geld bei <u>sich</u>?	Didn't you have enough money on you?

➤ Another use of reflexive pronouns in German is with transitive verbs where the action is performed for the benefit of the subject, as in the English phrase: I bought *myself* a new hat. The pronoun is not always translated in English.

Ich hole <u>mir</u> einen Kaffee.	I'm going to get (myself) a coffee.
Sie hat <u>sich</u> eine neue Jacke gekauft.	She bought (herself) a new jacket.

➤ Reflexive pronouns are usually used in German where *each other* and *one another* would be used in English.

Wir sind <u>uns</u> letzte Woche begegnet.	We met (each other) last week.

[i] Note that **einander**, (meaning *one another*, *each other*), which does not change in form, may be used instead of a reflexive pronoun in such cases.

Wir kennen <u>uns</u> schon. OR	
Wir kennen <u>einander</u> schon.	We already know each other.

➤ After prepositions, **einander** is always used instead of a reflexive pronoun. The preposition and **einander** are then joined to form one word.

Sie redeten <u>miteinander</u>.	They were talking to each other.

➤ In English, pronouns used for emphasis are the same as normal reflexive pronouns, for example, *I did it myself*. In German **selbst** or, in informal spoken language, **selber** are used instead of reflexive pronouns for emphasis. They never change their form and are always stressed, regardless of their position in the sentence:

Ich <u>selbst</u> habe es nicht gelesen, aber ...	I haven't read it *myself*, but ...

Key points

✔ German reflexive pronouns have two forms: accusative for the direct object pronoun and dative for the indirect object pronoun.

✔ Reflexive pronouns are also used after prepositions when the pronoun 'reflects back' to the subject of the sentence.

✔ Reflexive pronouns are usually used in German where *each other* or *one another* would be used in English, but **einander** can be used as an alternative and is always used after prepositions.

✔ **Selbst** or, in informal spoken German, **selber** are used instead of reflexive pronouns for emphasis.

Relative pronouns

What is a relative pronoun?

In English a **relative pronoun** is one of the words *who, which* and *that* (and the more formal *whom*). These pronouns are used to introduce information that makes it clear which person or thing is being talked about, for example, *The man who has just come in is Ann's boyfriend; The vase that you broke was quite valuable.*

Relative pronouns can also introduce further information about someone or something, for example, *Peter, who is a brilliant painter, wants to study art; Jane's house, which was built in 1890, needs a lot of repairs.*

➤ In German the most common relative pronouns **der, den, dessen, dem** etc have the same forms as the definite article, except in the dative plural and genitive singular and plural. They are declined as follows:

Case	Masculine Singular	Feminine Singular	Neuter Singular	All Genders Plural
Nominative	der	die	das	die
Accusative	den	die	das	die
Genitive	dessen	deren	dessen	deren
Dative	dem	der	dem	denen

➤ Relative pronouns must agree in gender and number with the noun to which they refer, but the case they have depends on their function in the relative clause. The relative clause is simply the part of the sentence in which the relative pronoun appears. Relative clauses are <u>ALWAYS</u> separated by commas from the rest of the sentence.

● In the following example, the relative pronoun **den** is in the accusative because it is the direct object in the relative clause.

Der Mann, <u>den</u> ich gestern gesehen habe, kommt aus Zürich.   The man that I saw yesterday comes from Zürich.

● In this second example, the relative pronoun **dessen** is in the genitive because it is used to show that something belongs to someone.

Das Mädchen, <u>dessen</u> Fahrrad gestohlen worden ist.   The girl whose bike was stolen.

Tip

In English we often miss out the object pronouns *who, which* and *that*.
For example, we can say both *the friends that I see most*, or *the friends
I see most*, and *the house which we want to buy*, or *the house we want to buy*.
In German you can NEVER miss out the relative pronoun in this way.

Die Frau, mit der ich gestern gesprochen habe, kennt deine Mutter.	The woman I spoke to yesterday knows your mother.

🛈 Note that the genitive forms are used in relative clauses in much the same way
as in English, but to translate *one of whom, some of whom* use the following
constructions.

Das Kind, dessen Fahrrad gestohlen worden war, fing an zu weinen.	The child whose bicycle had been stolen started to cry.
Die Kinder, von denen einige schon lesen konnten, ...	The children, some of whom could already read, ...
Meine Freunde, von denen einer ...	My friends, one of whom ...

Grammar Extra!

When a relative clause is introduced by a preposition, the relative pronoun can be replaced by
wo- or wor- if the noun or pronoun it stands for refers to an object or something abstract. The full
form of the pronoun plus preposition is much more common.

Das Buch, woraus ich vorgelesen
habe, gehört dir.

OR

Das Buch, aus dem ich vorgelesen habe, gehört dir.	The book I read aloud from belongs to you.

➤ In German wer and was are normally used as interrogative pronouns (meaning
who? and *what?*) to ask questions. They can also be the subject of a sentence or a
relative pronoun. For example, *he who, a woman who, anyone who, those who* etc.

Wer das glaubt, ist verrückt.	Anyone who believes that is mad.
Was du gestern gekauft hast, steht dir ganz gut.	The things you bought yesterday really suit you.

Note that **was** is the relative pronoun used in set expressions with certain neuter forms. For example:

alles, was ...	everything which
das, was ...	that which
nichts, was ...	nothing that
vieles, was ...	a lot that
wenig, was ...	little that
Nichts, <u>was</u> er sagte, hat gestimmt.	Nothing that he said was true.
Das, <u>was</u> du jetzt machst, ist unpraktisch.	What you are doing now is impractical.
Mit allem, <u>was</u> du gesagt hast, sind wir einverstanden.	We agree with everything you said.

Key points

✔ The most common relative pronouns **der, den, dessen, dem** etc have the same forms as the definite article, except in the dative plural and genitive singular and plural.

✔ Relative pronouns must agree in gender and number with the noun to which they refer, but take their case from their function in the relative clause.

✔ In German you can <u>NEVER</u> miss out the relative pronoun, unlike in English.

✔ Relative clauses are always separated by commas from the rest of the sentence.

✔ Wer and was are normally used as interrogative pronouns but can also be the subject of a sentence or a relative pronoun.

Interrogative pronouns

> **What is an interrogative pronoun?**
> This is one of the words *who*, *whose*, *whom*, *what* and *which* when they are used
> instead of a noun to ask questions, for example, *What's happening?; Who's coming?*

1 Wer? and was?

➤ Wer and was only have a singular form.

Case	Persons	Things
Nominative	wer?	was?
Accusative	wen?	was?
Genitive	wessen?	–
Dative	wem?	–

- They can be used in direct questions.

Wer hat es gemacht?	Who did it?
Mit **wem** bist du gekommen?	Who did you come with?
Wo ist der Kugelschreiber, mit **dem** du es geschrieben hast?	Where is the pen you wrote it with?

- They can also be used in indirect questions.

Ich weiß nicht, <u>wer</u> es gemacht hat.	I don't know who did it.
Sie wollte wissen, mit <u>wem</u> sie fahren sollte.	She wanted to know who she was to travel with.

2 Interrogative pronouns with prepositions

➤ When used with prepositions, **was** usually becomes **wo-** and is combined with
the preposition to form one word. Where the preposition begins with a vowel,
wor- is used instead.

<u>Wodurch</u> ist es zerstört worden?	How was it destroyed?
<u>Worauf</u> sollen wir sitzen? Es gibt keine Stühle.	What should we sit on? There aren't any chairs.

3 | Was für ein?, welcher?

➤ These are used to mean *what kind of ...?* and *which one?* and are declined like the definite article.

„Er hat jetzt ein Auto" –	"He has a car now." -
„<u>Was für eins</u> hat er gekauft?"	"What kind (of one) did he buy?"
<u>Welches</u> hast du gewollt?	Which one did you want?

⇨ *For more information on **Words declined like the definite article**, see page 31.*

➤ They can refer to people or things and require the appropriate endings.

Für <u>welchen</u> (e.g. **welchen Job, welchen Whisky** etc) **hat sie sich entschieden?** OR

Für <u>welches</u> (e.g. **welches Haus, welches Buch** etc) **hat sie sich entschieden?** OR

Für <u>welche</u> (e.g. **welche Person, welche Jacke** etc) **hat sie sich entschieden?**

Which one did she choose?

Key points

✔ The interrogative pronouns **wer** and **was** can be used for direct and indirect questions and only have a singular form.

✔ When used with prepositions, **was** becomes **wo-**, or **wor-** when the preposition begins with a vowel.

✔ **Was für ein?** and **welcher?** are used to mean *what kind of ...?* and *which one?*

VERBS

What is a verb?
A **verb** is a 'doing' word which describes what someone or something does, what someone or something is, or what happens to them, for example, *be, sing, live*.

Weak, strong and mixed verbs

➤ Verbs are usually used with a noun, with a pronoun such as *I, you* or *she*, or with somebody's name. They can relate to the present, the past and the future; this is called their <u>tense</u>.

⇨ For more information on **Nouns** and **Pronouns**, see pages 1 and 69.

➤ Verbs are either:
  ● <u>weak</u>: their forms follow a set pattern. These verbs may also be called <u>regular</u>.
  ● <u>strong</u> and <u>irregular</u>: their forms change according to different patterns.
  OR
  ● <u>mixed</u>: their forms follow a mixture of the patterns for weak and strong verbs.

➤ English verbs have a <u>base form</u> (the form of the verb without any endings added to it, for example, *walk*). This is the form you look up in a dictionary. The base form can have *to* in front of it, for example, *to walk*. This is called the <u>infinitive</u>.

➤ German verbs also have an infinitive, which is the form shown in a dictionary; most weak, strong and mixed verbs end in **-en**. For example, **holen** (meaning *to fetch*) is weak, **helfen** (meaning *to help*) is strong and **denken** (meaning *to think*) is mixed. All German verbs belong to one of these groups. We will look at each of these three groups in turn on the next few pages.

➤ English verbs have other forms apart from the base form and infinitive: a form ending in -s (*walks*), a form ending in -ing (*walking*), and a form ending in -ed (*walked*).

➤ German verbs have many more forms than this, which are made up of endings added to a <u>stem</u>. The stem of a verb can usually be worked out from the infinitive and can change, depending on the tense of the verb and who or what you are talking about.

➤ German verb endings also change, depending on who or what you are talking about: **ich** (*I*), **du** (*you* (informal)), **er/sie/es** (*he/she/it*), **Sie** (*you* (formal)) in the singular, or **wir** (*we*), **ihr** (*you* (informal)), **Sie** (*you* (formal)) and **sie** (*they*) in the plural. German verbs also have different forms depending on whether you are referring to the present, future or past.

⇨ For **Verb Tables**, see supplement.

Key points

✔ German verbs have different forms depending on what noun or pronoun they are used with, and on their tense.

✔ They are made up of a stem and an ending. The stem is based on the infinitive and can change in form.

✔ All German verbs fit into one of three patterns or conjugations: weak (and regular), strong (and irregular) or mixed (a mixture of the two).

The present tense

> **What is the present tense?**
> The **present tense** is used to talk about what is true at the moment, what happens regularly and what is happening now, for example, *I'm a student*, *I travel to college by train*, *I'm studying languages*.

1 Using the present tense

➤ In English there are two forms of the present tense. One is used to talk about things happening now and the other is used for things that happen all the time. In German, you use the same form for both of these.

- things that are happening now

Es **regnet**.	It's raining.
Sie **spielen** Fußball.	They're playing football.

- things that happen all the time, or things that you do as a habit

Hier **regnet** es viel.	It rains a lot here.
Samstags **spielen** sie Fußball.	They play football on Saturdays.

➤ In German there are three alternative ways of emphasizing that something is happening now:

- present tense + an adverb

Er kocht **gerade** das Abendessen. He's cooking dinner.

- beim + an infinitive being used as a noun

Ich bin **beim Bügeln**. I am ironing.

- eben/gerade dabei sein zu (meaning *to be in the process of*) + an infinitive

Sie **ist gerade dabei**, eine E-Mail zu schreiben. She is just writing an email.

➤ In English you can also use the present tense to talk about something that is going to happen in the near future. You can do the same in German.

Morgen **spiele** ich Tennis.	I'm going to play tennis tomorrow.
Wir **nehmen** den Zug um zehn Uhr.	We're getting the ten o'clock train.

> **Tip**
>
> Although English sometimes uses parts of the verb *to be* to form the present tense of other verbs (for example, *I am listening, she's talking*). German NEVER uses the verb **sein** in this way.
>
> When using **seit** or **seitdem** to describe an action which began in the past and is continuing in the present, the present tense is used in German, where in English a verb form with *have* or *has* is used.
>
> | | |
> |---|---|
> | Ich <u>wohne</u> <u>seit</u> drei Jahren hier. | I <u>have been living</u> here for three years. |
> | <u>Seit</u> er krank <u>ist</u>, hat er uns nicht besucht. | He hasn't visited us <u>since</u> he's <u>been</u> ill. |
> | <u>Seitdem</u> sie am Gymnasium <u>ist</u>, hat sie kaum mehr Zeit. | Since she's been going to grammar school, she's hardly had any time. |
>
> 🛈 Note that if the action is finished, the perfect tense is used in German.
>
> | | |
> |---|---|
> | <u>Seit</u> seinem Unfall <u>habe</u> ich ihn nur ein einziges Mal <u>gesehen</u>. | I <u>have</u> only <u>seen</u> him once since his accident. |

2 Forming the present tense of weak verbs

➤ Nearly all weak verbs in German end in **-en** in their infinitive form. This is the form of the verb you find in the dictionary, for example, **spielen, machen, holen**. Weak verbs are regular and their changes follow a set pattern or conjugation.

➤ To know which form of the verb to use in German, you need to work out what the stem of the verb is and then add the correct ending. The stem of most verbs in the present tense is formed by chopping the **-en** off the infinitive.

Infinitive	Stem (without -en)
spielen (to play)	spiel-
machen (to make)	mach-
holen (to fetch)	hol-

➤ Where the infinitive of a weak verb ends in **-eln** or **-ern**, only the **-n** is chopped off to form the stem.

Infinitive	Stem (without -n)
wandern (to hillwalk)	wander-
segeln (to sail)	segel-

➤ Now you know how to find the stem of a verb, you can add the correct ending. Which one you choose will depend on whether you are referring to **ich**, **du**, **er**, **sie**, **es**, **wir**, **ihr**, **Sie** or **sie**.

⇨ *For more information on* **Pronouns**, *see page 69.*

➤ Here are the present tense endings for weak verbs ending in **-en**:

Pronoun	Ending	Add to Stem, e.g. spiel-	Meanings
ich	-e	ich spiel<u>e</u>	I play I am playing
du	-st	du spiel<u>st</u>	you play you are playing
er sie es	-t	er spiel<u>t</u> sie spiel<u>t</u> es spiel<u>t</u>	he/she/it plays he/she/it is playing
wir	-en	wir spiel<u>en</u>	we play we are playing
ihr	-t	ihr spiel<u>t</u>	you (*plural*) play you are playing
sie	-en	sie spiel<u>en</u>	they play they are playing
Sie		Sie spiel<u>en</u>	you (*polite*) play you are playing

Sie <u>macht</u> ihre Hausaufgaben.		She's doing her homework.
Er <u>holt</u> die Kinder.		He's fetching the children.

i Note that you add **-n**, not **-en** to the stem of weak verbs ending in **-ern** and **-eln** to get the **wir**, **sie** and **Sie** forms of the present tense.

Pronoun	Ending	Add to Stem, e.g. wander-	Meanings
wir	-n	wir wander<u>n</u>	we hillwalk we are hillwalking
sie	-n	sie wander<u>n</u>	they hillwalk they are hillwalking
Sie		Sie wander<u>n</u>	you (*polite*) hillwalk you are hillwalking

Sie wander<u>n</u> gern, oder?	You like hillwalking, don't you?
Im Sommer wander<u>n</u> wir fast jedes Wochenende.	In the summer we go hillwalking most weekends.

➤ If the stem of a weak verb ends in -d or -t, an extra -e is added before the usual endings in the **du**, **er**, **sie**, **es** and **ihr** parts of the verb to make pronunciation easier.

Pronoun	Ending	Add to Stem, e.g. red-	Meanings
du	-est	du red<u>est</u>	you talk you are talking
er sie es	-et	er red<u>et</u> sie red<u>et</u> es red<u>et</u>	he/she/it talks he/she/it is talking
ihr	-et	ihr red<u>et</u>	you (*plural*) talk you are talking

Du red<u>est</u> doch die ganze Zeit über deine Arbeit!   You talk about your work all the time!

Pronoun	Ending	Add to Stem, e.g. arbeit-	Meanings
du	-est	du arbeit<u>est</u>	you work you are working
er sie es	-et	er arbeit<u>et</u> sie arbeit<u>et</u> es arbeit<u>et</u>	he/she/it works he/she/it is working
ihr	-et	ihr arbeit<u>et</u>	you (*plural*) work you are working

Sie arbeit<u>et</u> übers Wochenende.   She's working over the weekend.
Ihr arbeit<u>et</u> ganz schön viel.   You work a lot.

➤ If the stem of a weak verb ends in -m or -n, this extra -e is added to make pronunciation easier. If the -m or -n has a consonant in front of it, the -e is added, except if the consonant is **l**, **r** or **h**, for example **lernen**.

Pronoun	Ending	Add to Stem, e.g. atm-	Meanings
du	-est	du atm<u>est</u>	you breathe you are breathing
er sie es	-et	er atm<u>et</u> sie atm<u>et</u> es atm<u>et</u>	he/she/it breathes he/she/it is breathing
ihr	-et	ihr atm<u>et</u>	you (*plural*) breathe you are breathing

Du atm<u>est</u> ganz tief.   You're breathing very deeply.

For further explanation of grammatical terms, please see pages x-xiv.

Pronoun	Ending	Add to Stem, e.g. lern-	Meanings
du	-st	du lernst	you learn you are learning
er sie es	-t	er lernt sie lernt es lernt	he/she/it learns he/she/it is learning
ihr	-t	ihr lernt	you (plural) learn you are learning

Sie lernt alles ganz schnell.   She learns everything very quickly.

Key points

✔ Weak verbs are regular and most of them form their present tense stem by losing the -en from the infinitive.

✔ The present tense endings for weak verbs ending in -en are: -e, -st, -t, -en, -t, -en, -en.

✔ If the stem of a weak verb ends in -d, -t, -m or -n, an extra -e is added before the endings to make pronunciation easier.

3 Forming the present tense of strong verbs

➤ The present tense of most strong verbs is formed with the same endings that are used for weak verbs.

Pronoun	Ending	Add to Stem, e.g. sing-	Meanings
ich	-e	ich singe	I sing I am singing
du	-st	du singst	you sing you are singing
er sie es	-t	er singt sie singt es singt	he/she/it sings he/she/it is singing
wir	-en	wir singen	we sing we are singing
ihr	-t	ihr singt	you (plural) sing you are singing
sie Sie	-en	sie singen Sie singen	they sing they are singing you (polite) sing you are singing

Sie singen in einer Gruppe.   They sing in a band.

➤ However, the vowels in stems of most strong verbs change for the **du** and **er/sie/es** forms. The vowels listed below change as shown in nearly all cases:

long e	→	ie (*see* **sehen**)
short e	→	i (*see* **helfen**)
a	→	ä (*see* **fahren**)
au	→	äu (*see* **laufen**)
o	→	ö (*see* **stoßen**)

- long e → ie

Pronoun	Ending	Add to Stem, e.g. seh-	Meanings
ich	-e	ich sehe	I see I am seeing
du	-st	du siehst	you see you are seeing
er sie es	-t	er sieht sie sieht es sieht	he/she/it sees he/she/it is seeing
wir	-en	wir sehen	we see we are seeing
ihr	-t	ihr seht	you (*plural*) see you are seeing
sie Sie	-en	sie sehen Sie sehen	they see they are seeing you (*polite*) see you are seeing

Siehst du fern?   Are you watching TV?

- short e → i

Pronoun	Ending	Add to Stem, e.g. helf-	Meanings
ich	-e	ich helfe	I help I am helping
du	-st	du hilfst	you help you are helping
er sie es	-t	er hilft sie hilft es hilft	he/she/it helps he/she/it is helping
wir	-en	wir helfen	we help we are helping
ihr	-t	ihr helft	you (*plural*) help you are helping
sie Sie	-en	sie helfen Sie helfen	they help they are helping you (*polite*) help you are helping

Heute hilft er beim Kochen.   He's helping with the cooking today.

For further explanation of grammatical terms, please see pages x-xiv.

- a → ä

Pronoun	Ending	Add to Stem, e.g. fahr-	Meanings
ich	-e	ich fahre	I drive I am driving
du	-st	du fährst	you drive you are driving
er sie es	-t	er fährt sie fährt es fährt	he/she/it drives he/she/it is driving
wir	-en	wir fahren	we drive we are driving
ihr	-t	ihr fahrt	you (plural) drive you are driving
sie	-en	sie fahren	they drive they are driving
Sie		Sie fahren	you (polite) drive you are driving

Am Samstag fährt sie nach Italien.   She's driving to Italy on Saturday.

- au → äu

Pronoun	Ending	Add to Stem, e.g. lauf-	Meanings
ich	-e	ich laufe	I run I am running
du	-st	du läufst	you run you are running
er sie es	-t	er läuft sie läuft es läuft	he/she/it runs he/she/it is running
wir	-en	wir laufen	we run we are running
ihr	-t	ihr lauft	you (plural) run you are running
sie	-en	sie laufen	they run they are running
Sie		Sie laufen	you (polite) run you are running

Er läuft die 100 Meter in Rekordzeit.   He runs the 100 metres in record time.

● o → ö

Pronoun	Ending	Add to Stem, e.g. stoß-	Meanings
ich	-e	ich stoße	I push I am pushing
du	-st	du stößt	you push you are pushing
er sie es	-t	er stößt sie stößt es stößt	he/she/it pushes he/she/it is pushing
wir	-en	wir stoßen	we push we are pushing
ihr	-t	ihr stoßt	you (*plural*) push you are pushing
sie Sie	-en	sie stoßen Sie stoßen	they push they are pushing you (*polite*) push you are pushing

Pass auf, dass du nicht an den Tisch stößt.	Watch that you don't bump into the table.

ℹ️ Note that strong AND weak verbs whose stem ends in **-s**, **-z**, **-ss** or **-ß** (such as stoßen) add **-t** rather than **-st** to get the **du** form in the present tense. However, if the stem ends in **-sch**, the normal **-st** is added.

Verb	Stem	Du Form
wachsen	wachs-	wächst
waschen	wasch-	wäschst

Key points

✔ Strong verbs have the same endings in the present tense as weak verbs.

✔ The vowel or vowels of the stem of strong verbs change(s) in the present for the **du** and **er/sie/es** forms.

---

4 Forming the present tense of mixed verbs

➤ There are nine mixed verbs in German. They are very common and are formed according to a mixture of the rules already explained for weak and strong verbs.

➤ The nine mixed verbs are:

Mixed Verb	Meaning	Mixed Verb	Meaning	Mixed Verb	Meaning
brennen	to burn	kennen	to know	senden	to send
bringen	to bring	nennen	to name	wenden	to turn
denken	to think	rennen	to run	wissen	to know

➤ The present tense of mixed verbs has the same endings as weak verbs and has no vowel or consonant changes in the stem: **ich bringe, du bringst, er/sie/es bringt, wir bringen, ihr bringt, sie bringen, Sie bringen**.

Sie bringt mich nach Hause.	She's bringing me home.
Bringst du mir etwas mit?	Will you bring something for me?

🛈 Note that the present tense of the most important strong, weak and mixed verbs is shown in the Verb Tables.

⇨ For **Verb Tables**, see supplement.

Key points

✔ There are nine mixed verbs in German.

✔ The present tense of mixed verbs has the same endings as weak verbs and has no vowel or consonant changes in the stem.

Reflexive verbs

> **What is a reflexive verb?**
> A **reflexive verb** is one where the subject and object are the same, and where the action 'reflects back' on the subject. Reflexive verbs are used with a reflexive pronoun such as *myself*, *yourself* and *herself* in English, for example, *I washed myself*; *He shaved himself*.

1 Using reflexive verbs

➤ In German, reflexive verbs are much more common than in English, and many are used in everyday German. Reflexive verbs consist of two parts: the reflexive pronoun **sich** (meaning *himself*, *herself*, *itself*, *themselves* or *oneself*) and the infinitive of the verb.

⇨ For more information on **Reflexive pronouns**, see page 84.

2 Forming the present tense of reflexive verbs

➤ Reflexive verbs are often used to describe things you do (to yourself) every day or that involve a change of some sort (getting dressed, sitting down, getting excited, being in a hurry).

➤ The reflexive pronoun is either the direct object in the sentence, which means it is in the accusative case, or the indirect object in the sentence, which means it is in the dative case. Only the reflexive pronouns used with the **ich** and **du** forms of the verb have separate accusative and dative forms.

Accusative Form	Dative Form	Meaning
mich	mir	myself
dich	dir	yourself (*familiar*)
sich	sich	himself/herself/itself
uns	uns	ourselves
euch	euch	yourselves (*plural*)
sich	sich	themselves
sich	sich	yourself/yourselves (*polite*)

➤ The present tense forms of a reflexive verb work in just the same way as an ordinary verb, except that the reflexive pronoun is used as well.

➤ Below you will find the present tense of the common reflexive verbs **sich setzen** (meaning *to sit down*) which has its reflexive pronoun in the accusative and **sich erlauben** (meaning *to allow oneself*) which has its reflexive pronoun in the dative.

Reflexive Forms	Meaning
ich setze mich	I sit (myself) down
du setzt dich	you sit (yourself) down
er/sie/es setzt sich	he/she/it sits down
wir setzen uns	we sit down
ihr setzt euch	you (*plural familiar*) sit down
sie setzen sich	they sit down
Sie setzen sich	you (*polite form*) sit down

Ich setze **mich** neben dich.	I'll sit beside you.
Sie setzen **sich** aufs Sofa.	They sit down on the sofa.

Reflexive Forms	Meaning
ich erlaube mir	I allow myself
du erlaubst dir	you allow yourself
er/sie/es erlaubt sich	he/she/it allows himself/herself/itself
wir erlauben uns	we allow ourselves
ihr erlaubt euch	you (*plural familiar*) allow yourselves
sie erlauben sich	they allow themselves
Sie erlauben sich	you (*polite form*) allow yourself

Ich erlaube **mir** jetzt ein Bier.	Now I'm going to allow myself a beer.
Er erlaubt **sich** ein Stück Kuchen.	He's allowing himself a piece of cake.

➤ Some of the most common German reflexive verbs are listed here:

Reflexive Verb with Reflexive Pronoun in Accusative	Meaning
sich anziehen	to get dressed
sich aufregen	to get excited
sich beeilen	to hurry
sich beschäftigen mit	to be occupied with
sich bewerben um	to apply for
sich erinnern an	to remember
sich freuen auf	to look forward to
sich interessieren für	to be interested in
sich irren	to be wrong
sich melden	to report (for duty etc) *or* to volunteer
sich rasieren	to shave
sich setzen *or* hinsetzen	to sit down
sich trauen	to dare
sich umsehen	to look around

Ich **ziehe mich** schnell an und dann gehen wir.	I'll get dressed quickly and then we can go.
Wir müssen **uns beeilen**.	We must hurry.

Reflexive Verb with Reflexive Pronoun in Dative	Meaning
sich abgewöhnen	to give up (something)
sich ansehen	to have a look at
sich einbilden	to imagine (wrongly)
sich erlauben	to allow oneself
sich leisten	to treat oneself
sich vornehmen	to plan to do
sich vorstellen	to imagine
sich wünschen	to want

Ich muss <u>mir</u> das Rauchen abgewöhnen.	I must give up smoking.
Sie kann <u>sich</u> ein neues Auto nicht leisten.	She can't afford a new car.
Was <u>wünscht</u> ihr <u>euch</u> zu Weihnachten?	What do you want for Christmas?

[i] Note that a direct object reflexive pronoun changes to an indirect object pronoun if another direct object is present.

Ich wasche <u>mich</u>.	I'm having a wash.
mich = direct object reflexive pronoun	
Ich wasche <u>mir</u> die Hände.	I am washing my hands.
mir = indirect object reflexive pronoun	
die Hände = direct object	

⇨ *For more information on* **Pronouns***, see page* 69.

➤ Some German verbs which are not usually reflexive can be made reflexive by adding a reflexive pronoun.

Soll ich es melden?	Should I report it?
Ich habe <u>mich</u> gemeldet.	I volunteered.

⇨ *For more information on* **Reflexive pronouns***, see page* 84.

> **Key points**
> ✔ A reflexive verb is made up of a reflexive pronoun and a verb.
> ✔ The direct object pronouns in the accusative are mich, dich, sich, uns, euch, sich, sich.
> ✔ The indirect object pronouns in the dative are mir, dir, sich, uns, euch, sich, sich.

The imperative

> **What is the imperative?**
> An **imperative** is a form of the verb used when giving orders and instructions, for example, *Shut the door!; Sit down!; Don't go!*

1 Using the imperative

➤ In German, there are three main forms of the imperative that are used to give instructions or orders to someone. These correspond to the three different ways of saying *you*: **du**, **ihr** and **Sie**. However, it is only in the **Sie** form of the imperative that the pronoun usually appears – in the **du** and **ihr** forms, the pronoun is generally dropped, leaving only the verb.

Hör zu!	Listen!
Hören <u>Sie</u> zu!	Listen!

2 Forming the present tense imperative

➤ Most weak, strong and mixed verbs form the present tense imperative in the following way:

Pronoun	Form of Imperative	Verb Example	Meaning
du (*singular*)	verb stem (+ e)	hol(e)!	fetch!
ihr (*plural*)	verb stem + t	holt!	fetch!
Sie (*polite singular and plural*)	verb stem + en + Sie	holen Sie!	fetch!

i Note that the -e of the **du** form is often dropped, but NOT where the verb stem ends, for example, in **chn-**, **fn-**, or **tm-**. In such cases, the -e is kept to make the imperative easier to pronounce.

Hör zu!	Listen!
Hol es!	Fetch it!

BUT:	Öff<u>ne</u> die Tür!	Open the door!
	At<u>me</u> richtig durch!	Take a deep breath!
	Rech<u>ne</u> noch mal nach!	Do your sums again!

Grammar Extra!

Weak verbs ending in **-eln** or **-ern** also retain this **-e**, but the other **-e** in the stem itself is often dropped in spoken German.

Verb	Meaning	Imperative	Meaning
wandern	to walk	wand(e)re!	walk!
handeln	to act	hand(e)le!	act!

➤ Any vowel change in the present tense of a strong verb also occurs in the **du** form of its imperative and the **-e** mentioned above is generally not added. However, if this vowel change in the present tense involves adding an umlaut, this umlaut is NOT added to the **du** form of the imperative.

Verb	Meaning	2nd Person Singular	Meaning	2nd Person Singular Imperative	Meaning
nehmen	to take	du nimmst	you take	nimm!	take!
helfen	to help	du hilfst	you help	hilf!	help!
laufen	to run	du läufst	you run	lauf(e)!	run!
stoßen	to push	du stößt	you push	stoß(e)!	push!

3 | Word order with the imperative

➤ An object pronoun is a word like **es** (meaning *it*), **mir** (meaning *me*) or **ihnen** (meaning *them/to them*) that is used instead of a noun as the object of a sentence. In the imperative, the object pronoun comes straight after the verb. However, you can have orders and instructions containing both <u>direct object</u> and <u>indirect object</u> <u>pronouns</u>. In these cases, the direct object pronoun always comes before the indirect object pronoun.

Hol mir das Buch!	Fetch me that book!
Hol es mir!	Fetch me it!
Holt mir das Buch!	Fetch me that book!
Holt es mir!	Fetch me it!
Holen Sie mir das Buch!	Fetch me that book!
Holen Sie es mir!	Fetch me it!

⇨ For more information on **Word order with indirect object pronouns**, see page 77.

➤ In the imperative form of a reflexive verb such as **sich waschen** (meaning *to wash oneself*) or **sich setzen** (meaning *to sit down*), the reflexive pronoun comes immediately after the verb.

For further explanation of grammatical terms, please see pages x-xiv.

Reflexive verb	Meaning	Imperative Forms	Meaning
sich setzen	to sit down	setz dich!	sit down!
		setzt euch!	sit down!
		setzen Sie sich!	do sit down!

⇨ For more information on **Reflexive pronouns**, see page 84.

➤ In verbs which have separable prefixes, the prefix comes at the end of the imperative.

Verb with Separable Prefix	Meaning	Imperative Example	Meaning
zumachen	to close	**Mach die Tür zu!**	Close the door!
aufhören	to stop	**Hör aber endlich auf!**	Do stop it!

⇨ For more information on **Separable prefixes**, see page 109.

4 Other points about the imperative

➤ In German, imperatives are usually followed by an exclamation mark, unless they are not being used to give an order or instruction. For example, they can also be used where we might say *Can you...* or *Could you ...* in English.

Lass ihn in Ruhe!   Leave him alone!

Sagen Sie mir bitte, wie spät es ist.   Can you tell me what time it is please?

➤ The verb **sein** (meaning *to be*) is a strong, irregular verb. Its imperative forms are also irregular and the **du**, **Sie** and less common **wir** forms are not the same as the present tense forms of the verb.

Sei ruhig!   Be quiet!

Seid ruhig!   Be quiet!

Seien Sie ruhig!   Be quiet!

Tip

The words **auch**, **nur**, **mal** and **doch** are frequently used with imperatives to change their meanings in different ways, but are often not translated since they have no direct equivalent in English.

Geh doch!   Go on!/Get going!

Sag mal, wo warst du?   Tell me, where were you?

Versuchen Sie es mal!   Give it a try!

Komm schon!   Do come/Please come.

Mach es auch richtig!   Be sure to do it properly.

Grammar Extra!

There are some alternatives to using the imperative in German:

- Infinitives (the *to* form of a verb) are often used instead of the imperative in written instructions or public announcements

Einsteigen!	All aboard!
Zwiebeln abziehen und in Ringe schneiden.	Peel the onions and slice them.

- Nouns, adjectives or adverbs can also be used as imperatives

Ruhe!	Be quiet!/Silence!
Vorsicht!	Careful!/Look out!

Some of these have become set expressions

Achtung!	Listen!/Attention!
Rauchen verboten!	No smoking.

Key points

✔ The imperative has four forms: **du**, **ihr**, **Sie** and **wir**.

✔ The forms are the same as the **ihr**, **Sie** and **wir** forms of the present tense for most strong, weak and mixed verbs, but the **du** form drops the **-st** present tense ending and sometimes adds an -e on the end.

✔ Any vowel change in the stem of a strong verb also occurs in the imperative, except if it involves adding an umlaut.

✔ Object pronouns always go after the verb, with the direct object pronoun coming before the indirect object pronoun.

✔ Reflexive pronouns also come after the verb, while separable verb prefixes come at the end of the imperative sentence.

✔ **Sein** has irregular imperative forms.

Verb prefixes in the present tense

> **What is a verb prefix?**
> In English, a **verb prefix** is a word such as *up* or *down* which is used with verbs to create new verbs with an entirely different meaning.
>
>   get → get up → get down
>   put → put up → put down
>   shut → shut up → shut down

➤ In German there is a similar system, but the words are put before the infinitive and joined to it:

  zu (meaning *to*) + **geben** (meaning *to give*) = **zugeben** (meaning *to admit*)
  an (meaning *on, to, by*) + **ziehen** (meaning *to pull*) = **anziehen** (meaning *to put on* or *to attract*)

➤ Prefixes can be found in strong, weak and mixed verbs. Some prefixes are always joined to the verb and never separated from it – these are called inseparable prefixes. However, the majority are separated from the verb in certain tenses and forms, and come at the end of the sentence. They are called separable prefixes.

1 Inseparable prefixes

➤ There are eight inseparable prefixes in German, highlighted in the table of common inseparable verbs below:

Inseparable Verb	Meaning	Inseparable Verb	Meaning	Inseparable Verb	Meaning	Inseparable Verb	Meaning
beschreiben	to describe	enttäuschen	to disappoint	gehören	to belong	verlieren	to lose
empfangen	to receive	erhalten	to preserve	misstrauen	to mistrust	zerlegen	to dismantle

i Note that when you pronounce an inseparable verb, the stress is NEVER on the inseparable prefix:

  er**hal**ten
  ver**lie**ren
  emp**fang**en
  ver**gess**en

  Das muss ich wirklich nicht vergessen.   I really mustn't forget that.

2 Separable prefixes

➤ There are many separable prefixes in German and some of them are highlighted in the table below which shows a selection of the most common separable verbs:

Separable Verb	Meaning	Separable Verb	Meaning
a̲bfahren	to leave	mi̲tmachen	to join in
a̲nkommen	to arrive	na̲chgeben	to give way/in
a̲ufstehen	to get up	vo̲rziehen	to prefer
a̲usgehen	to go out	we̲glaufen	to run away
e̲insteigen	to get on	zu̲schauen	to watch
fe̲ststellen	to establish/see	zure̲chtkommen	to manage
fre̲ihalten	to keep free	zurü̲ckkehren	to return
he̲rkommen	to come (here)	zusa̲mmenpassen	to be well-suited; to go well together
hi̲nlegen	to put down		

Der Zug fährt in zehn Minuten a̲b.	The train is leaving in ten minutes.
Ich stehe jeden Morgen früh a̲uf.	I get up early every morning.
Sie gibt niemals na̲ch.	She'll never give in.

3 | Word order with separable prefixes

➤ In tenses consisting of one verb part only, for example the present and the imperfect, the separable prefix is placed at the end of the main clause.

Der Bus kam immer spät a̲n.　　The bus was always late.

⇨ *For more information on Separable prefixes in the perfect tense, see page 115.*

➤ In subordinate clauses, the prefix is attached to the verb, which is then placed at the end of the subordinate clause.

Weil der Bus spät a̲nkam, verpasste sie den Zug.　　Because the bus arrived late, she missed the train.

⇨ *For more information on **Subordinate clauses**, see page 177.*

➤ In infinitive phrases using **zu**, the **zu** is inserted between the verb and its prefix to form one word.

Um rechtzeitig au̲fzustehen, muss ich den Wecker stellen.　　In order to get up on time I'll have to set the alarm.

⇨ *For more information on the **Infinitive**, see page 134.*

For further explanation of grammatical terms, please see pages x-xiv.

4 Verb combinations

➤ Below you will see some other types of word which can be combined with verbs. These combinations are mostly written as two separate words (but some may also be written as one word) and behave like separable verbs:

- Noun + verb combinations

Ski fahren	to ski
Ich fahre gern Ski.	I like skiing.
Schlittschuh laufen	to ice-skate
Im Winter kann man Schlittschuh laufen.	You can ice-skate in winter.

- Infinitive + verb combinations

kennenlernen (or kennen lernen)	to meet or to get to know
Meine Mutter möchte dich kennenlernen.	My mother wants to meet you.
Er lernt sie nie richtig kennen.	He'll never get to know her properly.
sitzen bleiben (or sitzenbleiben)	to remain seated
Bleiben Sie bitte sitzen.	Please remain seated.
spazieren gehen (or spazierengehen)	to go for a walk
Er geht jeden Tag spazieren.	He goes for a walk every day.

- Adjective + verb combinations

bekannt machen	to announce
Die Regierung will das morgen bekannt machen.	The government plans to announce it tomorrow.

- Some adverb + verb combinations

gut riechen	to smell good
Das Essen riecht gut.	The food smells good.

- Verb combinations with -seits

abseitsstehen	to stand apart
Sie steht immer abseits von den anderen.	She always stands apart from the others.

- Prefix combinations with sein

auf sein	to be open or to be up
Das Fenster ist auf.	The window is open.
Die Geschäfte sind am Sonntag nicht auf.	The shops are closed on Sundays.
Sie ist noch nicht auf.	She isn't up yet.

zu sein	to be shut
Das Fenster <u>ist</u> <u>zu</u>.	The window is shut.

i Note that **auf** (meaning *open*) is another word for **geöffnet** and **zu** (meaning *shut* or *closed*) is another word for **geschlossen**.

Key points

✔ Prefixes can be found in strong, weak and mixed verbs.

✔ Eight prefixes are inseparable and are never separated from the verb.

✔ Most prefixes are separable and are separated from the verb in certain tenses and forms and come at the end of the sentence.

The perfect tense

> **What is the perfect tense?**
> The **perfect** is one of the verb tenses used to talk about the past, especially about a single, rather than a repeated action.
>
> Den Nachtisch habe ich schon gegessen.　　I've already eaten dessert.

1 Using the perfect tense

➤ The German perfect tense is the one generally used to translate an English form such as *I have finished*.

I <u>have</u> finished the book.　　Ich <u>habe</u> das Buch zu Ende <u>gelesen</u>.

➤ The perfect tense is also sometimes used to translate an English form such as *I gave*.

I gave him my phone number.　　Ich <u>habe</u> ihm meine Nummer <u>gegeben</u>.

> *Tip*
>
> When a specific time in the past is referred to, you use the perfect tense in German. In English you use the *-ed* form instead.
>
> Gestern Abend habe ich einen Krimi im Fernsehen gesehen.　　Last night I watched a thriller on TV.

➤ The perfect tense is used with **seit** or **seitdem** to describe a completed action in the past, whereas the present tense is used to describe an action which started in the past and is still continuing in the present.

Seit dem Unfall <u>habe</u> ich sie nur einmal <u>gesehen</u>.　　I've only seen her once since the accident.

⟹ For more information on this use of the **Present tense**, see page 94.

2 Forming the perfect tense

➤ Unlike the present and imperfect tenses, the perfect tense has <u>TWO</u> parts to it:

• the <u>present</u> tense of the irregular weak verb **haben** (meaning *to have*) or the irregular strong verb **sein** (meaning *to be*). They are also known as auxiliary verbs.

• a part of the main verb called the *past participle*, like *given, finished* and *done* in English.

➤ In other words, the perfect tense in German is like the form *I have done* in English.

Pronoun	Ending	Present Tense	Meanings
ich	-e	ich habe	I have
du	-st	du hast	you have
er sie es	-t	er hat sie hat es hat	he/she/it has
wir	-en	wir haben	we have
ihr	-t	ihr habt	you (*plural*) have
sie	-en	sie haben	they have
Sie		Sie haben	you (*polite*) have

Pronoun	Ending	Present Tense	Meanings
ich	–	ich bin	I am
du	–	du bist	you are
er sie es	–	er ist sie ist es ist	he/she/it is
wir	–	wir sind	we are
ihr	–	ihr seid	you (*plural*) are
sie	–	sie sind	they are
Sie	–	Sie sind	you (*polite*) are

3 | Forming the past participle

➤ To form the past participle of <u>weak</u> verbs, you add **ge-** to the beginning of the verb stem and **-t** to the end.

Infinitive	Take off -en	Add ge- and -t
holen (*to fetch*)	hol-	geholt
machen (*to do*)	mach-	gemacht

i Note that one exception to this rule is weak verbs ending in **-ieren**, which omit the **ge**.

studieren (*to study*)   studiert (*studied*)

➤ To form the past participle of <u>strong</u> verbs, you add **ge-** to the beginning of the verb stem and **-en** to the end. The vowel in the stem may also change.

Infinitive	Take off -en	Add ge- and -en
laufen (*to run*)	lauf-	gelaufen
singen (*to sing*)	sing-	gesungen

For further explanation of grammatical terms, please see pages x-xiv.

➤ To form the past participle of <u>mixed</u> verbs, you add **ge-** to the beginning of the verb stem and, like <u>weak</u> verbs, **-t** to the end. As with many strong verbs, the stem vowel may also change.

Infinitive	Take off -en	Add ge- and -t
bringen (to bring)	bring-	ge<u>bra</u>cht
denken (to think)	denk-	ge<u>da</u>cht

➤ The perfect tense of <u>separable</u> verbs is also formed in the above way, except that the separable prefix is joined on to the front of the **ge-**: **ich habe die Flasche aufgemacht, du hast die Flasche aufgemacht** and so on.

➤ With <u>inseparable</u> verbs, the only difference is that past participles are formed without the **ge-**: **ich habe Kaffee bestellt, du hast Kaffee bestellt** and so on.

⇨ For more information on **Separable** and **Inseparable verbs**, see page 109.

4 | Verbs that form their perfect tense with <u>haben</u>

➤ Most weak, strong and mixed verbs form their perfect tense with **haben**, for example **machen**:

Pronoun	haben	Past Participle	Meaning
ich	habe	gemacht	I did, I have done
du	hast	gemacht	you did, you have done
er sie es	hat	gemacht	he/she/it did, he/she/it has done
wir	haben	gemacht	we did, we have done
ihr	habt	gemacht	you (plural familiar) did, you have done
sie	haben	gemacht	they did, they have done
Sie	haben	gemacht	you (singular/plural formal) did, you have done

Sie hat ihre Hausaufgaben schon gemacht.	She has already done her homework.
Haben Sie gut geschlafen?	Did you sleep well?
Er hat fleißig gearbeitet.	He has worked hard.

5 haben or sein?

➤ MOST verbs form their perfect tense with **haben**.

Ich <u>habe</u> das schon <u>gemacht</u>.	I've already done that.
Wo <u>haben</u> Sie früher <u>gearbeitet</u>?	Where did you work before?

➤ With reflexive verbs the reflexive pronoun comes immediately after **haben**.

Ich <u>habe mich</u> heute Morgen geduscht.	I had a shower this morning.
Sie <u>hat sich</u> nicht daran erinnert.	She didn't remember.

⇨ *For more information on **Reflexive verbs**, see page 102.*

➤ There are two main groups of verbs which form their perfect tense with **sein** instead of **haben**, and most of them are strong verbs:

● verbs which take no direct object and are used mainly to talk about movement or a change of some kind, such as:

gehen	to go
kommen	to come
ankommen	to arrive
abfahren	to leave
aussteigen	to get off
einsteigen	to get on
sterben	to die
sein	to be
werden	to become
bleiben	to remain
begegnen	to meet
gelingen	to succeed
aufstehen	to get up
fallen	to fall

Gestern <u>bin</u> ich ins Kino <u>gegangen</u>.	I went to the cinema yesterday.
Sie <u>ist</u> heute Morgen ganz früh <u>abgefahren</u>.	She left really early this morning.
An welcher Haltestelle <u>sind</u> Sie <u>ausgestiegen</u>?	Which stop did you get off at?

● two verbs which mean *to happen*.

Was ist geschehen/passiert?	What happened?

⇨ Here are the perfect tense forms of a very common strong verb, gehen, in full:

Pronoun	sein	Past Participle	Meanings
ich	bin	gegangen	I went, I have gone
du	bist	gegangen	you went, you have gone
er sie es	ist	gegangen	he/she/it went, he/she/it has gone
wir	sind	gegangen	we went, we have gone
ihr	seid	gegangen	you (*plural familiar*) went, you have gone
sie	sind	gegangen	they went, they have gone
Sie	sind	gegangen	you (*singular/plural formal*) went, you have gone

i Note that the perfect tense of the most important strong, weak and mixed verbs is shown in the Verb Tables.

⇨ For **Verb Tables**, *see supplement*.

Key points

✔ The perfect tense describes things that happened and were completed in the past.

✔ The perfect tense is formed with the present tense of **haben** or **sein** and a past participle.

✔ The past participle begins in **ge-** and ends in -t for weak verbs, in **ge-** and -**en** for strong verbs, often with a stem vowel change, and in **ge-** and -**t** for mixed verbs, often with a stem vowel change.

✔ Most verbs take **haben** in the perfect tense. Many strong verbs, especially those referring to movement or change, take **sein**.

The imperfect tense

> **What is the imperfect tense?**
> The **imperfect tense** is one of the verb tenses used to talk about the past, especially in descriptions, and to say what used to happen, for example, It _was_ sunny at the weekend; I _used to walk_ to school.

1 | Using the imperfect tense

➤ The German imperfect tense is used:

- to describe actions in the past which the speaker feels have no link with the present

  Er _kam_ zu spät, um teilnehmen zu können.   He _arrived_ too late to take part.

- to describe what things were like and how people felt in the past

  Ich _war_ ganz traurig, als sie wegging.   I _was_ very sad when she left.

  Damals _gab_ es ein großes Problem mit Drogen.   There _was_ a big problem with drugs at that time.

- to say what used to happen or what you used to do regularly in the past

  Wir _machten_ jeden Tag einen Spaziergang.   We _used to go for a walk_ every day.

  Samstags _spielte_ ich Tennis.   I _used to play tennis_ on Saturdays.

> 🛈 Note that if you want to talk about an event or action that took place and was completed in the past, you normally use the _perfect tense_ in German conversation. The _imperfect tense_ is normally used in written German.
>
> **Was _hast_ du heute _gemacht_?**   What have you done today?

⇨ For more information on the **Perfect tense**, see page 113.

➤ When using **seit** or **seitdem** to describe something that _had_ happened or _had_ been true at a point in the past, the imperfect is used in German, where in English a verb form with _had_ is used.

   Sie _war_ seit ihrer Heirat als Lehrerin beschäftigt.   She _had_ been working as a teacher since her marriage.

⇨ For more information on the **Pluperfect tense**, see page 127.

> *Tip*
>
> Remember that you <u>NEVER</u> use the verb **sein** to translate *was* or *were* in forms like *was raining* or *were looking* and so on. You change the German verb ending instead.

2 | Forming the imperfect tense of weak verbs

➤ To form the imperfect tense of weak verbs, you use the same stem of the verb as for the present tense. Then you add the correct ending, depending on whether you are referring to **ich, du, er, sie, es, wir, ihr, sie** or Sie.

Pronoun	Ending	Add to Stem, e.g. spiel-	Meanings
ich	-te	ich spiel<u>te</u>	I played I was playing
du	-test	du spiel<u>test</u>	you played you were playing
er sie es	-te	er spiel<u>te</u> sie spiel<u>te</u> es spiel<u>te</u>	he/she/it played he/she/it played he/she/it were playing
wir	-ten	wir spiel<u>ten</u>	we played we were playing
ihr	-tet	ihr spiel<u>tet</u>	you (*plural*) played you were playing
sie Sie	-ten	sie spiel<u>ten</u> Sie spiel<u>ten</u>	they played they were playing you (*polite*) played you were playing

Sie holte ihn jeden Tag von der Arbeit ab.	She picked him up from work every day.
Normalerweise machte ich nach dem Abendessen meine Hausaufgaben.	I usually did my homework after dinner.

➤ As with the present tense, some weak verbs change their spellings slightly when they are used in the imperfect tense.

• If the stem ends in -d, -t, -m or -n an extra -e is added before the usual imperfect endings to make pronunciation easier.

Pronoun	Ending	Add to Stem, e.g. arbeit-	Meanings
ich	-ete	ich arbeit<u>ete</u>	I worked I was working
du	-etest	du arbeit<u>etest</u>	you worked you were working
er sie es	-ete	er arbeit<u>ete</u> sie arbeit<u>ete</u> es arbeit<u>ete</u>	he/she/it worked he/she/it was working
wir	-eten	wir arbeit<u>eten</u>	we worked we were working
ihr	-etet	ihr arbeit<u>etet</u>	you (*plural*) worked you were working
sie	-eten	sie arbeit<u>eten</u>	they worked they were working
Sie	-eten	Sie arbeit<u>eten</u>	you (*polite*) worked you (*polite*) were working

Sie arbeit<u>ete</u> übers Wochenende.   She was working over the weekend.

Ihr arbeit<u>etet</u> ganz schön viel.   You worked a lot.

- If the -m or -n has one of the consonants l, r or h in front of it, the -e is not added as shown in the du, er, sie and es, and ihr forms below.

Pronoun	Ending	Add to Stem, e.g. lern-	Meanings
du	-test	du lern<u>test</u>	you learned you were learning
er sie es	-te	er lern<u>te</u> sie lern<u>te</u> es lern<u>te</u>	he/she/it learned he/she/it was learning
ihr	-tet	ihr lern<u>tet</u>	you (*plural*) learned you were learning

Sie lern<u>te</u> alles ganz schnell.   She learned everything very quickly.

3 | Forming the imperfect tense of strong verbs

➤ The main difference between strong verbs and weak verbs in the imperfect is that strong verbs have a vowel change and take a different set of endings. For example, let's compare **sagen** and **rufen**:

	Infinitive	Meaning	Present	Imperfect
Weak	sagen	to say	er sagt	er sagte
Strong	rufen	to shout	er ruft	er rief

➤ To form the imperfect tense of strong verbs you add the following endings to the stem, which undergoes a vowel change.

Pronoun	Ending	Add to Stem, e.g. rief-	Meanings
ich	–	ich rief	I shouted I was shouting
du	-st	du riefst	you shouted you were shouting
er sie es	–	er rief sie rief es rief	he/she/it shouted he/she/it were shouting
wir	-en	wir riefen	we shouted we were shouting
ihr	-t	ihr rieft	you (*plural*) shouted you were shouting
sie Sie	-en	sie riefen Sie riefen	they shouted they were shouting you (*polite*) shouted you were shouting

Sie rief mich immer freitags an.	She always called me on Friday.
Sie liefen die Straße entlang.	They ran along the street.
Als Kind sangst du viel.	You used to sing a lot as a child.

➤ As in other tenses, the verb **sein** is a very irregular strong verb since the imperfect forms seem to have no relation to the infinitive form of the verb: **ich war, du warst, er/sie/es war, wir waren, ihr wart, sie/Sie waren.**

4 Forming the imperfect tense of mixed verbs

➤ The imperfect tense of mixed verbs is formed by adding the weak verb endings to a stem whose vowel has been changed as for a strong verb.

Pronoun	Ending	Add to Stem, e.g. kann-	Meanings
Ich	-te	ich kannte	I knew
du	-test	du kanntest	you knew
er sie es	-te	er kannte sie kannte es kannte	he/she/it knew
wir	-ten	wir kannten	we knew
ihr	-tet	ihr kanntet	you (*plural*) knew
sie Sie	-ten	sie kannten Sie kannten	they knew you (*polite*) knew

Er kannte die Stadt nicht.	He didn't know the town.

➤ **Bringen** (meaning *to bring*) and **denken** (meaning *to think*) have a vowel AND a consonant change in their imperfect forms

bringen (*to bring*)	**denken** (*to think*)
ich br<u>ach</u>te	ich d<u>ach</u>te
du br<u>ach</u>test	du d<u>ach</u>test
er/sie/es br<u>ach</u>te	er/sie/es d<u>ach</u>te
wir br<u>ach</u>ten	wir d<u>ach</u>ten
ihr br<u>ach</u>tet	ihr d<u>ach</u>tet
sie/Sie br<u>ach</u>ten	sie/Sie d<u>ach</u>ten

[*i*] Note that the imperfect tense of the most important strong, weak and mixed verbs is shown in the Verb Tables.

⇨ For **Verb Tables**, *see supplement.*

Key points

✔ The imperfect tense is generally used for things that happened regularly or for descriptions in the past, especially in written German.

✔ The imperfect of weak verbs is formed using the same stem of the verb as for the present tense + these endings: **-te**, **-test**, **-te**, **-ten**, **-tet**, **-ten**.

✔ If the stem of a weak verb ends in **-d**, **-t**, **-m** or **-n** an extra **-e** is added before the usual imperfect endings to make pronunciation easier. If the **-m** or **-n** has one of the consonants **l**, **r** or **h** in front of it, the **-e** is not added.

✔ The imperfect tense of strong verbs is formed by adding the following endings to the stem, which undergoes a vowel change: **-**, **-st**, **-**, **-en**, **-t**, **-en**.

✔ The imperfect tense of mixed verbs is formed by adding the weak verb endings to a stem whose vowel has been changed as for a strong verb. The verbs **bringen** and **denken** also have a consonant change.

The future tense

> **What is the future tense?**
> The **future tense** is a verb tense used to talk about something that will happen or will be true.

1 Using the future tense

➤ In English the future tense is often shown by *will* or its shortened form *'ll*.

> What <u>will</u> you do?
> The weather <u>will</u> be warm and dry tomorrow.
> He'<u>ll</u> be here soon.
> I'<u>ll</u> give you a call.

➤ Just as in English, you can use the present tense in German to refer to something that is going to happen in the future.

> Wir <u>fahren</u> nächstes Jahr nach Griechenland.   We're going to Greece next year.
>
> Ich nehme den letzten Zug heute Abend.   I'm taking the last train tonight.

➤ The future tense IS used however to:

- emphasize the future

> Das <u>werde</u> ich erst nächstes Jahr <u>machen können</u>.   I won't be able to do that until next year.

- express doubt or suppose something about the future

> Wenn sie zurückkommt, <u>wird</u> sie mir bestimmt <u>helfen</u>.   I'm sure she'll help me when she returns.

➤ In English we often use *going to* followed by an infinitive to talk about something that will happen in the immediate future. You CANNOT use the German verb **gehen** (meaning *to go*) followed by an infinitive in the same way. Instead, you use either the present or the future tense.

> Das <u>wirst</u> du bereuen.   You're going to regret that.
>
> Wenn er sich nicht beeilt, <u>verpasst</u> er den Zug.   He's going to miss the train if he doesn't hurry up.

2 Forming the future tense

➤ The future tense has <u>TWO</u> parts to it and is formed in the same way for all verbs, be they weak, strong or mixed:

- the present tense of the strong verb **werden** (meaning *to become*), which acts as an <u>auxiliary verb</u> like **haben** and **sein** in the perfect tense

Pronoun	Ending	Present Tense	Meanings
ich	-e	ich werde	I become
du	-st	du wirst	you become
er sie es	–	er wird sie wird es wird	he/she/it becomes
wir	-en	wir werden	we become
ihr	-t	ihr werdet	you (plural) become
sie	-en	sie werden	they become
Sie	-en	Sie werden	you (polite) become

- the infinitive of the main verb, which normally goes at the end of the clause or sentence.

Pronoun	Present Tense of werden	Infinitive of Main Verb	Meanings
ich	werde	holen	I will fetch
du	wirst	holen	you will fetch
er sie es	wird	holen	he/she/it will fetch
wir	werden	holen	we will fetch
ihr	werdet	holen	you (plural) will fetch
sie Sie	werden	holen	they will fetch you (polite) will fetch

Morgen **werde** ich mein Fahrrad <u>holen</u>.   I'll fetch my bike tomorrow.

Sie **wird** dir meine Adresse <u>geben</u>.   She'll give you my address.

Wir **werden** draußen <u>warten</u>.   We'll wait outside.

[*i*] Note that in reflexive verbs, the reflexive pronoun comes after the present tense of werden.

Ich <u>werde</u> mich nächste Woche <u>vorbereiten</u>.   I'll prepare next week.

Key points

✔ You can use a present tense in German to talk about something that will happen or be true in the future, just as in English.

✔ The future tense is formed from the present tense of **werden** and the infinitive of the main verb.

✔ You CANNOT use gehen with an infinitive to refer to things that will happen in the immediate future.

✔ The future tense is used to emphasize the future and express doubt or suppose something about the future.

For further explanation of grammatical terms, please see pages x-xiv.

The conditional

What is the conditional?

The **conditional** is a verb form used to talk about things that would happen or that would be true under certain conditions, for example, *I would help you if I could.* It is also used to say what you would like or need, for example, *Could you give me the bill?*

1 Using the conditional

➤ You can often recognize a conditional in English by the word *would* or its shortened form *'d*.

> I would be sad if you left.
>
> If you asked him, he'd help you.

➤ In German, the conditional is also used to express *would*.

Ich **würde** dir schon **helfen**, ich habe aber keine Zeit.	I would help you, but I don't have the time.
Was **würden** Sie an meiner Stelle **tun?**	What would you do in my position?

2 Forming the conditional

➤ The conditional has TWO parts to it and is formed in the same way for all verbs, be they weak, strong or mixed:

- the **würde** form or subjunctive of the verb **werden** (meaning *to become*)
- the infinitive of the main verb, which normally goes at the end of the clause.

Pronoun	Subjunctive of werden	Infinitive of Main Verb	Meanings
ich	würde	holen	I would fetch
du	würdest	holen	you would fetch
er sie es	würde	holen	he/she/it would fetch
wir	würden	holen	we would fetch
ihr	würdet	holen	you (*plural*) would fetch
sie	würden	holen	they would fetch
Sie			you (*polite*) would fetch

Das würde ich nie machen.	I would never do that.
Würdest du mir etwas Geld leihen?	Would you lend me some money?
Würden Sie jemals mit dem Rauchen aufhören?	Would you ever stop smoking?

i Note that you have to be careful not to mix up the present tense of **werden**, used to form the future tense, and the subjunctive of **werden**, used to form the conditional. They look similar.

FUTURE USE	CONDITIONAL USE
ich werde	ich würde
du wirst	du würdest
er/sie/es wird	er/sie/es würde
wir werden	wir würden
ihr werdet	ihr würdet
sie/Sie werden	sie/Sie würden

Key points

✔ The conditional tense is formed from the subjunctive or **würde** part of **werden** and the infinitive of the main verb.

✔ The future tense is often confused with the conditional.

The pluperfect tense

> **What is the pluperfect tense?**
> The **pluperfect** is a verb tense which describes something that had happened or had been true at a point in the past, for example, *I'd forgotten to finish my homework*.

1 Using the pluperfect tense

➤ You can often recognize a pluperfect tense in English by a form like *I had arrived, you'd fallen*.

Sie <u>waren</u> schon <u>weggefahren</u>.	They <u>had</u> already <u>left</u>.
Diese Bücher <u>hatten</u> sie schon <u>gelesen</u>.	They <u>had</u> already <u>read</u> these books.
Meine Eltern <u>waren</u> schon ins Bett <u>gegangen</u>.	My parents <u>had gone</u> to bed already.

[i] Note that when translating *had done/had been doing* in conjunction with **seit/seitdem**, you use the imperfect tense in German.

Sie <u>machte</u> es seit Jahren.   She <u>had been doing</u> it for years.

⇨ For more information on the *Imperfect tense*, see page 118.

2 Forming the pluperfect tense

➤ Like the perfect tense, the pluperfect tense in German has <u>two</u> parts to it:

- the <u>imperfect</u> tense of the verb **haben** (meaning *to have*) or **sein** (meaning *to be*)
- the past participle

➤ If a verb takes **haben** in the perfect tense, then it will take **haben** in the pluperfect too. If a verb takes **sein** in the perfect, then it will take **sein** in the pluperfect.

⇨ For more information on the *Imperfect tense* and the *Perfect tense*, see pages 118 and 113.

3 Verbs taking haben

➤ Here are the pluperfect tense forms of **holen** (meaning *to fetch*) in full.

Pronoun	haben	Past Participle	Meanings
ich	hatte	geholt	I had fetched
du	hattest	geholt	you had fetched
er sie es	hatte	geholt	he/she/it had fetched
wir	hatten	geholt	we had fetched
ihr	hattet	geholt	you (*plural*) had fetched
sie Sie	hatten	geholt	they had fetched you (*polite*) had fetched

Ich <u>hatte</u> schon mit ihm <u>gesprochen</u>.   I had already spoken to him.

4 Verbs taking sein

➤ Here are the pluperfect tense forms of reisen (meaning *to travel*) in full.

Pronoun	sein	Past Participle	Meanings
ich	war	gereist	I had travelled
du	warst	gereist	you had travelled
er sie es	war	gereist	he/she/it had travelled
wir	waren	gereist	we had travelled
ihr	wart	gereist	you (*plural*) had travelled
sie Sie	waren	gereist	they had travelled you (*polite*) had travelled

Sie <u>war</u> sehr spät <u>angekommen</u>.   She had arrived very late.

Key points

✔ The pluperfect tense describes things that had happened or were true at a point in the past before something else happened.

✔ It is formed with the imperfect tense of haben or sein and the past participle.

✔ Verbs which take haben in the perfect tense will take haben in the pluperfect tense and those which take sein in the perfect tense will take sein in the pluperfect tense.

The subjunctive

> **What is the subjunctive?**
> The **subjunctive** is a verb form that is used in certain circumstances to express some sort of feeling, or to show there is doubt about whether something will happen or whether something is true. It is only used occasionally in modern English, for example, *If I were you, I wouldn't bother; So be it.*

1 Using the subjunctive

➤ In German, subjunctive forms are used much more frequently than in English, to express uncertainty, speculation or doubt.

Es könnte doch wahr sein.	It could be true.

➤ Subjunctives are also commonly used in indirect speech, also known as reported speech. What a person asks or thinks can be reported directly:

Sie sagte: „Er kennt deine Schwester"	She said, "He knows your sister"

OR indirectly:

Sie sagte, er kenne meine Schwester.	She said he knew my sister.

[*i*] Note that the change from direct to indirect speech is indicated by a change of tense in English, but is shown by a change to the subjunctive form in German.

Grammar Extra!

➤ There are two ways of introducing indirect speech in German, as in English.

- The conjunction **dass** (meaning *that*) begins the clause containing the indirect speech and the verb goes to the end of the clause.

Sie hat uns gesagt, dass sie Italienisch spreche.	She told us that she spoke Italian.

- **dass** is dropped and normal word order applies in the second clause – the verb comes directly after the subject.

Sie hat uns gesagt, sie spreche Italienisch.	She told us she spoke Italian.

➤ If you want to express a possible situation in English, for example, *I would be happy if you came*, you use 'if' followed by the appropriate tense of the verb. In German you use the conjunction **wenn** followed by a subjunctive form of the verb.

[*i*] Note that the verb ALWAYS goes to the end of a clause beginning with **wenn**.

- **wenn** (meaning *if, whenever*)

  Wenn du käm(e)st (subjunctive), **wäre** (subjunctive) **ich froh.**

  OR

  Wenn du käm(e)st, würde ich froh sein.   I would be happy if you came.

[*i*] Note that the main clause can either have a subjunctive form or the conditional form.

  Wenn es mir nicht gefiele, würde ich es nicht bezahlen.

  OR

  Wenn es mir nicht gefiele, bezahlte (subjunctive) **ich es nicht.**   If I wasn't happy with it, I wouldn't pay for it.

Tip

The imperfect forms of **bezahlen**, and of all weak verbs, are exactly the same as the imperfect subjunctive forms, so it's better to use a conditional tense to avoid confusion.

➤ **wenn ... nur** (meaning *if only*), **selbst wenn** (meaning *even if* or *even though*) and **wie** (meaning *how*) work in the same way as **wenn**. This means that the normal word order is changed and the verb comes at the end of the clause.

- **wenn ... nur**

  Wenn wir nur erfolgreich wären!   If only we were successful!

- **selbst wenn**

  Selbst wenn er etwas wüsste, würde er nichts sagen.   Even if he knew about it, he wouldn't say anything.

- **wie**, expressing uncertainty

  Er wunderte sich, wie es ihr wohl ginge.   He wondered how she was.

➤ Unlike **wenn** and **wie** etc, the word order does not change after **als** (meaning *as if* or *as though*) when it is used in conditional clauses: it is immediately followed by the verb.

  Sie sah aus, als sei sie krank.   She looked as if she were ill.

Tip

It is quite common to hear the subjunctive used when someone is asking you something politely, for example, the person serving you in a shop might ask:

  Wäre da sonst noch etwas?   Will there be anything else?

---

2 | Forming the present subjunctive

➤ The three main forms of the subjunctive are the present subjunctive, the imperfect subjunctive and the pluperfect subjunctive.

➤ The present subjunctive of weak, strong and mixed verbs has the same endings:

Pronoun	Present Subjunctive: Weak and Strong Verb Endings
ich	-e
du	-est
er/sie/es	-e
wir	-en
ihr	-et
sie/Sie	-en

- holen (weak verb, meaning *to fetch*)

  ich hol**e**   I fetch
  du hol**est**   you fetch

- fahren (strong verb, meaning *to drive, to go*)

  Ich fahr**e**   I drive, I go
  du fahr**est**   you drive, you go

- denken (mixed verb, meaning *to think*)

  ich denk**e**   I think
  du denk**est**   you think

> **Tip**
>
> The present and the present subjunctive endings are exactly the same for the ich, wir and sie/Sie forms.

3 | Forming the imperfect subjunctive

➤ The imperfect subjunctive is very common and is not always used to describe actions in the past. It can, for example, express the future.

Wenn ich nur früher kommen könnte!   If only I could come earlier!

➤ The imperfect tense and the imperfect subjunctive of weak verbs are identical.

Pronoun	Imperfect/Imperfect Subjunctive	Meaning
ich	holte	I fetched
du	holtest	you fetched
er/sie/es	holte	he/she/it fetched
wir	holten	we fetched
ihr	holtet	you (plural) fetched
sie/Sie	holten	they/you (polite) fetched

➤ The imperfect subjunctive of strong verbs is formed by adding the following endings to the stem of the imperfect. If there is an a, o or u in this stem, an umlaut is also added to it.

Pronoun	Imperfect Subjunctive: Strong Verb Endings
ich	-e
du	-(e)st
er/sie/es	-e
wir	-en
ihr	-(e)t
sie/Sie	-en

ℹ️ Note that you add the -e to the du and ihr parts of the verb if it makes pronunciation easier, for example:

| du stießest | you pushed |
| ihr stießet | you pushed |

Pronoun	Imperfect Subjunctive	Meaning
ich	gäbe	I gave
du	gäb(e)st	you gave
er/sie/es	gäbe	he/she/it gave
wir	gäben	we gave
ihr	gäb(e)t	you (plural) gave
sie/Sie	gäben	they/you (polite) gave

➤ The imperfect subjunctive forms of the mixed verbs **brennen**, **kennen**, **senden**, **nennen**, **rennen** and **wenden** add weak verb imperfect endings to the stem of the verb, which DOES NOT change the vowel. The imperfect subjunctive forms of the remaining mixed verbs **bringen**, **denken** and **wissen** are also the same as the imperfect with one major difference: not only does the stem vowel change, but an umlaut is also added to the a or u. However, all of these forms are rare, with the conditional tense being used much more frequently instead.

Wenn ich du wäre, <u>würde</u> ich <u>rennen</u>.

INSTEAD OF

Wenn ich du wäre, <u>rennte</u> ich.　　　If I were you, I would run.

Ich <u>würde</u> so etwas nie <u>denken</u>!

INSTEAD OF

Ich <u>dächte</u> so etwas nie!　　　I would never think such a thing!

⇨ For more information on the **Conditional**, see page 125.

Grammar Extra!

The pluperfect subjunctive is formed from the imperfect subjunctive of haben or sein + the past participle. This subjunctive form is frequently used to translate the English structure 'If I had done something, ...'

Wenn ich Geld <u>gehabt hätte</u>,　　　If I had had money,
<u>wäre</u> ich <u>gereist</u>.　　　I would have travelled.

Key points

✔ In German, subjunctive forms are used much more frequently than in English, to express uncertainty, speculation or doubt.

✔ Subjunctive forms are commonly used in indirect speech and in conditional sentences.

✔ The present subjunctive of weak, strong and mixed verbs have the same endings.

✔ The imperfect tense and the imperfect subjunctive of weak verbs are identical.

✔ The imperfect subjunctive of strong verbs is formed by adding the endings -e, -(e)st, -e, -en, -(e)t, -en to the stem of the imperfect and often has an umlaut change.

✔ The imperfect subjunctive of mixed verbs is rare and the conditonal form of **würde** + infinitive is normally used instead.

The infinitive

> **What is the infinitive?**
> The **infinitive** is the 'to' form of the verb, for example, *to go*, and is the form you look up in a dictionary. It is the **-en** form of the verb in German.

Using the infinitive

➤ **zu** is used with the infinitive:

- after other verbs

  Ich versuchte <u>zu</u> kommen.   I tried <u>to come</u>.

- after adjectives

  Es war leicht <u>zu</u> sehen.   It was easy <u>to see</u>.

  Es ist schwierig <u>zu</u> verstehen.   It's hard <u>to understand</u>.

- after nouns

  Ich habe keine Zeit, <u>zu</u> gehen.   I don't have the time <u>to go</u>.

  Ich habe keine Lust, heute <u>zu</u> arbeiten.   I don't want to <u>work today</u>

➤ The infinitive is used <u>without</u> zu after the following:

- modal verbs, such as **können** (meaning *to be able*, *can*)

  Sie kann gut schwimmen.   She can swim very well.

⇨ *For more information on **Modal verbs**, see page 136.*

Tip

The English *–ing* form is often translated by the German infinitive, as shown in some of the examples below.

- the verbs **lassen** (meaning *to let, to leave*), **bleiben** (meaning *to stay*) and **gehen** (meaning *to go*)

  Sie <u>ließen</u> uns <u>warten</u>.   They kept us waiting.

  Sie <u>blieb</u> <u>sitzen</u>.   She remained seated.

  Er <u>ging</u> <u>einkaufen</u>.   He went shopping.

- verbs of perception such as **hören** (meaning *to hear, to listen (to)*) and **sehen** (meaning *to see, to watch*)

  Ich <u>sah</u> ihn <u>kommen</u>.   I saw him coming.

  Er <u>hörte</u> sie <u>singen</u>.   He heard her singing.

➤ The infinitive can be used to give an order or instruction.

Bitte nicht in diesen Zug einsteigen!   Please don't board this train!

➤ It can also be used as a noun with a capital letter. It is always neuter.

rauchen = to smoke

Sie hat das Rauchen aufgegeben.   She's given up smoking.

Key points

✔ The infinitive is the 'to' form of the verb, the one you look up in a dictionary.

✔ **zu** is used with the infinitive after other verbs, adjectives and nouns.

✔ The infinitive is used WITHOUT **zu** after certain verbs, mostly modal verbs.

✔ The infinitive can be used to give an order or instruction.

✔ It can be used as a noun with a capital letter and is always neuter.

Modal verbs

> **What are modal verbs?**
> **Modal verbs** are used to <u>modify</u> or <u>change</u> other verbs to show such things as *ability, permission* or *necessity*. For example, *He <u>can</u> swim; <u>May</u> I come?; We <u>ought to</u> go.*

1 Using modal verbs

➤ In German, the modal verbs are **dürfen, können, mögen, müssen, sollen** and **wollen**.

➤ Modal verbs are different from other verbs in their conjugation, which is shown in the Verb Tables.

⇨ For **Verb Tables**, see supplement.

➤ Here are the main uses of **dürfen**:

- Meaning *to be allowed to* or *may*
  <u>Darfst</u> du mit ins Kino kommen?   Are you allowed to/can you come to the cinema with us?

- Meaning *must not* or *may not*
  Ich <u>darf</u> keine Schokolade essen.   I mustn't eat any chocolate.

- Expressing politeness
  <u>Darf</u> ich?   May I?

➤ Here are the main uses of **können**:

- Meaning *to be able to* or *can*
  Wir <u>können</u> es nicht schaffen.   We can't make it.

- Meaning *would be able to* or *could*
  <u>Könntest</u> du morgen hinfahren?   Could you go there tomorrow?

- As a more common, informal alternative to **dürfen**, with the meaning *to be allowed to* or *can*
  <u>Kann</u> ich/<u>Darf</u> ich einen Kaffee haben?   Can I/May I have a coffee?

- Expressing possibility
  Das <u>kann</u> sein.   That may be so.
  Das <u>kann</u> nicht sein.   That can't be true.

➤ Here are the main uses of **mögen**:

- Meaning *to like*, when expressing likes and dislikes
  <u>Magst</u> du Schokolade?   Do you like chocolate?
  Sie <u>mögen</u> es nicht.   They don't like it.

- Meaning *would like to*, when expressing wishes and polite requests
  <u>Möchtest</u> du sie besuchen?   Would you like to visit her?
  <u>Möchten</u> Sie etwas trinken?   Would you like something to drink?

- Expressing possibility or probability

  Es **mag** sein, dass es falsch war.   It may well be that it was wrong.

➤ Here are the main uses of **müssen**:

- Meaning *to have to* or *must* or *need to*

  Sie **musste** jeden Tag um sechs aufstehen.   She had to get up at six o'clock every day.

- Certain common, informal uses

  Muss das sein?   Is that really necessary?

  Den Film **muss** man gesehen haben.   That film is worth seeing.

[*i*] Note that you can use a negative form of **brauchen** (meaning *to need*) instead of müssen for *don't have to* or *need not*

  Das **brauchst** du nicht zu sagen.   You don't have to say that.

➤ Here are the main uses of **sollen**:

- Meaning *ought to* or *should*

  Das **sollten** Sie sofort machen.   You ought to do that straight away.

  Sie wusste nicht, was sie tun **sollte**.   She didn't know what to do. (*what she should do*)

- Meaning *to be (supposed) to* where someone else has asked you to do something

  Du **sollst** deine Freundin anrufen.   You are to/should phone your girlfriend (*she has left a message asking you to ring*).

- Meaning *to be said to be*

  Sie **soll** sehr reich sein.   I've heard she's very rich/ She is said to be very rich.

➤ Here are the main uses of **wollen**:

- Meaning *to want* or *to want to*

  Sie **will** Lkw-Fahrerin werden.   She wants to be a lorry driver.

- As a common, informal alternative to **mögen**, meaning *to want* or *wish*

  Willst du eins?   Do you want one?

  Willst du/**Möchtest** du etwas trinken?   Do you Want/Would you like something to drink?

- Meaning *to be willing to*

  Er **will** nichts sagen.   He refuses to say anything.

- Expressing something you previously intended to do

  Ich **wollte** gerade anrufen.   I was just about to phone.

2 Modal verb forms

➤ Modal verbs have unusual present tenses:

dürfen	können	mögen
ich darf	ich kann	ich mag
du darfst	du kannst	du magst
er/sie/es darf	er/sie/es kann	er/sie/es mag
wir dürfen	wir können	wir mögen
ihr dürft	ihr könnt	ihr mögt
sie/Sie dürfen	sie/Sie können	sie/Sie mögen

müssen	sollen	wollen
ich muss	ich soll	ich will
du musst	du sollst	du willst
er/sie/es muss	er/sie/es soll	er/sie/es will
wir müssen	wir sollen	wir wollen
ihr müsst	ihr sollt	ihr wollt
sie/Sie müssen	sie/Sie sollen	sie/Sie wollen

➤ In tenses consisting of one verb part, the infinitive of the verb used with the modal comes at the end of the sentence or clause.

Sie <u>kann</u> sehr gut <u>schwimmen</u>. She is a very good swimmer.

Grammar Extra!

In sentences with modal verbs where the other verb expresses movement, it can be dropped if there is an adverb or adverbial phrase to show movement instead.

Ich <u>muss nach Hause</u>. I must go home.
Die Kinder <u>sollen</u> jetzt <u>ins Bett</u>. The children have to go to bed now.

⇨ *For more information on **Adverbs**, see page 57.*

Key points

✔ Modal verbs are used to <u>modify</u> the meaning of other verbs.

✔ In German, the modal verbs are **dürfen, können, mögen, müssen, sollen** and **wollen**.

✔ Modal verbs are different from other verbs in their conjugation.

For further explanation of grammatical terms, please see pages x–xiv.

Impersonal verbs

> **What is an impersonal verb?**
> An **impersonal verb** is one that does not relate to a real person or thing and
> where the subject is represented by *it*, for example, *It's going to rain; It's ten o'clock.*

➤ In German, <u>impersonal verbs</u> are used with **es** (meaning *it*) and the third person
singular form of the verb.

Es regnet.	It's raining.
Es gibt ein Problem.	There's a problem.

➤ Here are the most common impersonal verbs. In some of these expressions
it is possible to drop the **es**, in which case a personal pronoun such as **mich**
or **mir** begins the clause. For example:

Es ist mir egal, ob er mitkommt

OR

Mir ist egal, ob er mitkommt   I don't care if he comes with us.

⇨ *For more information on **Personal pronouns**, see page 70.*

➤ These expressions are marked with a * in the list below.

- **Es freut mich, dass/zu**   I am glad that/to.
  Es freut mich, dass du gekommen   I'm pleased that you have come.
  bist.

  Es freut mich, Sie in unserer Stadt   I'm pleased to welcome you to
  begrüßen zu dürfen.   our town.

- **Es gefällt mir.**   I like it.
  Es gefällt mir gar nicht.   I don't like it at all.

- **Es geht mir gut/schlecht.**   I'm fine/not too good.

- **Es geht nicht.**   It's not possible.

- **es geht um**   it's about
  Es geht um die Liebe.   It's about love.

- **es gelingt mir (zu)**   I succeed (in)
  Es ist <u>mir</u> gelungen, ihn zu überzeugen.   I managed to convince him.

- **es handelt sich um**   it's a question of
  Es handelt sich um Zeit und Geld.   It's a question of time and money.

- **Es hängt davon ab.**   It depends.
  Es hängt davon ab, ob ich arbeiten   It depends whether I have to
  muss.   work or not.

- Es hat keinen Zweck.

  There's no point.

- es ist mir egal (ob)*

  it's all the same to me (if)

  Es ist mir egal, ob du kommst oder nicht.

  I don't care if you come or not.

- es ist möglich(, dass)

  it's possible (that)

  Es is doch möglich, dass sie ihr Handy nicht dabei hat.

  It's always possible she doesn't have her mobile with her.

- es ist nötig

  it's necessary

  Es wird nicht nötig sein, mir Bescheid zu sagen.

  It won't be necessary to let me know.

- es ist schade(, dass)

  it's a pity (that)

  Es ist schade, dass sie nicht kommt.

  It's a pity (that) she isn't coming.

- Es ist mir warm OR Es ist mir kalt*.

  I'm warm OR I'm cold.

- Es klingelt.

  Someone's ringing the bell OR The phone is ringing.

  Es hat gerade geklingelt.

  The bell just went OR The phone just rang.

- Es klopft.

  Someone's knocking (at the door).

- es kommt darauf an(, ob)

  it all depends (whether)

  Es kommt darauf an, ob ich arbeiten muss.

  It all depends whether I have to work.

- Es lohnt sich (nicht).

  It's (not) worth it.

  Ich weiß nicht, ob es sich lohnt oder nicht.

  I don't know if it's worth it or not.

- Es macht nichts.

  It doesn't matter.

- es macht nichts aus

  it makes no difference

  Macht es dir etwas aus, wenn wir morgen gehen?

  Would you mind if we went tomorrow?

- es stimmt, dass ...

  it's true that ...

  Es stimmt, dass sie keine Zeit hat.

  It's true that she doesn't have any time.

- es tut mir leid(, dass) ...

  I'm sorry(that) ...

- Wie geht es (dir)?

  How are you?

- Mir wird schlecht*.

  I feel sick.

➤ All weather verbs are impersonal.

Infinitive	Expression	Meaning
donnern und blitzen	es donnert und blitzt	there's thunder and lightning
frieren	es friert	it's freezing
gießen	es gießt	it's pouring
regnen	es regnet	it's raining
schneien	es schneit	it's snowing
sein	es ist warm/kalt	it's cold/warm

Key points

✔ Impersonal verbs are used with **es** (meaning it) and the third person singular form of the verb.

✔ All weather verbs are impersonal.

There is/There are

➤ There are two main ways of expressing this in German.

1 Es gibt

- This is always used in the singular form and is followed by a singular or plural object in the accusative case.

Es gibt zu viele Probleme dabei.	There are too many problems involved.
Es gibt keinen besseren Wein.	There is no better wine.

- Es gibt is used to refer to things of a general nature.

Es gibt bestimmt Regen.	It's definitely going to rain.
Wenn wir zu spät kommen, gibt es Ärger.	If we arrive late, there'll be trouble.

- It is often used informally.

Was gibts (=gibt es) zu essen?	What is there to eat?
Was gibts?	What's wrong?, What's up?
So was gibts doch nicht!	That's impossible!

2 Es ist/es sind

- Here, the es simply introduces the real subject of the sentence, so if the subject is plural, es sind is used. The subject is in the nominative case.

Es sind kaum Leute da.	There are hardly any people there.

- Where the subject and verb swap places in the clause or sentence, the es is dropped.

Da sind kaum Leute.	There are hardly any people there.

[i] Note that es gibt is frequently used instead of es ist/es sind in the above two examples.

- Es ist or es sind are used to refer to a temporary situation.

Es war niemand da.	There was no-one there.

- They are also used to begin a story.

Es war einmal eine Königin.	Once upon a time there was a Queen ...

Key point

✔ In German there are two main ways of translating *there is/there are*: es gibt and es ist/es sind.

For further explanation of grammatical terms, please see pages x-xiv.

Use of es as an anticipatory object

➤ The object of many verbs can be a clause beginning with **dass** (meaning *that*) or an infinitive with **zu**.

Er wusste, <u>dass</u> wir pünktlich kommen würden.	He knew that we would come on time.
Sie fing an <u>zu</u> lachen.	She began to laugh.

➤ With some verbs, **es** is often used as the object to anticipate this clause or infinitive phrase.

Er hatte <u>es</u> abgelehnt, mitzukommen.	He refused to come.

➤ When the **dass** clause or infinitive phrase begins the sentence, **es** is not used in the main clause. Instead, it can be replaced by the pronoun **das** (meaning *that*).

<u>Dass</u> es Karla war, <u>das</u> haben wir ihr verschwiegen.	We did not tell her that it was Karla.

(i) Note that **dass** is a subordinating conjunction and **das** is a demonstrative pronoun.

⟹ For more information on **Subordinating conjunctions**, see page 172.

➤ The following common verbs <u>usually</u> have the **es** object.

- **es ablehnen, zu ...**   to refuse to

- **es aushalten, zu tun/dass ...**   to stand doing

  Ich halte <u>es</u> nicht mehr aus, bei ihnen zu arbeiten.   I can't stand working for them any longer.

- **es ertragen, zu tun/dass ...**   to bear doing

  Ich ertrage <u>es</u> nicht, dass sie mir widerspricht.   I can't bear her contradicting me.

- **es leicht haben, zu ...**   to find it easy to

  Sie hatte <u>es</u> nicht leicht, sie zu überreden.   She didn't have an easy job persuading them.

- **es nötig haben, zu ...**   to need to

  Ich habe <u>es</u> nicht nötig, mit dir darüber zu reden.   I don't have to talk to you about it.

- **es satt haben, zu ...**   to have had enough of (doing)

  Ich habe <u>es</u> satt, englische Verben zu lernen.   I've had enough of learning English verbs.

- **es verstehen, zu ...**   to know how to

  Sie versteht <u>es</u>, Autos zu reparieren.   She knows about repairing cars.

➤ The following common verbs <u>often</u> have the es object.

- es jemandem anhören/ansehen, dass ...

  to tell by listening to/looking at someone that

  Man hörte <u>es</u> ihm an, dass er kein Deutscher war.

  You could tell by listening to him that he wasn't German.

- es bereuen, zu tun/dass ...

  to regret doing/that

  Ich bereue <u>es</u> nicht, dass ich gekommen bin.

  I don't regret coming.

- es jemandem verbieten, zu ...

  to forbid someone to

  Ihre Mutter hat <u>es</u> ihr verboten, dort hinzugehen.

  Her mother forbade her to go there.

  es wagen zu ...

  to dare to

  Er wagte <u>es</u> nicht, ein neues Auto zu kaufen.

  He didn't dare buy a new car.

Key points

✔ The object of many verbs can be a clause beginning with **dass** (meaning *that*) or an infinitive with **zu**.

✔ With some verbs, **es** is used as the object to anticipate this clause or infinitive phrase.

✔ When the **dass** clause or infinitive phrase begins the sentence, **es** is not used in the main clause. Instead, it can be replaced by the pronoun **das** (meaning *that*).

For further explanation of grammatical terms, please see pages x-xiv.

Verbs followed by prepositions

➤ Some English verbs must be followed by prepositions for certain meanings, for example, *to wait for*, *to ask for*. This also happens in German:

sich sehnen <u>nach</u>	to long <u>for</u>
warten <u>auf</u>	to wait <u>for</u>
bitten <u>um</u>	to ask <u>for</u>

Tip

As you can see from the examples above, the preposition that is used in German is not always the same as the one that is used in English. Whenever you learn a new verb, try to learn which preposition is used after it too.

➤ As in English, using different prepositions with a verb creates completely different meanings.

bestehen	to pass (a test etc)
bestehen <u>aus</u>	to consist of
bestehen <u>auf</u>	to insist on
sich freuen <u>auf</u>	to look forward to
sich freuen <u>über</u>	to be pleased about

i Note that you occasionally need to use a preposition with a German verb whose English equivalent does not have one.

diskutieren <u>über</u>	to discuss

➤ Prepositions used with these verbs behave like normal prepositions and affect the case of the following noun in the normal way. For instance, with verbs followed by **für** the accusative case is always used.

sich interessieren für	to be interested in
Sie interessiert sich nicht <u>für den neuen</u> Wagen.	She isn't interested in the new car.

➤ A verb plus preposition is not always followed by a noun or pronoun. It can also be followed by a clause containing another verb. This is often used to translate an –*ing* form in English and is dealt with in one of two ways.

● If the verbs in both parts of the sentence have the same subject, **da-** or **dar-** is added to the beginning of the preposition and the following verb becomes an infinitive used with **zu**.

Ich freue mich sehr <u>dar</u>auf, mal wieder mit ihr <u>zu</u> arbeiten.	I am looking forward to working with her again.

- If the subject is not the same for both verbs, a **dass** (meaning *that*) clause is used.

Ich freue mich <u>darauf</u>, <u>dass</u> du morgen kommst.	I am looking forward to you com<u>ing</u> tomorrow.

1 Verbs followed by a preposition + the accusative case

➤ The following list contains the most common verbs followed by a preposition plus the accusative case:

- sich amüsieren über
  Sie haben sich <u>über ihn</u> amüsiert.

  to laugh at
  They laughed at him.

- sich ärgern über

  to get annoyed about/with

- sich bewerben um
  Sie hat sich <u>um die</u> Stelle als Direktorin beworben.

  to apply for
  She applied for the position of director.

- bitten um

  to ask for

- denken an
  <u>Daran</u> habe ich gar nicht mehr gedacht.

  to be thinking of
  I'd forgotten about that.

- denken über
  Wie denkt ihr <u>darüber</u>?

  to think about, hold an opinion of
  What do you think about it?

- sich erinnern an

  to remember

- sich freuen auf

  to look forward to

- sich freuen über
  Ich freue mich sehr über <u>den neuen</u> Job.

  to be pleased about
  I'm very pleased about the new job.

- sich gewöhnen an

  to get used to

- sich interessieren für
  Sie interessiert sich sehr <u>für</u> Politik.

  to be interested in
  She's very interested in politics.

- kämpfen um

  to fight for

- sich kümmern um
  Kannst du dich <u>um</u> meine Pflanzen kümmern?

  to take care of, see to
  Can you see to my plants?

- nachdenken über
  Er hatte schon lange <u>darüber</u> nachgedacht.

  to think about
  He had been thinking about it for a long time.

- sich unterhalten über

  to talk about

- sich verlassen auf
  Kann sie sich <u>auf</u> ihn verlassen?

  to rely on, depend on
  Can she rely on him?

- warten auf

  to wait for

For further explanation of grammatical terms, please see pages x–xiv.

2 Verbs followed by a preposition + the dative case

➤ The following list contains the most common verbs followed by a preposition plus the dative case:

- abhängen von
  Das hängt von der Zeit ab, die uns noch bleibt.

  to depend on
  That depends how much time we have left.

- sich beschäftigen mit
  Sie beschäftigen sich im Moment mit dem neuen Haus.

  to occupy oneself with
  They're busy with their new house at the moment.

- bestehen aus

  to consist of

- leiden an/unter
  Sie hat lange an dieser Krankheit gelitten.

  to suffer from
  She suffered from this illness for a long time.

- riechen nach

  to smell of

- schmecken nach
  Es schmeckt nach Zimt.

  to taste of
  It tastes of cinnamon.

- sich sehnen nach

  to long for

- sterben an
  Sie ist an Krebs gestorben.

  to die of
  She died of cancer.

- teilnehmen an
  Du solltest am Wettbewerb teilnehmen.

  to take part in
  You should take part in the competition.

- träumen von

  to dream of

- sich verabschieden von
  Ich habe mich noch nicht von ihm verabschiedet.

  to say goodbye to
  I haven't said goodbye to him yet.

- sich verstehen mit
  Sie versteht sich ganz gut mit ihr.

  to get along with, get on with
  She gets on really well with her.

Key points

✔ German prepositions after verbs are often not the same as the ones used in English.

✔ Using different prepositions with a verb creates completely different meanings.

✔ German verbs occasionally use prepositions where their English equivalents don't.

✔ Prepositions used with verbs behave like normal prepositions and affect the case of the following noun.

Verbs followed by the dative case

1 Verbs with a direct and indirect object

➤ Some verbs are generally used with a <u>direct object</u> and an <u>indirect object</u>. For example, in the English sentence, *She gave me a book*, the direct object of *gave* is *a book* and would be in the accusative case in German, and *me* (= *to me*) is the indirect object and would be in the dative case in German.

> **Sie gab mir ein Buch.**   She gave me a book.
> direct object = **ein Buch**
> indirect object = **mir**

➤ In German, as in English, this type of verb is usually concerned with giving or telling someone something, or with doing something for someone else.

> **Sie erzählte ihm eine Geschichte.**   She told him a story.
> direct object = **eine Geschichte**
> indirect object = **ihm**

> *i*   Note that the normal word order after such verbs is for the direct object to follow the indirect, EXCEPT where the direct object is a personal pronoun.

> **Kaufst du mir das Buch?**   Will you buy me the book?
> BUT
> **Kaufst du es mir?**   Will you buy it for me?

⟹ *For more information on* **Direct** *and* **Indirect object pronouns**, *see pages 74 and 76.*

➤ Here are some of the most common examples of verbs which are used with both a direct and an indirect object:

- **anbieten**   to offer
  Sie bot ihr die Arbeitsstelle an.   She offered her the job.

- **bringen**   to bring
  Bringst du mir eins?   Will you bring me one?

- **beweisen**   to prove
  Können Sie es mir beweisen?   Can you prove it to me?

- **fehlen**   to be absent *or* missing
  Mir fehlt das nötige Geld.   I don't have enough money.

- **geben**   to give
  Gib mir das sofort!   Give me that now!

- **schenken**   to give (as a present)
  Ich schenke _ihr_ einen Computer zum Geburtstag.   I'm giving her a computer for her birthday.

- **schreiben**   to write
  Schreib _ihm_ mal einen Brief.   Write him a letter sometime.

- **zeigen**   to show
  Zeig es _mir_!   Show me it!

2   Verbs with their object in the dative

➤ Certain verbs in German, such as **helfen** (meaning _to help_) can ONLY be followed by an object in the dative case.

➤ Here are some of the most common ones.

- **begegnen**   to bump into, meet
  Er ist _seinem_ Freund in der Stadt begegnet.   He bumped into his friend in town.

- **gehören**   to belong to
  Wem gehört dieses Buch?   Whose book is this?

- **helfen**   to help
  Er wollte _ihr_ nicht helfen.   He refused to help her.

- **danken**   to thank
  Ich danke _dir_!   Thank you!

- **schaden**   to damage
  Rauchen schadet _der_ Gesundheit   Smoking is bad for your health.

- **schmecken**   to taste
  Das Essen hat _ihnen_ gut geschmeckt.   They enjoyed the meal.

- **trauen**   to trust
  Ich traue _dir_ nicht.   I don't trust you.

Key points

✔ Some German verbs are usually used with a direct AND an indirect object.

✔ The indirect object is ALWAYS in the dative case.

✔ The normal word order after such verbs is for the direct object to follow the indirect, EXCEPT where the direct object is a personal pronoun.

✔ Certain German verbs can only be followed by an object in the dative case.

The passive

> **What is the passive?**
> The **passive** is the form of the verb that is used when the subject of the verb is the person or thing that is affected by the action, for example, *I was given, we were told, it had been made.*

1 Using the passive

➤ In a normal, or *active* sentence, the subject of the verb is the person or thing that carries out the action described by the verb. The object of the verb is the person or thing that the verb happens to.

Ryan (*subject*) hit (*active verb*) me (*object*).

➤ In English, as in German, you can turn an active sentence round to make a passive sentence.

I (*subject*) was hit (*passive verb*) by Ryan (*agent*).

➤ Very often, however, you cannot identify who is carrying out the action indicated by the verb.

I was hit in the face.
The trees will be chopped down.
I've been chosen to represent the school.

2 Forming the passive

➤ In English we use the verb *to be* with the past participle (*was hit, was given*) to form the passive and the word *by* usually introduces the agent. In German the passive is formed using **werden** and the past participle, while the agent is introduced by

- **von**, for a person or organisation
- **durch**, for a thing

Das Kind <u>wurde</u> <u>von</u> einem Hund <u>gebissen</u>.	The child was bitten by a dog.
Die Tür <u>wurde</u> <u>durch</u> den Wind <u>geöffnet</u>.	The door was opened by the wind.

⏩ *For more information on the **Past participle**, see page 114.*

➤ Here is the present tense of the verb **sehen** (meaning *to see*) in its passive form.

ich werde gesehen	I am seen
du wirst gesehen	you are seen
er/sie/es wird gesehen	he/she/it is seen
wir werden gesehen	we are seen
ihr werdet gesehen	you (*plural*) are seen
sie/Sie werden gesehen.	they/you (*formal*) are seen

Típ

There is/there are can be translated by a verb in the passive tense in German.

Es wird immer viel getrunken
auf seiner Party.

There is always a lot of
drinking at his party.

➤ You can form other tenses of the passive by changing the tense of the verb **werden**, for example, the imperfect passive.

ich wurde gesehen   I was seen

⇨ For more information on the **Imperfect tense**, see page 118.

Típ

There is a very important difference between German and English in sentences containing an <u>indirect object</u>. In English we can quite easily turn a normal (active) sentence with an indirect object into a passive sentence.

Active
Someone (*subject*) gave (*active verb*) me (*indirect object*) a book (*direct object*).

Passive
I (*subject*) was given (*passive verb*) a book (*direct object*).

In German, an indirect object can <u>NEVER</u> become the subject of a passive verb. Instead, the indirect object must remain in the dative case, with either the direct object becoming the subject of the passive sentence OR use of an impersonal passive construction.
Ein Buch (*subject*) **wurde mir geschenkt**.

3 Avoiding the passive

➤ Passives are not as common in German as in English. There are <u>three</u> main ways that German speakers express the same idea.

- by using the pronoun **man** (meaning *they* or *one*) with a normal, active verb

  <u>Man</u> hatte es mir schon gesagt. I had already been told.

  i Note that **man** is not always translated as *they* or *one*.

  <u>Man</u> hatte es schon verkauft. It had already been sold.

- by using **sich lassen** plus a verb in the infinitive

  Das <u>lässt</u> <u>sich</u> machen. That can be done.

- by using an active tense where the agent of the action is known

  Susi <u>schenkte</u> ihr ein Auto. Susi gave her a car.

  INSTEAD OF

  Ihr wurde von Susi ein Auto geschenkt. She was given a car by Susi.

Key points

✔ The present tense of the passive is formed by using the present tense of **werden** with the past participle.

✔ In German, an indirect object can <u>NEVER</u> become the subject of a passive verb.

✔ You can often avoid a passive construction by using the pronoun **man** or **sich lassen** plus an infinitive or an active tense where the agent is known.

PREPOSITIONS

What is a preposition?

A **preposition** is a word such as *at, for, with, into* or *from*, which is usually followed by a noun, pronoun or, in English, a word ending in *-ing*. Prepositions show how people and things relate to the rest of the sentence, for example, *She's at home; a tool for cutting grass; it's from David.*

Using prepositions

➤ Prepositions are used in front of nouns and pronouns (such as *me, him, the man* and so on), and show the relationship between the noun or pronoun and the rest of the sentence. Some prepositions can be used before verb forms ending in *-ing* in English.

> I showed my ticket <u>to</u> the inspector.
> Come <u>with</u> me.
> This brush is really good <u>for</u> cleaning shoes.

⇨ *For more information on **Nouns** and **Pronouns**, see pages 1 and 69.*

➤ In English, a preposition does not affect the word or phrase it introduces, for example:

the inspector	<u>to</u> the inspector
me	<u>with</u> me
cleaning shoes	<u>for</u> cleaning shoes

➤ In German, however, the noun following a preposition must be put into the accusative, genitive or dative case.

> *Tip*
>
> It is important to learn each preposition with the case or cases it governs.

---

1 Prepositions followed by the dative case

➤ Some of the most common prepositions taking the dative case are:
aus, außer, bei, gegenüber, mit, nach, seit, von, zu

- **aus**   *out of, from*

  Er trinkt **aus** der Flasche.   He is drinking out of the bottle.
  Sie kommt **aus** Essen.   She comes from Essen.

- **außer**   *out of; except*

Der Fahrstuhl war <u>außer</u> Betrieb.	The lift was out of order.
Der Patient ist jetzt <u>außer</u> Gefahr.	The patient is out of danger now.
Alle <u>außer</u> mir kamen zu spät.	All except me came too late.

- **bei**   *at the home/shop/work etc of; near*

Feiern wir <u>bei</u> uns?	Shall we celebrate at our house?
<u>Bei</u> uns in Schottland ist das kein Problem.	At home in Scotland that isn't a problem.
Er ist noch <u>beim</u> Friseur.	He is still at the hairdresser's.
Er wohnt immer noch <u>bei</u> seinen Eltern.	He still lives with his parents.
Riegel ist bei Freiburg.	Riegel is near Freiburg.

[i] Note that **bei** plus the definite article can be shortened to **beim**.

⇨ *For more information on **Shortened forms of prepositions**, see page 165.*

- **gegenüber**   *opposite; towards*

Er wohnt uns <u>gegenüber</u>.	He lives opposite us.
Sie ist mir <u>gegenüber</u> immer sehr freundlich gewesen.	She has always been very friendly towards me.

[i] Note that when used as a preposition, **gegenüber** is placed <u>AFTER</u> a pronoun, but can be placed <u>BEFORE</u> or <u>AFTER</u> a noun.

- **mit**   *with*

Er ging <u>mit</u> seinen Freunden spazieren.	He went for a walk with his friends.

- **nach**   *after; to*

<u>Nach</u> zwei Stunden kam er wieder.	He returned two hours later.
Sie ist <u>nach</u> London gereist.	She went to London.
Ihrer Sprache <u>nach</u> ist sie Süddeutsche.	From the way she talks I would say she is from southern Germany.

[i] Note that when **nach** means *according to*, as in the last example, it can be placed <u>AFTER</u> the noun.

- seit   *since; for (of time)*

Seit er krank ist, spielt er nicht mehr Fußball.	He's stopped playing football since he became ill.

i Note that after **seit**, meaning *for*, we use the present tense in German, but the perfect tense in English.

Ich wohne seit zwei Jahren in Frankfurt.	I've been living in Frankfurt for two years.
Sie arbeitet seit acht Jahren bei uns.	She's been working for us for eight years.

⇨ *For more information on **Tenses used with** seit see page 94.*

- von   *from; about; by (when used in the passive tense)*

Von Berlin sind wir weiter nach Krakau gefahren.	From Berlin we went on to Krakow.
Ich weiß nichts von ihm.	I know nothing about him.
Sie ist von unseren Argumenten überzeugt worden.	She was convinced by our arguments.

⇨ *For more information on the **Passive**, see page 150.*

i Note that von can be used as a common alternative to the genitive case.

Die Mutter von diesen Mädchen ist Künstlerin.	The mother of these girls is an artist.
Sie ist eine Freundin von Alexander.	She is a friend of Alexander's.

⇨ *For more information on the **Genitive case**, see page 11.*

- zu   *to; for*

Er ging zum Arzt.	He went to the doctor's.
Wir sind zum Essen eingeladen.	We're invited for a meal.

i Note that zu plus the definite article can be shortened to zum or zur.

⇨ *For more information on **Shortened forms of prepositions**, see page 165.*

Grammar Extra!

Some of the above prepositions are also used as separable verb prefixes, that is the part at the beginning of a separable German verb.

aushalten	to endure
Ich halte es nicht mehr <u>aus</u>.	I can't stand it any longer.
(jemandem) <u>bei</u>stehen	to stand by (somebody)
Er stand seinem Freund <u>bei</u>.	He stood by his friend.
<u>gegenüber</u>stehen	to have an attitude towards
Er steht ihnen kritisch <u>gegenüber</u>.	He has a critical attitude towards them.
jemanden <u>mit</u>nehmen	to give somebody a lift
Nimmst du mich bitte <u>mit</u>?	Will you give me a lift, please?
<u>nach</u>machen	to copy
Sie macht mir alles <u>nach</u>.	She copies everything I do.
<u>zu</u>machen	to shut
Mach die Tür <u>zu</u>!	Shut the door!

⇨ *For more information on **Separable verbs**, see page 109.*

Key points

✔ **gegenüber, aus, bei, mit, nach, seit, von, zu, außer** are the most common prepositions used with the dative case.

✔ Each of them has several different possible meanings, depending on the context they are used in.

✔ **aus, nach, mit, bei, gegenüber** and **zu** can also be used as separable verb prefixes.

2 Prepositions followed by the accusative case

➤ The most common prepositions taking the accusative case are:

durch, entlang, für, gegen, ohne, um, wider

Tip

If you want an easy way to remember which prepositions take the accusative case, you could think of the word DOGWUF, which can stand for the prepositions <u>d</u>urch <u>o</u>hne <u>g</u>egen <u>w</u>ider <u>u</u>m <u>f</u>ür.

For further explanation of grammatical terms, please see pages x-xiv.

- **durch**   *through*

  Sie guckte <u>durch</u> das Loch.

  <u>Durch</u> Zufall trafen sie sich wieder.

  She looked through the hole.

  They met again, by chance.

- **entlang**   *along*

  Die Kinder kommen die Straße <u>entlang</u>.

  The children are coming along the street.

[*i*] Note that **entlang** comes AFTER the noun in this meaning.

- **für**   *for; to*

  Ich habe es <u>für</u> dich getan.

  Das ist <u>für</u> ihn sehr wichtig.

  Was <u>für</u> eins hat er?

  Was <u>für</u> einen Wagen hat sie?

  Was <u>für</u> Äpfel sind das?

  I did it for you.

  That is very important to him.

  What kind (of one) does he have?

  What kind of car does she have?

  What kind of apples are they?

- **gegen**   *against; around*

  Stelle es <u>gegen</u> die Wand.

  Haben Sie etwas <u>gegen</u> Heuschnupfen?

  Wir sind <u>gegen</u> vier angekommen.

  Put it against the wall.

  Have you got something for hayfever?

  We arrived at around four o'clock.

- **ohne**   *without*

  <u>Ohne</u> sie gehts nicht.

  It won't work without her.

- **um**   *(a)round, round about; at (with time); by (with quantity)*

  Der Bahnhof liegt <u>um</u> die Ecke.

  Es fängt <u>um</u> neun Uhr an.

  Es ist <u>um</u> zehn Euro billiger.

  The station is round the corner.

  It begins at nine.

  It is cheaper by ten euros.

[*i*] Note that **um** is used after certain verbs.

  Sie baten <u>um</u> ein bisschen mehr Zeit.

  Es handelt sich <u>um</u> dein Benehmen.

  They asked for a bit more time.

  It's a question of your behaviour.

⇨ *For more information on **Verbs followed by prepositions**, see page 145.*

- **wider**   *contrary to, against*

  Das geht mir <u>wider</u> die Natur.

  That's against my nature.

Grammar Extra!

Some of the above prepositions are also used as separable verb prefixes, that is the part at the beginning of a separable German verb.

<u>durch</u>machen

Sie hat viel <u>durch</u>gemacht in ihrem Leben.   She's been through a lot in her life.

<u>entlang</u>gehen

Wir gingen die Straße <u>entlang</u>.   We went along the street.

um and **wider** are also used as separable or inseparable verb prefixes (<u>variable</u> verb prefixes), depending on the verb and meaning.

<u>um</u>armen	*inseparable*	to hug
Er hat sie <u>um</u>armt.		He gave her a hug.
<u>um</u>fallen	*separable*	to fall over
Sie ist <u>um</u>gefallen.		She fell over.
<u>wider</u>sprechen	*inseparable*	to go against
Das hat meinen Wünschen <u>wider</u>sprochen.		That went against my wishes.
(sich) <u>wider</u>spiegeln	*separable*	to reflect
Der Baum spiegelt sich im Wasser <u>wider</u>.		The tree is reflected in the water.

⇨ For more information on **Separable verbs** and **Inseparable verbs**, see page 109.

Key points

✔ **durch**, **entlang**, **für**, **gegen**, **ohne**, **um**, and **wider** are the most common prepositions used with the accusative case.

✔ Most of them have several different possible meanings, depending on the context they are used in.

✔ **durch**, **entlang** and **gegen** can also be used as separable verb prefixes.

✔ **um** and **wider** can also be used as variable verbal prefixes.

---

3 Prepositions followed by the accusative or the dative case

➤ There are a number of prepositions which can be followed by the accusative or the dative case. You use:

- the accusative case when there is some movement towards a different place
- the dative case when a location is described rather than movement, or when there is movement within the same place

➤ The most common prepositions in this category are:

an, auf, hinter, in, neben, über, unter, vor, zwischen

➤ You use **an**:

- with the <u>accusative</u> case

Die Lehrerin schrieb das Wort <u>an die</u> Tafel.	The teacher wrote the word on the board.
Ich habe einen Brief <u>an meine</u> Mutter geschrieben.	I wrote a letter to my mother.
Ich ziehe im Sommer <u>an die</u> Küste.	In the summer I move to the coast.

- with the <u>dative</u> case

Das Wort stand <u>an der</u> Tafel.	The word was written on the blackboard.
Wir treffen uns <u>am</u> Bahnhof.	We're meeting at the station.

[*i*] Note that **an** plus the definite article can be shortened to **am**.

⇨ *For more information on* **Shortened forms of prepositions**, *see page 165.*

➤ You use **auf**:

- with the <u>accusative</u> case

Stell die Suppe bitte <u>auf den</u> Tisch.	Put the soup on the table please.
Wir fahren morgen <u>aufs</u> Land.	We're going to the country tomorrow.
Er warf einen Blick <u>auf das</u> Buch.	He glanced at the book.

[*i*] Note that **auf** plus the definite article can be shortened to **aufs**.

⇨ *For more information on* **Shortened forms of prepositions**, *see page 165.*

- with the <u>dative</u> case

Die Suppe steht <u>auf dem</u> Tisch.	The soup's on the table.
<u>Auf dem</u> Land ist die Luft besser.	The air is better in the country.

➤ You use **hinter**:

- with the <u>accusative</u> case

Stell dich <u>hinter deinen</u> Bruder.	Stand behind your brother.

- with the <u>dative</u> case

Sie saß <u>hinter mir</u>.	She was sitting behind me.

➤ You use **in**:

- with the <u>accusative</u> case

| Sie ging <u>ins</u> Zimmer. | She entered the room. |
| Er wollte nicht <u>in die</u> Schule gehen. | He didn't want to go to school. |

- with the <u>dative</u> case

| Was hast du heute <u>in der</u> Schule gemacht? | What did you do at school today? |
| <u>Im</u> Zimmer warteten viele Leute auf ihn. | A lot of people were waiting for him in the room. |

[i] Note that **in** plus the definite article can be shortened to **im** or **ins**.

⇨ *For more information on **Shortened forms of prepositions**, see page 165.*

➤ You use **neben**:

- with the <u>accusative</u> case

| Stell dein Rad <u>neben</u> meines. | Put your bike next to mine. |

- with the <u>dative</u> case

| Dein Rad steht <u>neben</u> meinem. | Your bike's next to mine. |

➤ You use **über**:

- with the <u>accusative</u> case

Zieh den Pullover <u>über deinen</u> Kopf!	Pull the jumper over your head!
Sie ging quer <u>über das</u> Feld.	She went across the field.
Flugzeuge dürfen nicht <u>über dieses</u> Gebiet fliegen.	Planes are not allowed to fly over this area.

- with the <u>dative</u> case

| Die Lampe soll <u>über dem</u> Tisch hängen. | The lamp should hang over the table. |

[i] Note that when **über** means *about*, it is always followed by the accusative case, NOT the dative.

| Wir haben viel <u>über sie</u> gesprochen. | We talked about her a lot. |

➤ You use **unter**:

- with the <u>accusative</u> case

| Sie stellte sich <u>unter den</u> Baum. | She (came and) stood under the tree. |

For further explanation of grammatical terms, please see pages x-xiv.

- with the <u>dative</u> case

  Sie lebte dort <u>unter</u> Freunden.　　She lived there among friends.

➤ You use **vor**:

  - with the <u>accusative</u> case

    Stell den Stuhl <u>vor</u> das Fenster.　Put the chair in front of the
    　　　　　　　　　　　　　　　　window.

  - with the <u>dative</u> case

    Auf dem Foto stand sie <u>vor</u> <u>dem</u>　In the photo she was standing in
    Haus.　　　　　　　　　　　　　front of the house.
    Ich war <u>vor</u> ihm da.　　　　　　I was there before him.
    <u>Vor</u> <u>dem</u> Krankenhaus links abbiegen.　Turn left at the hospital.

➤ You use **zwischen**:

  - with the <u>accusative</u> case

    Er legte es <u>zwischen</u> <u>die</u> beiden　He put it between the two plates.
    Teller.

  - with the <u>dative</u> case

    Das Dorf liegt <u>zwischen</u> <u>den</u> Bergen.　The village lies between the
    　　　　　　　　　　　　　　　　mountains.

➤ Each of these prepositions can also be used with verbs and are then called
  <u>prepositional objects</u>.

    abhängen <u>von</u> + *dative*　　　　to depend on
    Das hängt <u>von</u> dir ab.　　　　That depends on you.

    schmecken <u>nach</u> + *dative*　　to taste of
    Der Nachtisch schmeckt <u>nach</u> Zimt.　The dessert tastes of cinnamon.

➤ When **auf** or **an** is used in this way, the case used depends on the verb – it's much
  easier to learn such examples together with the case which follows them.

    sich verlassen <u>auf</u> + *accusative*　to depend on
    Ich verlasse mich <u>auf</u> dich.　　I'm depending on you.

    bestehen <u>auf</u> + *dative*　　　to insist on
    Wir bestehen <u>auf</u> sofortiger　　We insist on immediate payment.
    Bezahlung.

    glauben <u>an</u> + *accusative*　　to believe in
    Sie glaubt <u>an</u> ihre Schwester.　She believes in her sister.

    leiden <u>an</u> + *dative*　　　　to suffer from
    Er leidet <u>an</u> einer tödlichen　　He is suffering from a terminal
    Krankheit.　　　　　　　　　　illness.

sich freuen <u>auf</u> + *accusative*	to look forward to
Ich freue mich <u>auf</u> die Sommerferien.	I'm looking forward to the summer holidays.
warten <u>auf</u> + *accusative*	to wait for
Er wartet jeden morgen <u>auf</u> den Bus.	Every morning he waits for the bus.

⇨ *For more information on **Verbs with prepositional objects**, see page 145.*

Grammar Extra!

Some of the above prepositions are also used as separable or inseparable verb prefixes.

<u>an</u>rechnen	*separable*	to charge for
Das wird Ihnen später <u>an</u>gerechnet.		You'll be charged for that later.
<u>auf</u>setzen	*separable*	to put on
Er setzte sich die Mütze <u>auf</u>.		He put his cap on.
<u>über</u>queren	*inseparable*	to cross
Sie hat die Straße <u>über</u>quert.		She crossed the street.

⇨ *For more information on **Separable verbs** and **Inseparable verbs**, see page 109.*

Key points

✔ **an, auf, hinter, in, neben, über, unter, vor** and **zwischen** are the most common prepositions which can be followed by the accusative or dative case.

✔ Most of them have several different possible meanings, depending on the context they are used in.

✔ Each of them can also be prepositional objects of certain verbs.

✔ Many of them can also be used as verb prefixes.

---

4 | Prepositions followed by the genitive case

➤ The following are some of the more common prepositions which take the genitive case:

außerhalb, infolge, innerhalb, statt, trotz, um ... willen, während, wegen

- **außerhalb**   *outside*

  Es liegt <u>außerhalb</u> der Stadt.   It's outside the town.

- **infolge**   *as a result of*

  <u>Infolge</u> des starken Regens kam   As a result of the heavy rain,
  es zu Überschwemmungen.   there were floods.

- **innerhalb**   *within, inside*

  Ich schaffe das nicht <u>innerhalb</u>   I won't manage that within the
  der gesetzten Frist.   deadline.

- **statt**   *instead of*

  Sie kam <u>statt</u> ihres Bruders.   She came instead of her brother.

- **trotz**   *in spite of*

  <u>Trotz</u> ihrer Krankheit ging sie   In spite of her illness, she went
  jeden Tag spazieren.   for a walk every day.

- **um ... willen**   *for ... sake, because of ...*

  Ich komme <u>um</u> deine<u>twillen</u>.   I'm coming for your sake.
  Tun Sie das bitte <u>um</u> meiner   Please do it, for my mother's sake.
  Mutter <u>willen</u>.

- **während**   *during*

  Was hast du <u>während</u> der Ferien   What did you do during the
  gemacht?   holidays?

- **wegen**   *because of, on account of*

  <u>Wegen</u> des schlechten Wetters   The event was cancelled because
  wurde die Veranstaltung abgesagt.   of bad weather.

i Note that **statt**, **trotz**, **während** and **wegen** can also be followed by the dative case.

Statt <u>dem</u> Abendessen musste   Instead of having dinner, I had
ich arbeiten.   to work.

Trotz <u>allem</u> will ich weiterstudieren.   In spite of everything, I want to
  continue studying.

Während <u>dem</u> Vortrag schlief er ein.   He fell asleep during the lecture.

Wegen <u>mir</u> musste sie früh nach   She had to go home early because
Hause.   of me.

Grammar Extra!

There are some other prepositions which take the genitive case.

- **beiderseits**   *on both sides of*
  Beiderseits des Flusses gibt es ein Ufer.   On both sides of the river there is a river bank.

- **diesseits**   *on this side of*
  Diesseits der Grenze spricht man Polnisch und Deutsch.   On this side of the border Polish and German are spoken.

- **... halber**
  Vorsichtshalber nehme ich heute meinen Regenschirm mit.   To be on the safe side I'm taking an umbrella today.
  Sicherheitshalber verschließt er die Tür.   For safety's sake he locks the door.

- **hinsichtlich**   *with regard to*
  Hinsichtlich Ihrer Beschwerde habe ich Ihren Brief an die zuständigen Behörden geschickt.   With regards to your complaint, I have passed on your letter to the relevant authorities.

- **jenseits**   *on the other side of*
  Das Dorf liegt 2 km **jenseits** der Grenze.   The village is 2km on the other side of the border.

Grammar Extra!

Special forms of the possessive and relative pronouns are used with **wegen**.

- **meinetwegen**
  Hat er sich **meinetwegen** so aufgeregt?   Did he get so upset on my account?

- **deinetwegen**
  Ich ging nicht **deinetwegen** nach Hause.   I didn't go home because of you.

- **seinetwegen**
  Ihr müsst **seinetwegen** nicht auf euren Urlaub verzichten.   You don't have to do without your holiday for his sake.

- **ihretwegen**
  Wir sind **ihretwegen** früher gegangen.   We went earlier because of them *or* her.

- **unsertwegen**
  Sie musste **unsertwegen** Strafe zahlen.   She had to pay a fine because of us.

- **euretwegen**
  Euretwegen durfte er nicht mitspielen.   Because of you he wasn't allowed to play.

- **Ihretwegen**
  Sollte es **Ihretwegen** Probleme geben, dann gehen wir alle nach Hause.   Should you cause any problems, then we'll all go home.

⇨   *For more information on **Possessive pronouns** and **Relative pronouns**, see pages 80 and 86.*

> **Key points**
> ✔ **außerhalb, beiderseits, diesseits, ... halber, hinsichtlich, infolge, innerhalb, jenseits, statt, trotz, um ... willen, während** and **wegen** are the most common prepositions which take the genitive case.
> ✔ **statt, trotz, während** and **wegen** can also take the dative case.
> ✔ Special forms of possessive and relative pronouns are used with **wegen**.

5 Shortened forms of prepositions

➤ After many German prepositions, a shortened or <u>contracted</u> form of the definite article can be merged with the preposition to make one word.

auf + das	→	aufs
bei + dem	→	beim
zu + der	→	zur

⇨ For more information on the **Definite article**, see page 25.

➤ This can be done with all of the following prepositions:

Preposition	+ das	+ den	+ dem	+ der
an	ans		am	
auf	aufs			
bei			beim	
durch	durchs			
für	fürs			
hinter	hinters	hintern	hinterm	
in	ins		im	
über	übers	übern	überm	
um	ums			
unter	unters	untern	unterm	
vor	vors		vorm	
von			vom	
zu			zum	zur

Er ging <u>ans</u> Fenster.	He went to the window.
Wir waren gestern <u>am</u> Meer.	We were at the seaside yesterday.
Er ist <u>beim</u> Friseur.	He's at the hairdresser's.
Wir gehen heute Abend <u>ins</u> Kino.	We're going to the cinema tonight.
Im Sommer lese ich gern <u>im</u> Garten.	In the summer I like reading in the garden.
Es ging immer <u>ums</u> Thema Geld.	It was always about the subject of money.
Der Hund lief <u>unters</u> Auto.	The dog ran under the car.
Der Ball rollte <u>untern</u> Tisch.	The ball rolled under the table.
Die Katze lag <u>unterm</u> Schreibtisch.	The cat lay under the desk.
Er erzählte <u>vom</u> Urlaub.	He talked about his holiday.
Sie fährt <u>zum</u> Bahnhof.	She drives to the station.
Er geht <u>zur</u> Schule.	He goes to school.

➤ The following shortened forms are normally only used in informal, spoken German:

- aufs

Wir fahren morgen <u>aufs</u> Land.	We're going to the country tomorrow.

- durchs

Sie flog <u>durchs</u> Abitur.	She failed her A-levels.

- fürs

Das ist <u>fürs</u> neue Haus.	That's for the new house.

- hinters, hintern, hinterm

Er lief <u>hinters</u> Auto.	He ran behind the car.
Stell es <u>hintern</u> Tisch.	Put it behind the table.
Es liegt <u>hinterm</u> Sofa.	It's behind the couch.

- übers, übern, überm

Sie legten ein Brett <u>übers</u> Loch.	They put a board over the hole.
Man muss das <u>übern</u> Kopf ziehen.	You have to pull it over your head.
<u>Überm</u> Tisch hängt eine Lampe.	There's a lamp hanging over the table.

- unters, untern, unterm

Die Katze ging <u>unters</u> Bett.	The cat went under the bed.
Der Ball rollte <u>untern</u> Tisch.	The ball rolled under the table.
Der Hund liegt <u>unterm</u> Tisch.	The dog is lying under the table.

- vors, vorm

  Stell den Stuhl <u>vors</u> Fenster.   Put the chair in front of the window.

  Er stand <u>vorm</u> Spiegel.   He stood in front of the mirror.

[*i*] Note that if you want to stress the article in a sentence, shortened forms are <u>NOT</u> used.

<u>In dem</u> Anzug kann ich mich nicht sehen lassen!   I can't go out in that suit!

➤ Shortened forms of prepositions can also be used:

- with personal pronouns representing inanimate objects, that is objects which are not living things

  Sie war <u>damit</u> zufrieden.   She was satisfied with that.

  Er hat es <u>darauf</u> angelegt, dass er die beste Note kriegen würde.   He was determined to get the best grade.

⇨ *For more information on **Personal pronouns**, see page 70.*

Key points

✔ It is often possible to combine the definite article and a preposition to create a shortened form.

✔ Some of these shortened forms should only be used in spoken German.

CONJUNCTIONS

What is a conjunction?
A **conjunction** is a linking word such as *and*, *but*, *if* and *because*, that links two words or phrases of a similar type, for example, *Diane and I have been friends for years*. Conjunctions also link two clauses, for example, *I left because I was bored*. In German there are two types of conjunctions, called **coordinating conjunctions** and **subordinating conjunctions**.

Coordinating conjunctions

➤ aber, denn, oder, sondern and und are the most important coordinating conjunctions.

- aber   *but*

  Wir wollten ins Kino, <u>aber</u> wir hatten kein Geld.   We wanted to go to the cinema, <u>but</u> we had no money.

[i] Note that you can't use **aber** after a negative to mean *not … but …*: you must use **sondern**.

- aber   *however*

  Ich wollte nach Hause, er <u>aber</u> wollte nicht mit.   I wanted to go home; however, he wouldn't come.

[i] Note that when **aber** means 'however', it comes between the subject and verb in the clause.

- denn   *because, since*

  Wir wollten heute fahren, <u>denn</u> montags ist weniger Verkehr.   We wanted to travel today because there is less traffic on Mondays.

- oder   *or*

  Sie hatte noch nie Whisky <u>oder</u> Schnaps getrunken.   She had never drunk whisky or schnapps.

  Willst du eins <u>oder</u> hast du vielleicht keinen Hunger?   Do you want one or aren't you hungry?

- sondern   *but*

  Es kostet nicht zwanzig, <u>sondern</u> fünfzig Euro.   It doesn't cost twenty euros, but fifty.

- und   *and*

  Susi <u>und</u> Oliver   Susi and Oliver

  Er ging in die Stadt <u>und</u> kaufte sich ein neues Hemd.   He went into town and bought himself a new shirt.

For further explanation of grammatical terms, please see pages x-xiv.

➤ If you use a coordinating conjunction, you do not put the verb at the end of the clause beginning with the conjunction.

Wir wollten ins Theater, <u>aber</u> <u>wir</u> <u>hatten</u> kein Geld.	We wanted to go to the theatre but we had no money.

wir = subject
hatten = verb

Coordinating conjunctions with two parts

➤ German, like English, also has conjunctions which have more than one part. Here are the most common ones.

- **sowohl ... als (auch)**   *both ... and*

  The verb is plural, whether the individual subjects are singular or plural.

Sowohl sein Vater **als auch** seine Mutter haben sich darüber gefreut.	Both his father and mother were pleased about it.
Sowohl unser Lehrkörper **als auch** unsere Schüler haben teilgenommen.	Both our staff and pupils took part.

- **weder ... noch**   *neither ... nor*

  With this conjunction, the verb is plural unless both subjects are singular, as shown below.

Weder die Lehrer **noch** die Schüler haben recht.	Neither the teachers nor the pupils are right.
Weder du **noch** ich würde es schaffen.	Neither you nor I would be able to do it.

  When **weder ... noch** is used to link clauses, the subject and verb are swapped round in BOTH clauses.

Weder mag ich ihn **noch** respektiere ich ihn.	I neither like nor respect him.

- **nicht nur ... sondern auch**   *not only ... but also*

  The verb agrees in number with the subject nearest to it.

Nicht nur sie, **sondern auch** ich habe es gehört.	They weren't the only ones to hear it – I heard it too.

  When **nicht nur ... sondern auch** is used to link clauses, the subject and verb are only swapped round in the first clause, not the second, BUT if **nicht nur** does not begin the clause, word order is normal.

  Nicht nur ist sie geschickt, **sondern auch** intelligent.

  OR

Sie ist **nicht nur** geschickt, **sondern auch** intelligent.	She is not only skilful but also intelligent.

- **entweder ... oder**   *either ... or*

  The verb agrees in number with the subject nearest to it. When **entweder ... oder** is used to link clauses, the subject and verb are only swapped round in the first clause, not the second.

Entweder du **oder** Karla muss es getan haben.	It must have been either you or Karla.
Entweder komme ich vorbei, **oder** ich rufe dich an.	I'll either drop in or I'll give you a ring.

For further explanation of grammatical terms, please see pages x–xiv.

Key points

✔ A conjunction is a word that links two words or clauses of a similar type, or two parts of a sentence.

✔ **Aber, denn, oder, sondern** and **und** are the most important coordinating conjunctions.

✔ Single-word coordinating conjunctions do not change the order of the subject and the verb in the clause.

Subordinating conjunctions

➤ The subordinate clause is always separated from the main clause by a comma. It is called a subordinate clause because it cannot stand on its own without the other clause in the sentence and is linked to this by a subordinating conjunction.

Sie ist zu Fuß gekommen, <u>weil</u> der Bus zu teuer ist.	She came on foot because the bus is too dear.
MAIN CLAUSE	= Sie ist zu Fuß gekommen
SUBORDINATE CLAUSE	= weil der Bus zu teuer ist

[*i*] Note that the verb comes at the end of the subordinate clause.

➤ **als, da, damit, dass, ob, obwohl, während, wenn, weil, um ... zu,** and **ohne ... zu** are some of the most important subordinating conjunctions.

- **als** *when*

  Es regnete, <u>als</u> ich in Glasgow ankam. It was raining when I arrived in Glasgow.

- **da** *as, since*

  <u>Da</u> du nicht kommen willst, gehe ich allein. Since you don't want to come, I'll go on my own.

- **damit** *so (that)*

  Ich sage dir das, <u>damit</u> du es weißt. I'm telling you so that you know.

- **dass** *that*

  Ich weiß, <u>dass</u> du besser in Mathe bist als ich. I know (that) you're better at maths than me.

- **ob** *if, whether*

  Sie fragt, <u>ob</u> du auch kommst. She wants to know if you're coming too.

- **obwohl** *although*

  Sie blieb lange auf, <u>obwohl</u> sie müde war. She stayed up late although she was tired.

- **während** *while*

  Sie sah fern, <u>während</u> sie ihre Hausaufgaben machte. She was watching TV while she was doing her homework.

- **wenn** *when, whenever, if*

  <u>Wenn</u> ich nach Hause komme, dusche ich erst mal. When I get home, the first thing I'm going to do is have a shower.

  <u>Wenn</u> er anruft, sag mir Bescheid. If he calls, tell me.

> ## Tip
> If translating *when* in a sentence which describes a single, completed action in the past, you use **als**, NOT **wenn**. You use **wenn** for single, momentary actions in the present or future.

- **weil** because

Morgen komme ich nicht, <u>weil</u> ich keine Zeit habe.	I'm not coming tomorrow because I don't have the time.

- **um ... zu** in order to ...

Um früh aufzustehen, musste sie den Wecker stellen.	In order to get up early, she had to set the alarm.

i   Note that **zu** is inserted between a separable verb and its prefix.

⇨ *For more information on **Separable verbs**, see page 109.*

- **ohne ... zu** without ...

Er verließ das Haus, <u>ohne</u> ein Wort <u>zu</u> sagen.	He left the house without saying a word.

i   Note that **um ... zu** and **ohne ... zu** are always used with infinitive constructions.

i   Note that with the subordinating conjunctions **als, da, damit, dass, ob, obwohl, während, wenn, weil, um ... zu**, and **ohne ... zu**, the subordinate clause can come <u>BEFORE</u> the main clause, as seen in the example with **da**. When this happens, the verb and subject of the main clause swap places.

⇨ *For more information on the **Infinitive**, see page 134.*

➤ In tenses which only have one verb part, such as the present and imperfect, the verb comes last in the subordinate clause.

<u>Wenn</u> er mich <u>sah</u>, lief er davon.	Whenever he saw me, he ran away.

➤ In tenses which have two verb parts, such as the perfect tense, it is the form of **haben, sein** or **werden** which comes last in the subordinate clause, after the past participle.

Sie will nicht ausgehen, <u>weil</u> sie noch nichts <u>gegessen</u> <u>hat</u>.	She doesn't want to go out because she hasn't eaten anything yet.

⇨ *For more information on the **Perfect** and **Imperfect tenses**, see pages 113 and 118.*

➤ Any modal verb, for example **mögen** (meaning *to like*) and **können** (meaning *can, to be able to*), used in a subordinate clause is placed last in the clause.

Sie wusste nicht, <u>ob</u> sie kommen <u>konnte</u>.	She didn't know if she could come.

⇨ *For more information on **Modal verbs**, see page 136.*

Key points

✔ Subordinating conjunctions link the main clause and subordinating clause in a sentence.

✔ After subordinating conjunctions, verbs go to the end of the clause.

✔ Als, da, damit, dass, ob, obwohl, während, wenn, weil, um ... zu, and ohne ... zu are some of the most important subordinating conjunctions.

✔ The subordinate clause can come before the main clause. When this happens, the verb and subject of the main clause swap places.

✔ In tenses which only have one verb part, the verb comes last in the subordinate clause. In tenses which have two verb parts, haben, sein or werden comes last in the subordinate clause, after the past participle.

WORD ORDER

➤ Here is a ready-reference guide to the key points of German word order.

1 Main clauses

➤ In a main clause the subject comes first and is followed by the verb, as in English.

Seine Mutter (subject) **trinkt** (verb) **Whisky.**	His mother (subject) drinks (verb) whisky.

➤ In tenses with more than one verb element, such as the perfect tense and the passive, **haben**, **sein** or **werden** comes after the subject, and the past participle or infinitive goes to the end of the clause.

Sie <u>hat</u> mir nichts <u>gesagt</u>.	She told me nothing.
Er <u>ist</u> spät <u>angekommen</u>.	He arrived late.
Es <u>wurde</u> für ihn <u>gekauft</u>.	It was bought for him.

➤ A direct object usually follows an indirect object, except where the direct object is a personal pronoun.

Ich gab **dem Mann** (indirect object) **das Geld** (direct object).	I gave the man the money.
Ich gab **ihm** (indirect object) **das Geld** (direct object).	I gave him the money.
BUT	
Ich gab **es** (direct object) **ihm** (indirect object).	I gave it to him.

[i] Note that the indirect object can also be placed last for emphasis, providing it is NOT a pronoun.

Er gab das Geld seiner Schwester.	He gave the money to his sister.

⇨ For more information on **Direct** and **Indirect objects**, see pages 9 and 13.

⇨ For more information on **Using direct** and **Indirect object pronouns**, see pages 74 and 76.

➤ As a general rule, adverbs are placed next to the words to which they refer.

- Adverbs of <u>time</u> often come first in the clause, but this is not fixed.

  <u>Gestern</u> gingen wir ins Theater.
  OR
  Wir gingen <u>gestern</u> ins Theater.   We went to the theatre yesterday.

- Adverbs of <u>place</u> can also come first in the clause when you want to emphasize something.

  <u>Dort</u> haben sie Fußball gespielt.   That's where they played football.

- Adverbs of <u>manner</u> comment on verbs and so are likely to come immediately after the verb they refer to.

  Sie spielen <u>gut</u> Fußball.   They play football well.

- Where there is more than one adverb, a useful rule of thumb is: 'TIME, MANNER, PLACE'

  Wir haben <u>gestern gut hierhin</u> gefunden.   We found our way here all right yesterday.

  gestern = adverb of time
  gut = adverb of manner
  hierhin = adverb of place

- If there is a pronoun object (a word like *her, it, me* or *them*) in the clause, it comes before all adverbs.

  Sie haben <u>es</u> gestern sehr billig gekauft.   They bought it very cheaply yesterday.

➤ The normal word order in a main clause is subject followed by verb. The subject can be replaced as the first element by any of the words and phrases below. In such cases, the verb is the second element in the clause.

- an adverb

  <u>Gestern</u> sind wir ins Theater gegangen.   We went to the theatre yesterday.

- a direct or indirect object

  <u>Seinen Freunden</u> wollte er es nicht zeigen.   He wouldn't show it to his friends.

- an infinitive phrase

  <u>Ihren Freunden zu helfen</u>, hat sie nicht versucht.   She didn't try to help her friends.

- another noun or pronoun

  <u>Deine Schwester</u> war es.   It was your sister.
  <u>Sie</u> war es.   It was her.

- a past participle

  <u>Geraucht</u> hatte er nie.   He had never, ever smoked.

- a phrase with a preposition

  <u>In diesem Haus</u> bin ich auf die Welt gekommen.   I was born in this house.

- a clause which acts as the object of the verb

  <u>Was mit ihm los war</u>, haben wir nie herausgefunden.   We never found out what was wrong with him.

For further explanation of grammatical terms, please see pages x-xiv.

- a subordinate clause

<u>Nachdem ich ihn gesehen hatte,</u>
ging ich nach Hause.

I went home after seeing him.

2 | Subordinate clauses

➤ A subordinate clause may be introduced by a relative pronoun (a word such as der, die or dessen) or a subordinating conjunction (a word such as da, als or ob).

Die Kinder, <u>die</u> wir gesehen haben ...

The children whom we saw ...

<u>Da</u> sie nicht schwimmen wollte, ist sie nicht mitgekommen.

As she didn't want to swim, she didn't come.

➤ The subject follows the conjunction or relative pronoun.

Ich weiß nicht, <u>ob er</u> kommt.

I don't know if he's coming.

➤ The main verb ALMOST ALWAYS goes to the end of a subordinate clause.

<u>Als</u> ich nach Hause <u>kam</u>, war ich ganz müde.

When I came home I was really tired.

Grammar Extra!

The exceptions to this are:

- A clause which normally begins with wenn, but from which it can be left out.

<u>Findest</u> du mein Handy, so ruf mich bitte an.
INSTEAD OF
<u>Wenn</u> du mein Handy findest, ruf mich bitte an.

If you find my mobile, please give me a call.

- Indirect speech without the conjunction dass (meaning *that*).

Sie meint, sie <u>werde</u> es innerhalb einer Stunde schaffen.
INSTEAD OF
Sie meint, <u>dass</u> sie es innerhalb einer Stunde schaffen wird.

She thinks (that) she will manage it inside an hour.

➤ The rules applying to the order of articles, nouns, adjectives, adverbs, direct and indirect objects are the same in subordinate clauses as in main clauses, EXCEPT that all these words are placed between the subject of the clause and the relevant verb part.

MAIN CLAUSE:

Sie ist <u>gestern mit ihrer Mutter in die Stadt</u> gefahren.

She went into town with her mother yesterday.

SUBORDINATE CLAUSE:

<u>Da</u> sie <u>gestern mit ihrer Mutter in die Stadt</u> gefahren ist...

Since she went into town with her mother yesterday...

Tip

The rule 'time, manner, place' applies equally to subordinate clauses, EXCEPT that the verb goes to the end.

⇨ *For more information on **Subordinate clauses**, see page 193.*

➤ Word order in the imperative, in direct and indirect speech and in verbs with separable prefixes is covered in the relevant chapters:

⇨ *For more information on the **Imperative**, see page 105.*

⇨ *For more information on **Direct** and **Indirect speech**, see page 129.*

⇨ *For more information on **Verbs with separable prefixes**, see page 109.*

NEGATIVES

What is a negative?
A **negative** question or statement is one which contains a word such as *not*, *never* or *nothing* and is used to say that something is not happening, is not true or is absent.

1 Using negatives

➤ In English we use words like *not, no, nothing* and *never* to show a negative.

> I'm <u>not</u> very pleased.
> Dan <u>never</u> rang me.
> Nothing <u>ever</u> happens here!
> There's <u>no</u> milk left.

➤ In German, if you want to make something negative, you generally add **nicht** (meaning *not*) or **nie** (meaning *never*) next to the phrase or word referred to.

Ich will <u>nicht</u> mitgehen.	I <u>don't</u> want to come.
Sie fährt <u>nie</u> mit ans Meer.	She <u>never</u> comes with us to the seaside.

➤ Here is a list of the other common German negatives:

- **nein**   *no*

<u>Nein</u>, ich habe keine Zeit.	No, I don't have any time.

- **nichts**   *nothing*

Sie hat <u>nichts</u> damit zu tun.	She has nothing to do with it.

- **nicht mehr**   *not ... any more, no longer*

Ich rauche <u>nicht mehr</u>.	I don't smoke any more/ I no longer smoke.
Sie geht <u>nicht mehr</u> hin.	She doesn't go any more.

[i] Note that **nicht** and **mehr** always appear next to each other.

kein *none*	
<u>Keiner</u> meiner Freunde wollte kommen.	None of my friends wanted to come.
Wo ist die Milch? – Es ist <u>keine</u> mehr da.	Where is the milk? – There is none left.

> ### Tip
> **Nicht** applies to verbs. Remember that when you want to make a negative statement about a noun, you must use **kein**. If you want to say *I don't drink milk any more*, you would say **Ich trinke <u>keine</u> Milch <u>mehr</u>**.

⇨ *For more information on the **Indefinite article in negative sentences** and on **Indefinite pronouns**, see pages 36 and 82.*

- **niemand**   *nobody or no one*

  Es war niemand im Büro.   There was nobody in the office.

⇨ *For more information on **Indefinite pronouns**, see page 82.*

- **nirgendwo** or **nirgends**   *nowhere, not ... anywhere*

  Nirgends sonst gibt es so schöne Blumen.   Nowhere else will you find such beautiful flowers.

  Hier gibts nirgendwo ein Schwimmbad.   There isn't a swimming pool anywhere here.

- **weder noch**   *neither of two things*

  Karotten oder Erbsen? – Weder noch, danke.   Carrots or peas? – Neither, thanks.

- **weder ... noch**   *neither ... nor*

  Weder Sabina noch Oliver kommen zur Party.   Neither Sabina nor Oliver are coming to the party.

⇨ *For more information on **Coordinating conjunctions with two parts**, see page 170.*

- **... auch nicht** *neither have I, nor does he, nor are we etc*

  Ich mag ihn nicht. – Ich auch nicht!   I don't like him. – Neither do I!

  Er war noch nie in Spanien. – Sie auch nicht!   He's never been to Spain. – Neither has she!

2 Word order with negatives

➤ In a sentence with only one verb part, such as the present tense, **nicht** and **nie** usually come directly after the verb. However, in direct questions, the negative word comes after the subject.

  Du arbeitest nicht.   You're not working.
  BUT
  Arbeitest du nicht?   Aren't you working?

➤ In a sentence with two verb parts, such as the perfect tense and the passive, **haben**, **sein** or **werden** come after the subject and the negative word usually comes directly before the past participle or infinitive. The position of the negative doesn't change in direct questions.

  Sie haben es nicht gemacht.   You haven't done it.
  Haben Sie es nicht gemacht?   Haven't you done it?

For further explanation of grammatical terms, please see pages x–xiv.

➤ You can change the emphasis in a sentence by moving the position of the negative. For example, **nie** can be placed at the start of the sentence. The subject and verb then swap positions.

Nie waren sie glücklicher gewesen.	They had <u>never</u> been happier.
Nie im Leben hatte er so etwas gesehen.	<u>Never</u> in his life had he seen such a thing.

➤ **nicht** comes at the end of a negative imperative, except if the verb is separable, in which case it comes before the separable prefix.

Iss das <u>nicht</u>!	Don't eat that!
Setzen Sie sich <u>nicht</u>!	Don't sit down!
BUT	
Geh <u>nicht</u> weg!	Don't go away!

➤ **nicht** + the indefinite article **ein** is usually replaced by forms of **kein**.

Gibt es **keine** Plätzchen?	Aren't there any biscuits?
Kein einziger Student hatte die Arbeit gemacht.	Not a single student had done the work.

⇨ *For more information on the **Indefinite article**, see page 35.*

➤ To contradict a negative statement, **doch** is used instead of **ja**, to mean *yes*.

Du kommst nicht mit. – <u>Doch</u>, ich komme mit.	You're not coming. – Yes I am.
Das ist nicht wahr. – <u>Doch</u>!	That isn't true! – Yes it is!

➤ **nicht ... sondern** (meaning *not ... but*) is used to correct a wrong idea or false impression.

<u>Nicht</u> Susi, <u>sondern</u> ihr Bruder war es.	It wasn't Susi, it was her brother.

Key points

✔ A statement is usually made negative by adding **nicht** (meaning *not*) or **nie** (meaning *never*).

✔ The most common German negatives are: **nicht, nein, nie, nichts, nicht mehr, kein, niemand, nirgends** or **nirgendwo, weder noch, weder ... noch** and **... auch nicht**.

✔ **Nicht** comes at the end of a negative imperative, except if the verb is separable, in which case it comes before the separable prefix.

✔ **Nicht** + the indefinite article **ein** is usually replaced by forms of **kein**.

✔ To contradict a negative statement, **doch** is used instead of **ja**, to mean *yes*.

✔ **Nicht ... sondern** (meaning *not ... but*) is used to correct a wrong idea or false impression.

QUESTIONS

What is a question?

A **question** is a sentence which is used to ask someone about something and which in English normally has the verb in front of the subject. Question words such as *why, where, who, which* or *how* are also used to ask a question.

How to ask a question in German

1 The basic rules

➤ There are three ways of asking direct questions in German:
- by changing round the order of words in a sentence
- by adding **nicht, nicht wahr, oder** or **doch** (meaning *isn't it*) to a sentence
- by using a question word

2 Asking a question by changing word order

➤ Many questions are formed in German by simply changing the normal word order of a sentence. You swap round the subject and verb, and add a question mark.

Magst *(verb)* du *(subject)* ihn?	Do you like him?
Gehst *(verb)* du *(subject)* ins Kino?	Do you go to the cinema? OR Are you going to the cinema?

➤ In tenses with more than one verb, such as the perfect tense and the passive, **haben, sein** or **werden** come <u>BEFORE</u> the subject, and the past participle or infinitive goes to the end of the clause.

<u>Haben</u> Sie es <u>gesehen</u>?	Did you see it?

3 Asking a question by adding nicht, nicht wahr, oder or doch

➤ A statement can be made into a question by adding **nicht, nicht wahr, oder** or **doch**, in the same way as *isn't it, won't you* etc is added in English. You'd normally expect the answer to such questions to be a simple *yes* or *no*.

Das stimmt, <u>nicht wahr</u>?	That's true, isn't it?
Das Essen ist fertig, <u>nicht</u>?	The food's ready, isn't it?
Sie machen das, <u>oder</u>?	They'll do it, won't they?
Das schaffst du <u>doch</u>?	You'll manage, won't you?

➤ When a question is put in the negative, **doch** can be used to answer it more positively than **ja**.

Glaubst du mir nicht? – Doch!	Don't you believe me? – Yes, I do!

For further explanation of grammatical terms, please see pages x–xiv.

4 | Asking a question by using a question word

➤ A question word is a word like *when* or *how* that is used to ask for information. In German, these words are a mixture of interrogative adverbs, pronouns and adjectives. Listed below are the most common question words:

wie? (*how?*)	**wo?** (*where?*)	**wem?** (*whom?*)
was? (*what?*)	**welcher?** (*which?*)	**wessen?** (*whose?*)
wann? (*when?*)	**wer?** (*who?*)	**warum?** (*why?*)

i Note that **wer** means *who*, NOT *where*.

➤ When questions are formed with interrogative adverbs like **wann, wo, wie** and **warum**, normal word order changes and the subject and verb swap places.

Wann ist er gekommen?	When did he come?
Wo willst du hin?	Where are you off to?
Wie haben Sie das gemacht?	How did you do that?
Warum ist sie so spät aufgestanden?	Why did she get up so late?

> *Tip*
>
> Remember to use **woher** and **wohin** when direction is involved.
>
> | | |
> |---|---|
> | **Woher** kommst du? | Where do you come from? |
> | **Wohin** fahren Sie? | Where are you going? |

➤ When questions are formed with interrogative pronouns and adjectives, word order is normal if the interrogative pronoun or adjective is the subject of the verb at the beginning of the clause.

Wer (*subject*) hat (*verb*) das gemacht?	Who did that?

➤ If the interrogative pronoun or adjective is NOT the subject of the verb at the beginning of the clause, the subject and verb swap places.

Wem hast (*verb*) du (*subject*) es geschenkt?	Who did you give it to?

⇨ For more information on **Interrogative pronouns**, see page 89.

i Note that in indirect questions, that is questions following verbs of *asking* and *wondering*, the verb comes at the end of the question.

Sie fragte, ob du mitkommen wolltest.	She asked if you wanted to come.

Key points

✔ There are three basic ways of asking direct questions in German: changing the word order; adding **nicht**, **nicht wahr**, **oder** or **doch**; and using a question word.

✔ When a question is put in the negative, **doch** can be used to answer it more positively than **ja**.

✔ The most common question words are the interrogative adverbs **wann**, **wo**, **wie** and **warum**, the interrogative pronouns **was**, **wer**, **wem** and **wessen**, and the interrogative adjective **welcher**.

NUMBERS

0	null
1	eins
2	zwei
3	drei
4	vier
5	fünf
6	sechs
7	sieben
8	acht
9	neun
10	zehn
11	elf
12	zwölf
13	dreizehn
14	vierzehn
15	fünfzehn
16	sechzehn
17	siebzehn
18	achtzehn
19	neunzehn
20	zwanzig
21	einundzwanzig
22	zweiundzwanzig
30	dreißig
40	vierzig
50	fünfzig
60	sechzig
70	siebzig
80	achtzig
90	neunzig
a hundred	hundert
one hundred	einhundert
101	hunderteins
102	hundertzwei
121	hunderteinundzwanzig
200	zweihundert
a thousand	tausend
one thousand	eintausend
1001	tausendeins
2000	zweitausend
100,000	hunderttausend
1,000,000	eine Million

ℹ️ Note that **zwo** often replaces **zwei** in speech, to distinguish it clearly from **drei**.

> *Tip*
>
> In German, spaces or full stops are used with large numbers where English uses a comma. Decimals are written with a comma instead of a full stop.
>
> 1,000,000   **1.000.000** *or* **1 000 000**
>
> 7.5 (*seven point five*)   **7,5 (sieben Komma fünf)**

1st	1.	der erste
2nd	2.	der zweite
3rd	3.	der dritte
4th	4.	der vierte
5th	5.	der fünfte
6th	6.	der sechste
7th	7.	der siebte
8th	8.	der achte
9th	9.	der neunte
10th	10.	der zehnte
11th	11.	der elfte
12th	12.	der zwölfte
13th	13.	der dreizehnte
14th	14.	der vierzehnte
15th	15.	der fünfzehnte
16th	16.	der sechzehnte
17th	17.	der siebzehnte
18th	18.	der achtzehnte
19th	19.	der neunzehnte
20th	20.	der zwanzigste
21st	21.	der einundzwanzigste
22nd	22.	der zweiundzwanzigste
30th	30.	der dreißigste
40th	40.	der vierzigste
50th	50.	der fünfzigste
60th	60.	der sechzigste
70th	70.	der siebzigste
80th	80.	der achtzigste
90th	90.	der neunzigste
100th	100.	der hundertste
101st	101.	der hunderterste
102nd	102.	der hundertzweite
121st	121.	der hunderteinundzwanzigste
200th	200.	der zweihundertste

1000th	1000.	der tausendste
1001st	1001.	der tausenderste
2000th	2000.	der zweitausendste
100,000th	100 000.	der hunderttausendste
1,000,000th	1 000 000.	der millionste

> ## Tip
> When these numbers are used as nouns, they are written with a capital letter.
>
> **Sie ist die Zehnte.**   She's the tenth.

half	$\frac{1}{2}$	halb, die Hälfte
third	$\frac{1}{3}$	das Drittel
two thirds	$\frac{2}{3}$	zwei Drittel
quarter	$\frac{1}{4}$	das Viertel
three quarters	$\frac{3}{4}$	drei Viertel
one and a half	$1\frac{1}{2}$	anderthalb, eineinhalb
two and a half	$2\frac{1}{2}$	zweieinhalb

BEISPIELE	EXAMPLES
Sie hat zwei Autos.	She has two cars.
Er ist zwanzig Jahre alt.	He is twenty years old.
Sie wohnt im dritten Stock.	She lives on the third floor.
Er hat am 31. August Geburtstag.	His birthday is on the 31st of August.
Ich brauche anderthalb Stunden, um nach Hause zu kommen.	I need an hour and a half or one and a half hours to get home.
Sie aß zwei Drittel von dem Kuchen.	She ate two thirds of the cake.

Note that ordinal numbers (**erste, zweite**, and so on) are declined according to the number, case and gender of the noun.

Ich habe gerade mein erstes Auto gekauft.	I've just bought my first car.
Sie kam zum zweiten Mal mit Verspätung an.	She arrived late for the second time.

DIE ZEIT	THE TIME
Wie spät ist es? *or*	What time is it?
Wie viel Uhr ist es?	
Es ist ...	It's ...
Mitternacht *or* null Uhr *or*	midnight *or* twelve o'clock
vierundzwanzig Uhr *or* zwölf Uhr	
zehn (Minuten) nach zwölf *or*	ten (minutes) past twelve
null Uhr zehn	
Viertel nach zwölf *or*	quarter past twelve
null Uhr fünfzehn	
halb eins *or* null Uhr dreißig	half past twelve
zwanzig (Minuten) vor eins *or*	twenty (minutes) to one
null Uhr vierzig	
Viertel vor eins *or* drei viertel eins *or*	quarter to one
null Uhr fünfundvierzig	
ein Uhr	one o'clock
zehn (Minuten) nach eins *or*	ten (minutes) past one
ein Uhr zehn	
Viertel nach eins *or* ein Uhr fünfzehn	quarter past one
halb zwei *or* ein Uhr dreißig	half past one
zwanzig (Minuten) vor zwei *or*	twenty (minutes) to two
ein Uhr vierzig	
Viertel vor zwei *or* drei viertel zwei *or*	quarter to two
ein Uhr fünfundvierzig	
zehn (Minuten) vor zwei *or*	ten (minutes) to two
ein Uhr fünfzig	
zwölf Uhr	twelve o'clock (midday)
halb eins *or* zwölf Uhr dreißig	half past twelve
ein Uhr *or* dreizehn Uhr	one o'clock
halb fünf *or* sechzehn Uhr dreißig	half past four
zehn Uhr *or* zweiundzwanzig Uhr *or*	ten o'clock
zwoundzwanzig Uhr	
Um wie viel Uhr?	At what time?
Wann?	**When?**
morgen um halb drei	tomorrow at half past two
um drei Uhr (nachmittags)	at three (pm)
kurz vor zehn Uhr	just before ten o'clock
gegen vier Uhr (nachmittags)	around four o'clock
	(in the afternoon)
erst um halb neun	not until half past-eight
ab neun Uhr	from nine o'clock onwards
morgen früh	tomorrow morning
morgen Abend	tomorrow evening

For further explanation of grammatical terms, please see pages x-xiv.

DAS DATUM	THE DATE
WOCHENTAGE	**DAYS OF THE WEEK**

Montag	Monday
Dienstag	Tuesday
Mittwoch	Wednesday
Donnerstag	Thursday
Freitag	Friday
Samstag	Saturday
Sonntag	Sunday

Wann? — **When?**

Montag	(on) Monday
montags	(on) Mondays
jeden Montag	every Monday
letzten Dienstag	last Tuesday
nächsten Freitag	next Friday
Samstag in einer Woche or in acht Tagen	a week on Saturday
Samstag in zwei Wochen	two weeks on Saturday

MONATE	**MONTHS**
Januar	January
Februar	February
März	March
April	April
Mai	May
Juni	June
Juli	July
August	August
September	September
Oktober	October
November	November
Dezember	December

Wann? — **When?**

im Dezember	in December
im April	in April
nächsten Januar	next January
letzten August	last August
Anfang/Ende September	at the beginning/ end of September

Der Wievielte is heute?	What's the date today?
Welches Datum haben wir heute?	

Heute ist ...
der zwanzigste März
der Zwanzigste

It's ...
the twentieth of March
the twentieth

Heute haben wir ...
den zwanzigsten März
den Zwanzigsten

It's ...
the twentieth of March
the twentieth

Am Wievielten findet es statt?
am ersten April ...
am Ersten ...
(am) Montag, den ersten April *or*
Montag, den 1. April

When does it take place?
... on the first of April
... on the first
on Monday, the first of April *or*
April 1st

JAHRESZEITEN

im Winter
im Sommer
im Herbst
im Frühling

SEASONS

in winter
in summer
in autumn
in spring

NÜTZLICHE VOKABELN

Wann?

heute
heute Morgen
heute Nachmittag
heute Abend
(im Jahr(e)) 2015

USEFUL VOCABULARY

When?

today
this morning
this afternoon
this evening
in 2015

Wie oft?

jeden Tag
alle zwei Tage
einmal in der Woche/pro Woche
zweimal pro Woche
einmal im Monat/pro Monat

How often?

every day
every other day
once a week
twice a week
once a month

Wann ist das passiert?	**When did it happen?**
am Morgen/Vormittag	in the morning
morgens/vormittags	in the mornings
am Abend	in the evening
abends	in the evenings
gestern	yesterday
gestern Abend	yesterday evening
vorgestern	the day before yesterday
vor einer Woche	a week ago
vor zwei Wochen	two weeks ago
letztes Jahr	last year

Wann passiert das?	**When is it going to happen?**
morgen	tomorrow
morgen früh	tomorrow morning
übermorgen	the day after tomorrow
in zwei Tagen	in two days
in einer Woche	in a week
in vierzehn Tagen/zwei Wochen	in two weeks
nächsten Monat	next month
nächstes Jahr	next year

i Note that to talk about the year in which something happens, you don't use **in** in German.

Das findet 2016 statt.	That's taking place in 2016.
Sie wurde 1990 geboren.	She was born in 1990.
Ich ging 2001 für ein Jahr nach Deutschland.	I went to Germany for a year in 2001.

SOME COMMON DIFFICULTIES

General problems

➤ You can't always translate German into English and English into German word for word. While occasionally it is possible to do this, often it is not. For example:

- Sentences which contain a verb and preposition in English might <u>NOT</u> contain a preposition in German.

jemanden/etwas ansehen	to look <u>at</u> somebody/something
jemandem/etwas zuhören	to listen <u>to</u> somebody/something

- However, many sentences which contain a verb and preposition in German <u>DO</u> contain a preposition in English.

sich interessiern <u>für</u>	to be interested <u>in</u>
denken <u>über</u>	to think <u>about</u>

➤ Remember that German prepositions are of two types:

- Some are only ever used with one case, such as **gegen** (accusative), **bei** (dative) and **außerhalb** (genitive). For all of these it is useful to learn the preposition and its case by heart.

- The second type are used either with the accusative or the dative, according to whether movement from one place to another is involved or not. The translation of the same preposition from the last group can change according to the case being used.

Sie schrieb einen Brief <u>an</u> ihren Bruder.	She wrote a letter <u>to</u> her brother.
Wir treffen uns <u>am</u> Bahnhof.	We're meeting <u>at</u> the station.

⇨ *For more information on **Prepositions**, see page 153.*

➤ A word which is plural in English may not be in German.

eine Brille	glasses, spectacles
eine Schere	scissors
eine Hose	trousers

i Note that they are only used in the plural in German to mean more than one pair, for example, **zwei Hosen** = two pairs of trousers.

➤ In English, you use 's to show who or what something belongs to; in German you generally either use the genitive case or **von** + the dative case.

> **das Auto meiner Schwester**
>
> , OR
>
> **das Auto von meiner Schwester**   my sister's car

⇨ *For more information on the Genitive case, see page 11.*

➤ German punctuation differs from English in several ways.

- Decimal places are always shown by a comma, NOT a full stop.

  3,4 (drei Komma vier)   3.4 (three point four)

- Large numbers are separated by means of a space or a full stop, NOT a comma.

  20 000

  OR: **20.000 (zwanzigtausend)**   20,000 (twenty thousand)

- Subordinate clauses are always separated from the rest of the sentence by a comma.

  Er bleibt gesund, obwohl er zu viel trinkt.   He stays healthy, even though he drinks too much.

⇨ *For more information on Subordinate clauses, see page 177.*

- When two main clauses are linked by **und** (meaning *and*) or **oder** (meaning *or*), no comma is required.

  Wir gehen ins Kino oder wir bleiben zu Hause.   We'll go to the cinema or stay at home.

Specific problems

1 Nouns with capital letters

➤ Unlike English, <u>ALL</u> German nouns start with a capital letter, not just proper names.

der Tisch	the table
die Politikerin	the politician
die Königin	the Queen

(i) Note that this also applies to verbs being used as nouns.

Sie hat ihr <u>Können</u> bewiesen.	She has proved her ability.

2 Three forms of you

➤ In English we have only <u>one</u> way of saying *you*. In German, there are <u>three</u> words: **du**, **ihr** and **Sie**. You use:

- the familiar **du** if talking to one person <u>you know well</u>, such as a friend, someone younger than you or a relative

Kommst <u>du</u> mit ins Kino?	Are you coming to the cinema?

- the familiar **ihr** if talking to more than one person <u>you know well</u>.

Also, was wollt <u>ihr</u> heute Abend machen?	So, what do you want to do tonight?

- the formal or polite **Sie** if talking to one or more people <u>you do not know so well</u>, such as your teacher, your boss or a stranger

Was haben <u>Sie</u> gemacht?	What did you do?

3 -ing

➤ Although English sometimes uses parts of the verb *to be* to form the present tense of other verbs (for example, *I am listening*, *she's talking*), German <u>NEVER</u> uses the verb **sein** in this way. Instead, it uses the normal present tense of the verb.

Ich <u>spiele</u> Tennis.	I play tennis.
	OR
	I am playing tennis.

For further explanation of grammatical terms, please see pages x-xiv.

4 To be

➤ The verb *to be* is generally translated by **sein**.

Es **ist** spät.	It's late.
Das **ist** nicht möglich.	That's not possible.

➤ When you are talking about the physical position of something you can use **liegen**. You may also come across **sich befinden** in more formal contexts.

Wo **liegt/befindet sich** der Bahnhof?	Where's the station?

➤ In certain set phrases which describe how you are feeling or a state you are in, the verb **haben** is used.

Hunger haben	to be hungry
Durst haben	to be thirsty
Angst haben	to be afraid
unrecht haben	to be wrong
recht haben	to be right

[i] Note that to say *I am hot* or *I am cold* etc, you use a personal pronoun in the dative case followed by **sein**.

Mir **ist** heiß.	I am hot.
NOT	
Ich bin heiß.	
Ihr is kalt.	She is cold.
NOT	
Sie ist kalt.	

➤ When talking about your health, use the following forms of the verb **gehen**.

Wie geht es dir/Ihnen?	How are you?
Es geht mir gut	
OR	
Mir geht es gut.	I'm fine.

5 It

➤ There are three ways of saying *it* in German: **er**, **sie** and **es**. These correspond to the three different genders, masculine, feminine and neuter.

Wo ist der Wagen? – **Er** steht da drüben.	Where is the car? – **It**'s over there.
Ich finde meine Uhr nicht. Hast du **sie** gesehen?	I can't find my watch. Have you seen **it**?
Was hältst du von meinem Haus? – **Es** ist ganz schön.	What do you think of my house? – **It**'s really nice.

⟹ *For more information on **Gender**, see page 3.*

6 Date and time

➤ When talking about a particular day or date, use the preposition **an** + the dative case in the following constructions:

Ich fahre <u>am Montag</u> nach Hause.	I'm going home <u>on Monday</u>.
Sie wurde <u>am Dienstag, den 1. April</u> aus dem Krankenhaus entlassen.	She was discharged from hospital <u>on Tuesday, the 1st of April</u>.
Meine Nichte hat <u>am 6. September</u> Geburtstag.	My niece's birthday is <u>on the 6th of September</u>.

➤ When stating the time of a particular event, use the preposition **um** + the accusative case in the following construction.

Ich bin <u>um 9 Uhr</u> aufgestanden.	I got up <u>at 9 o'clock</u>.
Der Zug ist <u>um 22.30 Uhr</u> abgefahren.	The train left <u>at 10.30 hours</u>.

⇨ *For more information on **Prepositions**, see page 153.*

7 There is, there are

➤ Both *there is* and *there are* are translated by **es gibt**.

Hier <u>gibt es</u> ein schönes Freibad.	<u>There's</u> a lovely open-air pool here.
In Stuttgart <u>gibt es</u> viele Parks.	<u>There are</u> lots of parks in Stuttgart.

8 The imperfect of modal verbs

➤ Modal verbs never have an umlaut in the imperfect tense.

können (*can, to be able to*)	konnte
müssen (*must, to have to*)	musste
mögen (*to like*)	mochte
dürfen (*to be allowed to*)	durfte
sollen (*to ought to*)	sollte
wollen (*to want*)	wollte

⇨ *For more information on **Modal verbs**, see page 136.*

For further explanation of grammatical terms, please see pages x-xiv.

TIPS **197**

9 Er/sie/es parts of strong verbs in the imperfect

➤ You do NOT add a –t to the er/sie/es parts of the imperfect tense of strong verbs.

er/sie/es ging   he/she/it went
NOT
er/sie/es gingt

er/sie/es sang   he/she/it sang
NOT
er/sie/es sangt

⇨ *For more information on the* **Imperfect tense**, *see page 118.*

10 Inseparable verbs in the perfect tense

➤ Inseparable verbs have no ge- added to beginning of the past participle in the perfect tense.

Das habe ich schon <u>be</u>zahlt.   I've already paid for that.
Er hat sich endlich <u>ent</u>schlossen.   He's finally decided.

⇨ *For more information on* **Inseparable verbs**, *see page 109.*

11 Can, to be able to

➤ If you want to say *could*, meaning *was able to*, you use **konnte**, the imperfect form of **können**, you do NOT use the conditional form **könnte**.

Sie <u>konnte</u> nicht kommen.   She couldn't make it.
Er <u>konnte</u> das einfach nicht.   He just wasn't able to do it.

ALPHABET

➤ The German alphabet is pronounced differently from the way it is pronounced in English. Use the list below to help you sound out the letters.

A, a	[aː]	(ah)	
Ä, ä	[ɛː]	(eh)	
B, b	[beː]	(bay)	
C, c	[tseː]	(tsay)	
D, d	[deː]	(day)	
E, e	[eː]	(ay)	
F, f	[ɛf]	(ef)	
G, g	[geː]	(gay)	
H, h	[haː]	(hah)	
I, i	[iː]	(ee)	
J, j	[jɔt]	(yot)	
K, k	[kaː]	(kah)	
L, l	[ɛl]	(el)	
M, m	[ɛm]	(em)	
N, n	[ɛn]	(en)	
O, o	[oː]	(oh)	
Ö, ö	[ø]	(ö)	like ö in 'ökonomisch'
P, p	[peː]	(pay)	
Q, q	[kuː]	(koo)	
R, r	[ɛr]	(air)	
S, s	[ɛs]	(es)	
T, t	[teː]	(tay)	
U, u	[uː]	(oo)	
Ü, ü	[yː]	(ü)	like ü in 'über'
V, v	[fau]	(fow)	
W, w	[veː]	(vay)	
X, x	[iks]	(ix)	
Y, y	[ʏpsilɔn]	(üpsilon)	like 'ü' in 'über'
Z, z	[tsɛt]	(tset)	

For further explanation of grammatical terms, please see pages x-xiv.

VERB TABLES

Introduction

The **Verb Tables** in the following section contain 97 tables of German verbs (strong, weak and mixed) in alphabetical order. Each table shows you the following forms: **Present, Perfect, Future, Present Subjunctive, Imperfect, Conditional, Imperative** and the **Present** and **Past Participles**. For more information on these tenses, how they are formed, when they are used and so on, you should look at the section on **Verbs** in the main text on pages 91-152.

In order to help you use the verbs shown in the **Verb Tables** correctly, there are also a number of example phrases at the bottom of each page to show the verb as it is used in context.

In German there are **weak** verbs (their forms follow regular patterns), **strong** verbs (their forms follow irregular patterns) and **mixed** verbs (their forms follow a mixture of regular and irregular patterns). Two of the weak verbs in these tables are **holen** (to fetch) and **machen** (to do, to make). All weak, strong and mixed verbs are shown in full.

The **Verb Index** at the end of this section contains around 1000 verbs, each of which is cross-referred to one of the verbs given in the Verb Tables. The table shows the patterns that the verb listed in the index follows.

▶ annehmen (to accept) strong, separable, *formed with* haben

PRESENT

ich	nehme an
du	nimmst an
er/sie/es	nimmt an
wir	nehmen an
ihr	nehmt an
sie/Sie	nehmen an

PRESENT SUBJUNCTIVE

ich	nehme an
du	nehmest an
er/sie/es	nehme an
wir	nehmen an
ihr	nehmet an
sie/Sie	nehmen an

PERFECT

ich	habe angenommen
du	hast angenommen
er/sie/es	hat angenommen
wir	haben angenommen
ihr	habt angenommen
sie/Sie	haben angenommen

IMPERFECT

ich	nahm an
du	nahmst an
er/sie/es	nahm an
wir	nahmen an
ihr	nahmt an
sie/Sie	nahmen an

FUTURE

ich	werde annehmen
du	wirst annehmen
er/sie/es	wird annehmen
wir	werden annehmen
ihr	werdet annehmen
sie/Sie	werden annehmen

CONDITIONAL

ich	würde annehmen
du	würdest annehmen
er/sie/es	würde annehmen
wir	würden annehmen
ihr	würdet annehmen
sie/Sie	würden annehmen

IMPERATIVE

nimm an!/nehmen wir an!/
nehmt an!/nehmen Sie an!

PAST PARTICIPLE

angenommen

PRESENT PARTICIPLE

annehmend

EXAMPLE PHRASES

Ich **nehme an**, dass er heute nicht mehr kommt. I assume that he isn't coming today.
Sie **hatte angenommen**, dass sie zu der Party gehen darf. She had assumed that she
   was allowed to go to the party.
Nehmen Sie unsere Einladung **an**? Will you accept our invitation?

---

ich = I **du** = you **er** = he/it **sie** = she/it **es** = it/he/she **wir** = we **ihr** = you **sie** = they **Sie** = you

▶ arbeiten (to work)

weak, *formed with* haben

PRESENT

ich	arbeite
du	arbeitest
er/sie/es	arbeitet
wir	arbeiten
ihr	arbeitet
sie/Sie	arbeiten

PRESENT SUBJUNCTIVE

ich	arbeite
du	arbeitest
er/sie/es	arbeite
wir	arbeiten
ihr	arbeitet
sie/Sie	arbeiten

PERFECT

ich	habe gearbeitet
du	hast gearbeitet
er/sie/es	hat gearbeitet
wir	haben gearbeitet
ihr	habt gearbeitet
sie/Sie	haben gearbeitet

IMPERFECT

ich	arbeitete
du	arbeitetest
er/sie/es	arbeitete
wir	arbeiteten
ihr	arbeitetet
sie/Sie	arbeiteten

FUTURE

ich	werde arbeiten
du	wirst arbeiten
er/sie/es	wird arbeiten
wir	werden arbeiten
ihr	werdet arbeiten
sie/Sie	werden arbeiten

CONDITIONAL

ich	würde arbeiten
du	würdest arbeiten
er/sie/es	würde arbeiten
wir	würden arbeiten
ihr	würdet arbeiten
sie/Sie	würden arbeiten

IMPERATIVE

arbeite!/arbeiten wir!/arbeitet!/
arbeiten Sie!

PAST PARTICIPLE

gearbeitet

PRESENT PARTICIPLE

arbeitend

EXAMPLE PHRASES

Er **arbeitet** seit einem Jahr bei der Computerfirma. He has been working for the computer firm for a year.

Er **hat** früher als Elektriker **gearbeitet**. He used to work as an electrician.

Ich **würde** nicht gern sonntags **arbeiten**. I wouldn't like to work on Sundays.

---

ich = I **du** = you **er** = he/it **sie** = she/it **es** = it/he/she **wir** = we **ihr** = you **sie** = they **Sie** = you

▶ atmen (to breathe)

weak, *formed with* **haben**

PRESENT

ich	atme
du	atmest
er/sie/es	atmet
wir	atmen
ihr	atmet
sie/Sie	atmen

PRESENT SUBJUNCTIVE

ich	atme
du	atmest
er/sie/es	atme
wir	atmen
ihr	atmet
sie/Sie	atmen

PERFECT

ich	habe geatmet
du	hast geatmet
er/sie/es	hat geatmet
wir	haben geatmet
ihr	habt geatmet
sie/Sie	haben geatmet

IMPERFECT

ich	atmete
du	atmetest
er/sie/es	atmete
wir	atmeten
ihr	atmetet
sie/Sie	atmeten

FUTURE

ich	werde atmen
du	wirst atmen
er/sie/es	wird atmen
wir	werden atmen
ihr	werdet atmen
sie/Sie	werden atmen

CONDITIONAL

ich	würde atmen
du	würdest atmen
er/sie/es	würde atmen
wir	würden atmen
ihr	würdet atmen
sie/Sie	würden atmen

IMPERATIVE

atme!/atmen wir!/atmet!/
atmen Sie!

PAST PARTICIPLE

geatmet

PRESENT PARTICIPLE

atmend

EXAMPLE PHRASES

Sie konnte wieder frei **atmen**. She was able to breathe freely again.
Wir **atmeten** *tief ein und aus.* We took deep breaths.
Er **hat** *ganz normal* **geatmet**. He breathed normally.

---

ich = I **du** = you **er** = he/it **sie** = she/it **es** = it/he/she **wir** = we **ihr** = you **sie** = they **Sie** = you

▶ ausreichen (to be enough) weak, separable, *formed with* haben

PRESENT

ich	reiche aus
du	reichst aus
er/sie/es	reicht aus
wir	reichen aus
ihr	reicht aus
sie/Sie	reichen aus

PRESENT SUBJUNCTIVE

ich	reiche aus
du	reichest aus
er/sie/es	reiche aus
wir	reichen aus
ihr	reichet aus
sie/Sie	reichen aus

PERFECT

ich	habe ausgereicht
du	hast ausgereicht
er/sie/es	hat ausgereicht
wir	haben ausgereicht
ihr	habt ausgereicht
sie/Sie	haben ausgereicht

IMPERFECT

ich	reichte aus
du	reichtest aus
er/sie/es	reichte aus
wir	reichten aus
ihr	reichtet aus
sie/Sie	reichten aus

FUTURE

Ich	werde ausreichen
du	wirst ausreichen
er/sie/es	wird ausreichen
wir	werden ausreichen
ihr	werdet ausreichen
sie/Sie	werden ausreichen

CONDITIONAL

ich	würde ausreichen
du	würdest ausreichen
er/sie/es	würde ausreichen
wir	würden ausreichen
ihr	würdet ausreichen
sie/Sie	würden ausreichen

IMPERATIVE

reich(e) aus!/reichen wir aus!/
reicht aus!/reichen Sie aus!

PAST PARTICIPLE

ausgereicht

PRESENT PARTICIPLE

ausreichend

EXAMPLE PHRASES

*Das Geld hat nicht **ausgereicht**.* There wasn't enough money.
***Reicht** dir das **aus**?* Is that enough for you?
*Die Zeit **reichte** nie **aus**.* There was never enough time.

---

ich = I **du** = you **er** = he/it **sie** = she/it **es** = it/he/she **wir** = we **ihr** = you **sie** = they **Sie** = you

▶ beginnen (to begin)   strong, inseparable, *formed with* haben

PRESENT

ich	beginne
du	beginnst
er/sie/es	beginnt
wir	beginnen
ihr	beginnt
sie/Sie	beginnen

PRESENT SUBJUNCTIVE

ich	beginne
du	beginnest
er/sie/es	beginne
wir	beginnen
ihr	beginnet
sie/Sie	beginnen

PERFECT

ich	habe begonnen
du	hast begonnen
er/sie/es	hat begonnen
wir	haben begonnen
ihr	habt begonnen
sie/Sie	haben begonnen

IMPERFECT

ich	begann
du	begannst
er/sie/es	begann
wir	begannen
ihr	begannt
sie/Sie	begannen

FUTURE

ich	werde beginnen
du	wirst beginnen
er/sie/es	wird beginnen
wir	werden beginnen
ihr	werdet beginnen
sie/Sie	werden beginnen

CONDITIONAL

ich	würde beginnen
du	würdest beginnen
er/sie/es	würde beginnen
wir	würden beginnen
ihr	würdet beginnen
sie/Sie	würden beginnen

IMPERATIVE

beginn(e)!/beginnen wir!/
beginnt!/beginnen Sie!

PAST PARTICIPLE

begonnen

PRESENT PARTICIPLE

beginnend

EXAMPLE PHRASES

Sie **begann** *mit der Arbeit*. She started working.
Die Vorstellung **beginnt** *gleich*. The performance is about to begin.
Er **hat** *als Lehrling* **begonnen**. He started off as an apprentice.

---

ich = I **du** = you **er** = he/it **sie** = she/it **es** = it/he/she **wir** = we **ihr** = you **sie** = they **Sie** = you

▶ **beißen** (to bite)

strong, *formed with* **haben**

PRESENT

ich	beiße
du	beißt
er/sie/es	beißt
wir	beißen
ihr	beißt
sie/Sie	beißen

PRESENT SUBJUNCTIVE

ich	beiße
du	beißest
er/sie/es	beiße
wir	beißen
ihr	beißet
sie/Sie	beißen

PERFECT

ich	habe gebissen
du	hast gebissen
er/sie/es	hat gebissen
wir	haben gebissen
ihr	habt gebissen
sie/Sie	haben gebissen

IMPERFECT

ich	biss
du	bissest
er/sie/es	biss
wir	bissen
ihr	bisst
sie/Sie	bissen

FUTURE

ich	werde beißen
du	wirst beißen
er/sie/es	wird beißen
wir	werden beißen
ihr	werdet beißen
sie/Sie	werden beißen

CONDITIONAL

ich	würde beißen
du	würdest beißen
er/sie/es	würde beißen
wir	würden beißen
ihr	würdet beißen
sie/Sie	würden beißen

IMPERATIVE

beiß(e)!/beißen wir!/beißt!/
beißen Sie!

PAST PARTICIPLE

gebissen

PRESENT PARTICIPLE

beißend

EXAMPLE PHRASES

*Der Hund **hat** mich **gebissen**.* The dog bit me.
*Sie **biss** in den Apfel.* She bit into the apple.
*Rosa **beißt** sich mit Orange.* Pink clashes with orange.

---

ich = I **du** = you **er** = he/it **sie** = she/it **es** = it/he/she **wir** = we **ihr** = you **sie** = they **Sie** = you

▶ **bestellen** (to order)

weak, inseparable, *formed with* **haben**

PRESENT

ich	bestelle
du	bestellst
er/sie/es	bestellt
wir	bestellen
ihr	bestellt
sie/Sie	bestellen

PRESENT SUBJUNCTIVE

ich	bestelle
du	bestellest
er/sie/es	bestelle
wir	bestellen
ihr	bestellet
sie/Sie	bestellen

PERFECT

ich	habe bestellt
du	hast bestellt
er/sie/es	hat bestellt
wir	haben bestellt
ihr	habt bestellt
sie/Sie	haben bestellt

IMPERFECT

ich	bestellte
du	bestelltest
er/sie/es	bestellte
wir	bestellten
ihr	bestelltet
sie/Sie	bestellten

FUTURE

ich	werde bestellen
du	wirst bestellen
er/sie/es	wird bestellen
wir	werden bestellen
ihr	werdet bestellen
sie/Sie	werden bestellen

CONDITIONAL

ich	würde bestellen
du	würdest bestellen
er/sie/es	würde bestellen
wir	würden bestellen
ihr	würdet bestellen
sie/Sie	würden bestellen

IMPERATIVE

bestell(e)!/bestellen wir!/
bestellt!/bestellen Sie!

PAST PARTICIPLE

bestellt

PRESENT PARTICIPLE

bestellend

EXAMPLE PHRASES

Wir **bestellten** einen Tisch für zwei. We reserved a table for two.
Ich **würde** die Karten gern im Voraus **bestellen**. I'd like to book the tickets in advance.
Haben Sie schon **bestellt**? Have you ordered yet?

ich = I **du** = you **er** = he/it **sie** = she/it **es** = it/he/she **wir** = we **ihr** = you **sie** = they **Sie** = you

▶ **bieten** (to offer)

strong, *formed with* **haben**

PRESENT

ich	biete
du	bietest
er/sie/es	bietet
wir	bieten
ihr	bietet
sie/Sie	bieten

PRESENT SUBJUNCTIVE

ich	biete
du	bietest
er/sie/es	biete
wir	bieten
ihr	bietet
sie/Sie	bieten

PERFECT

ich	habe geboten
du	hast geboten
er/sie/es	hat geboten
wir	haben geboten
ihr	habt geboten
sie/Sie	haben geboten

IMPERFECT

ich	bot
du	bot(e)st
er/sie/es	bot
wir	boten
ihr	botet
sie/Sie	boten

FUTURE

ich	werde bieten
du	wirst bieten
er/sie/es	wird bieten
wir	werden bieten
ihr	werdet bieten
sie/Sie	werden bieten

CONDITIONAL

ich	würde bieten
du	würdest bieten
er/sie/es	würde bieten
wir	würden bieten
ihr	würdet bieten
sie/Sie	würden bieten

IMPERATIVE

biet(e)!/bieten wir!/bietet!/
bieten Sie!

PAST PARTICIPLE

geboten

PRESENT PARTICIPLE

bietend

EXAMPLE PHRASES

Er **bot** ihm die Hand. He held out his hand to him.
Für das Bild **wurden** 2000 Euro **geboten**. There was a bid of 2000 euros for the painting.
Diese Stadt hat nichts zu **bieten**. This town has nothing to offer.

ich = I **du** = you **er** = he/it **sie** = she/it **es** = it/he/she **wir** = we **ihr** = you **sie** = they **Sie** = you

▶ **bitten** (to request) strong, *formed with* **haben**

PRESENT

ich	bitte
du	bittest
er/sie/es	bittet
wir	bitten
ihr	bittet
sie/Sie	bitten

PRESENT SUBJUNCTIVE

ich	bitte
du	bittest
er/sie/es	bitte
wir	bitten
ihr	bittet
sie/Sie	bitten

PERFECT

ich	habe gebeten
du	hast gebeten
er/sie/es	hat gebeten
wir	haben gebeten
ihr	habt gebeten
sie/Sie	haben gebeten

IMPERFECT

ich	bat
du	bat(e)st
er/sie/es	bat
wir	baten
ihr	batet
sie/Sie	baten

FUTURE

ich	werde bitten
du	wirst bitten
er/sie/es	wird bitten
wir	werden bitten
ihr	werdet bitten
sie/Sie	werden bitten

CONDITIONAL

ich	würde bitten
du	würdest bitten
er/sie/es	würde bitten
wir	würden bitten
ihr	würdet bitten
sie/Sie	würden bitten

IMPERATIVE

bitt(e)!/bitten wir!/bittet!/
bitten Sie!

PAST PARTICIPLE

gebeten

PRESENT PARTICIPLE

bittend

EXAMPLE PHRASES

*Sie **bat** ihn um Hilfe.* She asked him for help.
*Herr Müller lässt **bitten**.* Mr Müller will see you now.
*Man **hat** die Bevölkerung um Mithilfe **gebeten**.* The public was asked for assistance.

---

ich = I **du** = you **er** = he/it **sie** = she/it **es** = it/he/she **wir** = we **ihr** = you **sie** = they **Sie** = you

▶ bleiben (to remain)

strong, *formed with* sein

PRESENT

ich	bleibe
du	bleibst
er/sie/es	bleibt
wir	bleiben
ihr	bleibt
sie/Sie	bleiben

PRESENT SUBJUNCTIVE

ich	bleibe
du	bleibest
er/sie/es	bleibe
wir	bleiben
ihr	bleibet
sie/Sie	bleiben

PERFECT

ich	bin geblieben
du	bist geblieben
er/sie/es	ist geblieben
wir	sind geblieben
ihr	seid geblieben
sie/Sie	sind geblieben

IMPERFECT

ich	blieb
du	bliebst
er/sie/es	blieb
wir	blieben
ihr	bliebt
sie/Sie	blieben

FUTURE

ich	werde bleiben
du	wirst bleiben
er/sie/es	wird bleiben
wir	werden bleiben
ihr	werdet bleiben
sie/Sie	werden bleiben

CONDITIONAL

ich	würde bleiben
du	würdest bleiben
er/sie/es	würde bleiben
wir	würden bleiben
ihr	würdet bleiben
sie/Sie	würden bleiben

IMPERATIVE

bleib(e)!/bleiben wir!/bleibt!/
bleiben Sie!

PAST PARTICIPLE

geblieben

PRESENT PARTICIPLE

bleibend

EXAMPLE PHRASES

*Hoffentlich **bleibt** das Wetter schön.* I hope the weather will stay fine.
*Vom Kuchen **ist** nur noch ein Stück **geblieben**.* There's only one piece of cake left.
*Dieses Erlebnis **blieb** in meiner Erinnerung.* This experience stayed with me.

---

ich = I **du** = you **er** = he/it **sie** = she/it **es** = it/he/she **wir** = we **ihr** = you **sie** = they **Sie** = you

▶ brechen (to break)

strong, *formed with* **haben/sein***

PRESENT

ich	breche
du	brichst
er/sie/es	bricht
wir	brechen
ihr	brecht
sie/Sie	brechen

PRESENT SUBJUNCTIVE

ich	breche
du	brechest
er/sie/es	breche
wir	brechen
ihr	brechet
sie/Sie	brechen

PERFECT

ich	habe gebrochen
du	hast gebrochen
er/sie/es	hat gebrochen
wir	haben gebrochen
ihr	habt gebrochen
sie/Sie	haben gebrochen

IMPERFECT

ich	brach
du	brachst
er/sie/es	brach
wir	brachen
ihr	bracht
sie/Sie	brachen

FUTURE

ich	werde brechen
du	wirst brechen
er/sie/es	wird brechen
wir	werden brechen
ihr	werdet brechen
sie/Sie	werden brechen

CONDITIONAL

ich	würde brechen
du	würdest brechen
er/sie/es	würde brechen
wir	würden brechen
ihr	würdet brechen
sie/Sie	würden brechen

IMPERATIVE

brich!/brechen wir!/brecht!/
brechen Sie!

PAST PARTICIPLE

gebrochen

PRESENT PARTICIPLE

brechend

EXAMPLE PHRASES

*Mir **bricht** das Herz.* It's breaking my heart.
*Der Sturz **brach** ihm fast den Arm.* The fall almost broke his arm.
*Sie **hat** ihr Versprechen **gebrochen**.* She broke her promise.
*Das Eis **ist gebrochen**.* The ice is broken.

*When **brechen** is used with no direct object, it is formed with **sein**.

ich = I **du** = you **er** = he/it **sie** = she/it **es** = it/he/she **wir** = we **ihr** = you **sie** = they **Sie** = you

▶ **brennen** (to burn)

mixed, *formed with* haben

PRESENT

ich	brenne
du	brennst
er/sie/es	brennt
wir	brennen
ihr	brennt
sie/Sie	brennen

PRESENT SUBJUNCTIVE

ich	brenne
du	brennest
er/sie/es	brenne
wir	brennen
ihr	brennet
sie/Sie	brennen

PERFECT

ich	habe gebrannt
du	hast gebrannt
er/sie/es	hat gebrannt
wir	haben gebrannt
ihr	habt gebrannt
sie/Sie	haben gebrannt

IMPERFECT

ich	brannte
du	branntest
er/sie/es	brannte
wir	brannten
ihr	branntet
sie/Sie	brannten

FUTURE

ich	werde brennen
du	wirst brennen
er/sie/es	wird brennen
wir	werden brennen
ihr	werdet brennen
sie/Sie	werden brennen

CONDITIONAL

ich	würde brennen
du	würdest brennen
er/sie/es	würde brennen
wir	würden brennen
ihr	würdet brennen
sie/Sie	würden brennen

IMPERATIVE

brenn(e)!/brennen wir!/brennt!/
brennen Sie!

PAST PARTICIPLE

gebrannt

PRESENT PARTICIPLE

brennend

EXAMPLE PHRASES

*Das ganze Haus **brannte**.* The entire house was on fire.
*Wir **werden** diese CD zuerst **brennen**.* We'll burn this CD first.
*Das Streichholz **brennt** nicht.* The match won't light.

---

ich = I **du** = you **er** = he/it **sie** = she/it **es** = it/he/she **wir** = we **ihr** = you **sie** = they **Sie** = you

▶ **bringen** (to bring)

mixed, *formed with* **haben**

PRESENT

ich	bringe
du	bringst
er/sie/es	bringt
wir	bringen
ihr	bringt
sie/Sie	bringen

PRESENT SUBJUNCTIVE

ich	bringe
du	bringest
er/sie/es	bringe
wir	bringen
ihr	bringet
sie/Sie	bringen

PERFECT

ich	habe gebracht
du	hast gebracht
er/sie/es	hat gebracht
wir	haben gebracht
ihr	habt gebracht
sie/Sie	haben gebracht

IMPERFECT

ich	brachte
du	brachtest
er/sie/es	brachte
wir	brachten
ihr	brachtet
sie/Sie	brachten

FUTURE

ich	werde bringen
du	wirst bringen
er/sie/es	wird bringen
wir	werden bringen
ihr	werdet bringen
sie/Sie	werden bringen

CONDITIONAL

ich	würde bringen
du	würdest bringen
er/sie/es	würde bringen
wir	würden bringen
ihr	würdet bringen
sie/Sie	würden bringen

IMPERATIVE

bring(e)!/bringen wir!/bringt!/
bringen Sie!

PAST PARTICIPLE

gebracht

PRESENT PARTICIPLE

bringend

EXAMPLE PHRASES

Kannst du mich zum Flughafen **bringen**? Can you take me to the airport?
Max **hat** *mir Blumen* **gebracht**. Max brought me flowers.
Das **brachte** *mich auf eine Idee*. It gave me an idea.

▶ denken (to think)

mixed, *formed with* **haben**

PRESENT

ich	denke
du	denkst
er/sie/es	denkt
wir	denken
ihr	denkt
sie/Sie	denken

PRESENT SUBJUNCTIVE

ich	denke
du	denkest
er/sie/es	denke
wir	denken
ihr	denket
sie/Sie	denken

PERFECT

ich	habe gedacht
du	hast gedacht
er/sie/es	hat gedacht
wir	haben gedacht
ihr	habt gedacht
sie/Sie	haben gedacht

IMPERFECT

ich	dachte
du	dachtest
er/sie/es	dachte
wir	dachten
ihr	dachtet
sie/Sie	dachten

FUTURE

ich	werde denken
du	wirst denken
er/sie/es	wird denken
wir	werden denken
ihr	werdet denken
sie/Sie	werden denken

CONDITIONAL

ich	würde denken
du	würdest denken
er/sie/es	würde denken
wir	würden denken
ihr	würdet denken
sie/Sie	würden denken

IMPERATIVE

denk(e)!/denken wir!/denkt!/
denken Sie!

PAST PARTICIPLE

gedacht

PRESENT PARTICIPLE

denkend

EXAMPLE PHRASES

Wie **denken** Sie darüber? What do you think about it?
Das **war** für ihn **gedacht**. It was meant for him.
Es war das Erste, woran ich **dachte**. It was the first thing I thought of.

---

ich = I **du** = you **er** = he/it **sie** = she/it **es** = it/he/she **wir** = we **ihr** = you **sie** = they **Sie** = you

▶ durchsetzen (to enforce)   weak, separable, *formed with* haben

PRESENT

ich	setze durch
du	setzt durch
er/sie/es	setzt durch
wir	setzen durch
ihr	setzt durch
sie/Sie	setzen durch

PRESENT SUBJUNCTIVE

ich	setze durch
du	setzest durch
er/sie/es	setze durch
wir	setzen durch
ihr	setzet durch
sie/Sie	setzen durch

PERFECT

ich	habe durchgesetzt
du	hast durchgesetzt
er/sie/es	hat durchgesetzt
wir	haben durchgesetzt
ihr	habt durchgesetzt
sie/Sie	haben durchgesetzt

IMPERFECT

ich	setzte durch
du	setztest durch
er/sie/es	setzte durch
wir	setzten durch
ihr	setztet durch
sie/Sie	setzten durch

FUTURE

ich	werde durchsetzen
du	wirst durchsetzen
er/sie/es	wird durchsetzen
wir	werden durchsetzen
ihr	werdet durchsetzen
sie/Sie	werden durchsetzen

CONDITIONAL

ich	würde durchsetzen
du	würdest durchsetzen
er/sie/es	würde durchsetzen
wir	würden durchsetzen
ihr	würdet durchsetzen
sie/Sie	würden durchsetzen

IMPERATIVE

setz(e) durch!/setzen wir durch!/
setzt durch!/setzen Sie durch!

PAST PARTICIPLE

durchgesetzt

PRESENT PARTICIPLE

durchsetzend

EXAMPLE PHRASES

*Sie **setzt** immer ihren Willen **durch**.* She always gets her own way.
*Er kann sich nicht **durchsetzen**.* He doesn't know how to assert himself.
*Ich **habe** mich mit meinem Vorschlag **durchgesetzt**.* They accepted my suggestion.

---

ich = I **du** = you **er** = he/it **sie** = she/it **es** = it/he/she **wir** = we **ihr** = you **sie** = they **Sie** = you

▶ dürfen (to be allowed to)

modal, *formed with* haben

PRESENT

ich	darf
du	darfst
er/sie/es	darf
wir	dürfen
ihr	dürft
sie/Sie	dürfen

PRESENT SUBJUNCTIVE

ich	dürfe
du	dürfest
er/sie/es	dürfe
wir	dürfen
ihr	dürfet
sie/Sie	dürfen

PERFECT

ich	habe gedurft/dürfen
du	hast gedurft/dürfen
er/sie/es	hat gedurft/dürfen
wir	haben gedurft/dürfen
ihr	habt gedurft/dürfen
sie/Sie	haben gedurft/dürfen

IMPERFECT

ich	durfte
du	durftest
er/sie/es	durfte
wir	durften
ihr	durftet
sie/Sie	durften

FUTURE

ich	werde dürfen
du	wirst dürfen
er/sie/es	wird dürfen
wir	werden dürfen
ihr	werdet dürfen
sie/Sie	werden dürfen

CONDITIONAL

ich	würde dürfen
du	würdest dürfen
er/sie/es	würde dürfen
wir	würden dürfen
ihr	würdet dürfen
sie/Sie	würden dürfen

PAST PARTICIPLE

gedurft/dürfen*

PRESENT PARTICIPLE

dürfend

This form is used when combined with another infinitive.

EXAMPLE PHRASES

Darf ich ins Kino? Can I go to the cinema?
Das **würde** ich zu Hause nicht **dürfen**. I wouldn't be allowed to do that at home.
Das **dürfen** Sie mir glauben. You can take my word for it.

---

ich = I **du** = you **er** = he/it **sie** = she/it **es** = it/he/she **wir** = we **ihr** = you **sie** = they **Sie** = you

▶ **empfehlen** (to recommend) strong, inseparable, *formed with* **haben**

PRESENT		PRESENT SUBJUNCTIVE	
ich	empfehle	ich	empfehle
du	empfiehlst	du	empfehlest
er/sie/es	empfiehlt	er/sie/es	empfehle
wir	empfehlen	wir	empfehlen
ihr	empfehlt	ihr	empfehlet
sie/Sie	empfehlen	sie/Sie	empfehlen

PERFECT		IMPERFECT	
ich	habe empfohlen	ich	empfahl
du	hast empfohlen	du	empfahlst
er/sie/es	hat empfohlen	er/sie/es	empfahl
wir	haben empfohlen	wir	empfahlen
ihr	habt empfohlen	ihr	empfahlt
sie/Sie	haben empfohlen	sie/Sie	empfahlen

FUTURE		CONDITIONAL	
ich	werde empfehlen	ich	würde empfehlen
du	wirst empfehlen	du	würdest empfehlen
er/sie/es	wird empfehlen	er/sie/es	würde empfehlen
wir	werden empfehlen	wir	würden empfehlen
ihr	werdet empfehlen	ihr	würdet empfehlen
sie/Sie	werden empfehlen	sie/Sie	würden empfehlen

IMPERATIVE

empfiehl!/empfehlen wir!/
empfehlt!/empfehlen Sie!

PAST PARTICIPLE

empfohlen

PRESENT PARTICIPLE

empfehlend

EXAMPLE PHRASES

*Ich **würde** Ihnen **empfehlen**, zu gehen.* I would advise you to go.
*Was **empfiehlst** du mir zu tun?* What would you recommend I do?
*Dieses Restaurant **wurde** uns **empfohlen**.* This restaurant has been recommended
   to us.

ich = I **du** = you **er** = he/it **sie** = she/it **es** = it/he/she **wir** = we **ihr** = you **sie** = they **Sie** = you

▶ entdecken (to discover) weak, inseparable, *formed with* haben

PRESENT

ich	entdecke
du	entdeckst
er/sie/es	entdeckt
wir	entdecken
ihr	entdeckt
sie/Sie	entdecken

PRESENT SUBJUNCTIVE

ich	entdecke
du	entdeckest
er/sie/es	entdecke
wir	entdecken
ihr	entdecket
sie/Sie	entdecken

PERFECT

ich	habe entdeckt
du	hast entdeckt
er/sie/es	hat entdeckt
wir	haben entdeckt
ihr	habt entdeckt
sie/Sie	haben entdeckt

IMPERFECT

ich	entdeckte
du	entdecktest
er/sie/es	entdeckte
wir	entdeckten
ihr	entdecktet
sie/Sie	entdeckten

FUTURE

ich	werde entdecken
du	wirst entdecken
er/sie/es	wird entdecken
wir	werden entdecken
ihr	werdet entdecken
sie/Sie	werden entdecken

CONDITIONAL

ich	würde entdecken
du	würdest entdecken
er/sie/es	würde entdecken
wir	würden entdecken
ihr	würdet entdecken
sie/Sie	würden entdecken

IMPERATIVE

entdeck(e)!/entdecken wir!/
entdeckt!/entdecken Sie!

PAST PARTICIPLE

entdeckt

PRESENT PARTICIPLE

entdeckend

EXAMPLE PHRASES

Kolumbus **hat** *Amerika* **entdeckt**. Columbus discovered America.
Ich **entdecke** *im Park oft neue Insekten.* I often discover new insects in the park.
Er **entdeckte** *sie in der Menge.* He spotted her in the crowd.

---

ich = I **du** = you **er** = he/it **sie** = she/it **es** = it/he/she **wir** = we **ihr** = you **sie** = they **Sie** = you

▶ **erzählen** (to tell)   weak, inseparable, *formed with* haben

PRESENT

ich	erzähle
du	erzählst
er/sie/es	erzählt
wir	erzählen
ihr	erzählt
sie/Sie	erzählen

PRESENT SUBJUNCTIVE

ich	erzähle
du	erzählest
er/sie/es	erzähle
wir	erzählen
ihr	erzählet
sie/Sie	erzählen

PERFECT

ich	habe erzählt
du	hast erzählt
er/sie/es	hat erzählt
wir	haben erzählt
ihr	habt erzählt
sie/Sie	haben erzählt

IMPERFECT

ich	erzählte
du	erzähltest
er/sie/es	erzählte
wir	erzählten
ihr	erzähltet
sie/Sie	erzählten

FUTURE

ich	werde erzählen
du	wirst erzählen
er/sie/es	wird erzählen
wir	werden erzählen
ihr	werdet erzählen
sie/Sie	werden erzählen

CONDITIONAL

ich	würde erzählen
du	würdest erzählen
er/sie/es	würde erzählen
wir	würden erzählen
ihr	würdet erzählen
sie/Sie	würden erzählen

IMPERATIVE

erzähl(e)!/erzählen wir!/
erzählt!/erzählen Sie!

PAST PARTICIPLE

erzählt

PRESENT PARTICIPLE

erzählend

EXAMPLE PHRASES

Er **hat** mir **erzählt**, dass er schon oft in dieser Pizzeria war. He told me that he has often been to this pizzeria.

Sie **erzählte** uns ihren Traum. She told us about her dream.

Man **erzählt** sich, dass er Millionär ist. People say that he is a millionaire.

---

ich = I **du** = you **er** = he/it **sie** = she/it **es** = it/he/she **wir** = we **ihr** = you **sie** = they **Sie** = you

▶ **essen** (to eat)

strong, *formed with* **haben**

PRESENT

ich	esse
du	isst
er/sie/es	isst
wir	essen
ihr	esst
sie/Sie	essen

PRESENT SUBJUNCTIVE

ich	esse
du	essest
er/sie/es	esse
wir	essen
ihr	esset
sie/Sie	essen

PERFECT

ich	habe gegessen
du	hast gegessen
er/sie/es	hat gegessen
wir	haben gegessen
ihr	habt gegessen
sie/Sie	haben gegessen

IMPERFECT

ich	aß
du	aßest
er/sie/es	aß
wir	aßen
ihr	aßt
sie/Sie	aßen

FUTURE

ich	werde essen
du	wirst essen
er/sie/es	wird essen
wir	werden essen
ihr	werdet essen
sie/Sie	werden essen

CONDITIONAL

ich	würde essen
du	würdest essen
er/sie/es	würde essen
wir	würden essen
ihr	würdet essen
sie/Sie	würden essen

IMPERATIVE

iss!/essen wir!/esst!/essen Sie!

PAST PARTICIPLE

gegessen

PRESENT PARTICIPLE

essend

EXAMPLE PHRASES

Ich **esse** kein Fleisch. I don't eat meat.
Wir **haben** nichts **gegessen**. We haven't had anything to eat.
Ich möchte etwas **essen**. I'd like something to eat.

---

ich = I **du** = you **er** = he/it **sie** = she/it **es** = it/he/she **wir** = we **ihr** = you **sie** = they **Sie** = you

▶ fahren (to drive; to go)

strong, *formed with* **haben/sein***

PRESENT

ich	fahre
du	fährst
er/sie/es	fährt
wir	fahren
ihr	fahrt
sie/Sie	fahren

PRESENT SUBJUNCTIVE

ich	fahre
du	fahrest
er/sie/es	fahre
wir	fahren
ihr	fahret
sie/Sie	fahren

PERFECT

ich	bin gefahren
du	bist gefahren
er/sie/es	ist gefahren
wir	sind gefahren
ihr	seid gefahren
sie/Sie	sind gefahren

IMPERFECT

ich	fuhr
du	fuhrst
er/sie/es	fuhr
wir	fuhren
ihr	fuhrt
sie/Sie	fuhren

FUTURE

ich	werde fahren
du	wirst fahren
er/sie/es	wird fahren
wir	werden fahren
ihr	werdet fahren
sie/Sie	werden fahren

CONDITIONAL

ich	würde fahren
du	würdest fahren
er/sie/es	würde fahren
wir	würden fahren
ihr	würdet fahren
sie/Sie	würden fahren

IMPERATIVE

fahr(e)!/fahren wir!/fahrt!/
fahren Sie!

PAST PARTICIPLE

gefahren

PRESENT PARTICIPLE

fahrend

EXAMPLE PHRASES

Sie **fahren** mit dem Bus in die Schule. They go to school by bus.
Rechts **fahren**! Drive on the right!
Ich **bin** mit der Familie nach Spanien **gefahren**. I went to Spain with my family.
Sie **hat** das Auto **gefahren**. She drove the car.

*When fahren is used with a direct object, it is formed with haben.

ich = I **du** = you **er** = he/it **sie** = she/it **es** = it/he/she **wir** = we **ihr** = you **sie** = they **Sie** = you

▶ fallen (to fall)

strong, *formed with* **sein**

PRESENT

ich	falle
du	fällst
er/sie/es	fällt
wir	fallen
ihr	fallt
sie/Sie	fallen

PRESENT SUBJUNCTIVE

ich	falle
du	fallest
er/sie/es	falle
wir	fallen
ihr	fallet
sie/Sie	fallen

PERFECT

ich	bin gefallen
du	bist gefallen
er/sie/es	ist gefallen
wir	sind gefallen
ihr	seid gefallen
sie/Sie	sind gefallen

IMPERFECT

ich	fiel
du	fielst
er/sie/es	fiel
wir	fielen
ihr	fielt
sie/Sie	fielen

FUTURE

ich	werde fallen
du	wirst fallen
er/sie/es	wird fallen
wir	werden fallen
ihr	werdet fallen
sie/Sie	werden fallen

CONDITIONAL

ich	würde fallen
du	würdest fallen
er/sie/es	würde fallen
wir	würden fallen
ihr	würdet fallen
sie/Sie	würden fallen

IMPERATIVE

fall(e)!/fallen wir!/fallt!/
fallen Sie!

PAST PARTICIPLE

gefallen

PRESENT PARTICIPLE

fallend

EXAMPLE PHRASES

*Er **fiel** vom Fahrrad.* He fell off his bike.
*Ich **bin** durch die Prüfung **gefallen**.* I failed my exam.
*Die Aktien **fielen** im Kurs.* Share prices fell.

ich = I **du** = you **er** = he/it **sie** = she/it **es** = it/he/she **wir** = we **ihr** = you **sie** = they **Sie** = you

▶ **fangen** (to catch)

strong, *formed with* **haben**

PRESENT

ich	fange
du	fängst
er/sie/es	fängt
wir	fangen
ihr	fangt
sie/Sie	fangen

PRESENT SUBJUNCTIVE

ich	fange
du	fangest
er/sie/es	fange
wir	fangen
ihr	fanget
sie/Sie	fangen

PERFECT

ich	habe gefangen
du	hast gefangen
er/sie/es	hat gefangen
wir	haben gefangen
ihr	habt gefangen
sie/Sie	haben gefangen

IMPERFECT

ich	fing
du	fingst
er/sie/es	fing
wir	fingen
ihr	fingt
sie/Sie	fingen

FUTURE

ich	werde fangen
du	wirst fangen
er/sie/es	wird fangen
wir	werden fangen
ihr	werdet fangen
sie/Sie	werden fangen

CONDITIONAL

ich	würde fangen
du	würdest fangen
er/sie/es	würde fangen
wir	würden fangen
ihr	würdet fangen
sie/Sie	würden fangen

IMPERATIVE

fang(e)!/fangen wir!/
fangt!/fangen Sie!

PAST PARTICIPLE

gefangen

PRESENT PARTICIPLE

fangend

EXAMPLE PHRASES

*Ich **fing** den Ball.* I caught the ball.
*Die Polizei **hat** die Verbrecher **gefangen**.* The police caught the criminals.
*Die Katze **fing** die Maus.* The cat caught the mouse.

---

ich = I **du** = you **er** = he/it **sie** = she/it **es** = it/he/she **wir** = we **ihr** = you **sie** = they **Sie** = you

▶ finden (to find)

strong, *formed with* haben

PRESENT

ich	finde
du	findest
er/sie/es	findet
wir	finden
ihr	findet
sie/Sie	finden

PRESENT SUBJUNCTIVE

ich	finde
du	findest
er/sie/es	finde
wir	finden
ihr	findet
sie/Sie	finden

PERFECT

ich	habe gefunden
du	hast gefunden
er/sie/es	hat gefunden
wir	haben gefunden
ihr	habt gefunden
sie/Sie	haben gefunden

IMPERFECT

ich	fand
du	fand(e)st
er/sie/es	fand
wir	fanden
ihr	fandet
sie/Sie	fanden

FUTURE

ich	werde finden
du	wirst finden
er/sie/es	wird finden
wir	werden finden
ihr	werdet finden
sie/Sie	werden finden

CONDITIONAL

ich	würde finden
du	würdest finden
er/sie/es	würde finden
wir	würden finden
ihr	würdet finden
sie/Sie	würden finden

IMPERATIVE

find(e)!/finden wir!/findet!/
finden Sie!

PAST PARTICIPLE

gefunden

PRESENT PARTICIPLE

findend

EXAMPLE PHRASES

Hast du deine Brieftasche gefunden? Have you found your wallet?
Er fand den Mut, sie zu fragen. He found the courage to ask her.
Ich finde, sie ist eine gute Lehrerin. I think she's a good teacher.

---

ich = I du = you er = he/it sie = she/it es = it/he/she wir = we ihr = you sie = they Sie = you

► **fliegen** (to fly)

strong, formed with **haben/sein***

PRESENT

ich	fliege
du	fliegst
er/sie/es	fliegt
wir	fliegen
ihr	fliegt
sie/Sie	fliegen

PRESENT SUBJUNCTIVE

ich	fliege
du	fliegest
er/sie/es	fliege
wir	fliegen
ihr	flieget
sie/Sie	fliegen

PERFECT

ich	bin geflogen
du	bist geflogen
er/sie/es	ist geflogen
wir	sind geflogen
ihr	seid geflogen
sie/Sie	sind geflogen

IMPERFECT

ich	flog
du	flogst
er/sie/es	flog
wir	flogen
ihr	flogt
sie/Sie	flogen

FUTURE

ich	werde fliegen
du	wirst fliegen
er/sie/es	wird fliegen
wir	werden fliegen
ihr	werdet fliegen
sie/Sie	werden fliegen

CONDITIONAL

ich	würde fliegen
du	würdest fliegen
er/sie/es	würde fliegen
wir	würden fliegen
ihr	würdet fliegen
sie/Sie	würden fliegen

IMPERATIVE

flieg(e)!/fliegen wir!/fliegt!/
fliegen Sie!

PAST PARTICIPLE

geflogen

PRESENT PARTICIPLE

fliegend

EXAMPLE PHRASES

Wir **flogen** zusammen nach Spanien. We flew together to Spain.
Die Zeit **fliegt**. Time flies.
Er **ist** von der Schule **geflogen**. He was thrown out of school.

*When **fliegen** is used with a direct object, it is formed with **haben**.

ich = I **du** = you **er** = he/it **sie** = she/it **es** = it/he/she **wir** = we **ihr** = you **sie** = they **Sie** = you

▶ fliehen (to flee)

strong, formed with **haben/sein***

PRESENT

ich	fliehe
du	fliehst
er/sie/es	flieht
wir	fliehen
ihr	flieht
sie/Sie	fliehen

PRESENT SUBJUNCTIVE

ich	fliehe
du	fliehest
er/sie/es	fliehe
wir	fliehen
ihr	fliehet
sie/Sie	fliehen

PERFECT

ich	bin geflohen
du	bist geflohen
er/sie/es	ist geflohen
wir	sind geflohen
ihr	seid geflohen
sie/Sie	sind geflohen

IMPERFECT

ich	floh
du	flohst
er/sie/es	floh
wir	flohen
ihr	floht
sie/Sie	flohen

FUTURE

ich	werde fliehen
du	wirst fliehen
er/sie/es	wird fliehen
wir	werden fliehen
ihr	werdet fliehen
sie/Sie	werden fliehen

CONDITIONAL

ich	würde fliehen
du	würdest fliehen
er/sie/es	würde fliehen
wir	würden fliehen
ihr	würdet fliehen
sie/Sie	würden fliehen

IMPERATIVE

flieh(e)!/fliehen wir!/flieht!/
fliehen Sie!

PAST PARTICIPLE

geflohen

PRESENT PARTICIPLE

fliehend

EXAMPLE PHRASES

Sie **floh** *vor der Polizei.* She fled from the police.
Es gelang ihm, aus dem Gefängnis zu **fliehen**. He managed to escape from prison.
Sie **sind** *aus Afghanistan* **geflohen**. They are refugees from Afghanistan.

*When **fliehen** is used with a direct object, it is formed with **haben**.

ich = I **du** = you **er** = he/it **sie** = she/it **es** = it/he/she **wir** = we **ihr** = you **sie** = they **Sie** = you

▶ fließen (to flow)

strong, formed with sein

PRESENT

ich	fließe
du	fließt
er/sie/es	fließt
wir	fließen
ihr	fließt
sie/Sie	fließen

PRESENT SUBJUNCTIVE

ich	fließe
du	fließest
er/sie/es	fließe
wir	fließen
ihr	fließet
sie/Sie	fließen

PERFECT

ich	bin geflossen
du	bist geflossen
er/sie/es	ist geflossen
wir	sind geflossen
ihr	seid geflossen
sie/Sie	sind geflossen

IMPERFECT

ich	floss
du	flossest
er/sie/es	floss
wir	flossen
ihr	flosst
sie/Sie	flossen

FUTURE

ich	werde fließen
du	wirst fließen
er/sie/es	wird fließen
wir	werden fließen
ihr	werdet fließen
sie/Sie	werden fließen

CONDITIONAL

ich	würde fließen
du	würdest fließen
er/sie/es	würde fließen
wir	würden fließen
ihr	würdet fließen
sie/Sie	würden fließen

IMPERATIVE

fließ(e)!/fließen wir!/fließt!/
fließen Sie!

PAST PARTICIPLE

geflossen

PRESENT PARTICIPLE

fließend

EXAMPLE PHRASES

Welcher Fluss **fließt** *durch Hamburg?* Which river flows through Hamburg?
Die Tränen **flossen** *in Strömen.* There were floods of tears.
Es **ist** *genug Blut* **geflossen**. Enough blood has been spilled.

---

ich = I **du** = you **er** = he/it **sie** = she/it **es** = it/he/she **wir** = we **ihr** = you **sie** = they **Sie** = you

▶ geben (to give)

strong, formed with haben

PRESENT

ich	gebe
du	gibst
er/sie/es	gibt
wir	geben
ihr	gebt
sie/Sie	geben

PRESENT SUBJUNCTIVE

ich	gebe
du	gebest
er/sie/es	gebe
wir	geben
ihr	gebet
sie/Sie	geben

PERFECT

ich	habe gegeben
du	hast gegeben
er/sie/es	hat gegeben
wir	haben gegeben
ihr	habt gegeben
sie/Sie	haben gegeben

IMPERFECT

ich	gab
du	gabst
er/sie/es	gab
wir	gaben
ihr	gabt
sie/Sie	gaben

FUTURE

ich	werde geben
du	wirst geben
er/sie/es	wird geben
wir	werden geben
ihr	werdet geben
sie/Sie	werden geben

CONDITIONAL

ich	würde geben
du	würdest geben
er/sie/es	würde geben
wir	würden geben
ihr	würdet geben
sie/Sie	würden geben

IMPERATIVE

gib!/geben wir!/gebt!/
geben Sie!

PAST PARTICIPLE

gegeben

PRESENT PARTICIPLE

gebend

EXAMPLE PHRASES

Er **gab** mir das Geld für die Bücher. He gave me the money for the books.
Was **gibt** es im Kino? What's on at the cinema?
Wir **würden** alles darum **geben**, ins Finale zu kommen. We would give anything
   to reach the finals.

---

ich = I **du** = you **er** = he/it **sie** = she/it **es** = it/he/she **wir** = we **ihr** = you **sie** = they **Sie** = you

▶ gehen (to go)

strong, *formed with* **sein**

PRESENT

ich	gehe
du	gehst
er/sie/es	geht
wir	gehen
ihr	geht
sie/Sie	gehen

PRESENT SUBJUNCTIVE

ich	gehe
du	gehest
er/sie/es	gehe
wir	gehen
ihr	gehet
sie/Sie	gehen

PERFECT

ich	bin gegangen
du	bist gegangen
er/sie/es	ist gegangen
wir	sind gegangen
ihr	seid gegangen
sie/Sie	sind gegangen

IMPERFECT

ich	ging
du	gingst
er/sie/es	ging
wir	gingen
ihr	gingt
sie/Sie	gingen

FUTURE

ich	werde gehen
du	wirst gehen
er/sie/es	wird gehen
wir	werden gehen
ihr	werdet gehen
sie/Sie	werden gehen

CONDITIONAL

ich	würde gehen
du	würdest gehen
er/sie/es	würde gehen
wir	würden gehen
ihr	würdet gehen
sie/Sie	würden gehen

IMPERATIVE

geh(e)!/gehen wir!/geht!/
gehen Sie!

PAST PARTICIPLE

gegangen

PRESENT PARTICIPLE

gehend

EXAMPLE PHRASES

Die Kinder **gingen** *ins Haus.* The children went into the house.
Wie **geht** *es dir?* How are you?
Wir **sind** *gestern schwimmen* **gegangen**. We went swimming yesterday.

ich = I **du** = you **er** = he/it **sie** = she/it **es** = it/he/she **wir** = we **ihr** = you **sie** = they **Sie** = you

▶ gewinnen (to win)

strong, inseparable, *formed with* **haben**

PRESENT

ich	gewinne
du	gewinnst
er/sie/es	gewinnt
wir	gewinnen
ihr	gewinnt
sie/Sie	gewinnen

PRESENT SUBJUNCTIVE

ich	gewinne
du	gewinnest
er/sie/es	gewinne
wir	gewinnen
ihr	gewinnet
sie/Sie	gewinnen

PERFECT

ich	habe gewonnen
du	hast gewonnen
er/sie/es	hat gewonnen
wir	haben gewonnen
ihr	habt gewonnen
sie/Sie	haben gewonnen

IMPERFECT

ich	gewann
du	gewannst
er/sie/es	gewann
wir	gewannen
ihr	gewannt
sie/Sie	gewannen

FUTURE

ich	werde gewinnen
du	wirst gewinnen
er/sie/es	wird gewinnen
wir	werden gewinnen
ihr	werdet gewinnen
sie/Sie	werden gewinnen

CONDITIONAL

ich	würde gewinnen
du	würdest gewinnen
er/sie/es	würde gewinnen
wir	würden gewinnen
ihr	würdet gewinnen
sie/Sie	würden gewinnen

IMPERATIVE

gewinn(e)!/gewinnen wir!/
gewinnt!/gewinnen Sie!

PAST PARTICIPLE

gewonnen

PRESENT PARTICIPLE

gewinnend

EXAMPLE PHRASES

Er **hat** den ersten Preis **gewonnen**. He won first prize.
Am liebsten **würde** ich im Lotto **gewinnen**. What I'd love most is to win the lottery.
Das Flugzeug **gewann** an Höhe. The plane gained altitude.

ich = I **du** = you **er** = he/it **sie** = she/it **es** = it/he/she **wir** = we **ihr** = you **sie** = they **Sie** = you

▶ grüßen (to greet)

weak, formed with haben

PRESENT

ich	grüße
du	grüßt
er/sie/es	grüßt
wir	grüßen
ihr	grüßt
sie/Sie	grüßen

PRESENT SUBJUNCTIVE

ich	grüße
du	grüßest
er/sie/es	grüße
wir	grüßen
ihr	grüßet
sie/Sie	grüßen

PERFECT

ich	habe gegrüßt
du	hast gegrüßt
er/sie/es	hat gegrüßt
wir	haben gegrüßt
ihr	habt gegrüßt
sie/Sie	haben gegrüßt

IMPERFECT

ich	grüßte
du	grüßtest
er/sie/es	grüßte
wir	grüßten
ihr	grüßtet
sie/Sie	grüßten

FUTURE

ich	werde grüßen
du	wirst grüßen
er/sie/es	wird grüßen
wir	werden grüßen
ihr	werdet grüßen
sie/Sie	werden grüßen

CONDITIONAL

ich	würde grüßen
du	würdest grüßen
er/sie/es	würde grüßen
wir	würden grüßen
ihr	würdet grüßen
sie/Sie	würden grüßen

IMPERATIVE

grüß(e)!/grüßen wir!/grüßt!/
grüßen Sie!

PAST PARTICIPLE

gegrüßt

PRESENT PARTICIPLE

grüßend

EXAMPLE PHRASES

Unsere Nachbarin **grüßt** *uns jeden Morgen.* Our neighbour greets us every morning.
Er **hat** *mich nicht* **gegrüßt.** He didn't say hello to me.
Oliver lässt dich **grüßen.** Oliver sends his regards.

---

ich = I **du** = you **er** = he/it **sie** = she/it **es** = it/he/she **wir** = we **ihr** = you **sie** = they **Sie** = you

▶ haben (to have)

strong, *formed with* haben

PRESENT

ich	habe
du	hast
er/sie/es	hat
wir	haben
ihr	habt
sie/Sie	haben

PRESENT SUBJUNCTIVE

ich	habe
du	habest
er/sie/es	habe
wir	haben
ihr	habet
sie/Sie	haben

PERFECT

ich	habe gehabt
du	hast gehabt
er/sie/es	hat gehabt
wir	haben gehabt
ihr	habt gehabt
sie/Sie	haben gehabt

IMPERFECT

ich	hatte
du	hattest
er/sie/es	hatte
wir	hatten
ihr	hattet
sie/Sie	hatten

FUTURE

ich	werde haben
du	wirst haben
er/sie/es	wird haben
wir	werden haben
ihr	werdet haben
sie/Sie	werden haben

CONDITIONAL

ich	würde haben
du	wurdest haben
er/sie/es	würde haben
wir	würden haben
ihr	würdet haben
sie/Sie	würden haben

IMPERATIVE

hab(e)!/haben wir!/habt!/
haben Sie!

PAST PARTICIPLE

gehabt

PRESENT PARTICIPLE

habend

EXAMPLE PHRASES

Hast du eine Schwester? Have you got a sister?
Er **hatte** Hunger. He was hungry.
Sie **hat** heute Geburtstag. It's her birthday today.

---

ich = I **du** = you **er** = he/it **sie** = she/it **es** = it/he/she **wir** = we **ihr** = you **sie** = they **Sie** = you

▶ halten (to hold)

strong, *formed with* **haben**

PRESENT

ich	halte
du	hältst
er/sie/es	hält
wir	halten
ihr	haltet
sie/Sie	halten

PRESENT SUBJUNCTIVE

ich	halte
du	haltest
er/sie/es	halte
wir	halten
ihr	haltet
sie/Sie	halten

PERFECT

ich	habe gehalten
du	hast gehalten
er/sie/es	hat gehalten
wir	haben gehalten
ihr	habt gehalten
sie/Sie	haben gehalten

IMPERFECT

ich	hielt
du	hielt(e)st
er/sie/es	hielt
wir	hielten
ihr	hieltet
sie/Sie	hielten

FUTURE

ich	werde halten
du	wirst halten
er/sie/es	wird halten
wir	werden halten
ihr	werdet halten
sie/Sie	werden halten

CONDITIONAL

ich	würde halten
du	würdest halten
er/sie/es	würde halten
wir	würden halten
ihr	würdet halten
sie/Sie	würden halten

IMPERATIVE

halt(e)!/halten wir!/haltet!/
halten Sie!

PAST PARTICIPLE

gehalten

PRESENT PARTICIPLE

haltend

EXAMPLE PHRASES

Kannst du das mal **halten**? Can you hold that for a moment?
Der Bus **hielt** *vor dem Rathaus.* The bus stopped in front of the town hall.
Ich **habe** *sie für deine Mutter* **gehalten**. I took her for your mother.

---

ich = I **du** = you **er** = he/it **sie** = she/it **es** = it/he/she **wir** = we **ihr** = you **sie** = they **Sie** = you

▶ handeln (to trade; to act)

weak, *formed with* haben

PRESENT

ich	handle
du	handelst
er/sie/es	handelt
wir	handeln
ihr	handelt
sie/Sie	handeln

PRESENT SUBJUNCTIVE

ich	handle
du	handlest
er/sie/es	handle
wir	handeln
ihr	handlet
sie/Sie	handeln

PERFECT

ich	habe gehandelt
du	hast gehandelt
er/sie/es	hat gehandelt
wir	haben gehandelt
ihr	habt gehandelt
sie/Sie	haben gehandelt

IMPERFECT

ich	handelte
du	handeltest
er/sie/es	handelte
wir	handelten
ihr	handeltet
sie/Sie	handelten

FUTURE

ich	werde handeln
du	wirst handeln
er/sie/es	wird handeln
wir	werden handeln
ihr	werdet handeln
sie/Sie	werden handeln

CONDITIONAL

ich	würde handeln
du	würdest handeln
er/sie/es	würde handeln
wir	würden handeln
ihr	würdet handeln
sie/Sie	würden handeln

IMPERATIVE

handle!/handeln wir!/handelt!/
handeln Sie!

PAST PARTICIPLE

gehandelt

PRESENT PARTICIPLE

handelnd

EXAMPLE PHRASES

Die Geschichte **handelte** *von einem alten Mann.* The story was about an old man.
Wir müssen schnell **handeln**. We must act quickly.
Er **hat** *früher in Gebrauchtwagen* **gehandelt**. He used to deal in used cars.

ich = I **du** = you **er** = he/it **sie** = she/it **es** = it/he/she **wir** = we **ihr** = you **sie** = they **Sie** = you

▶ hängen* (to hang)

strong, *formed with* haben

PRESENT

ich	hänge
du	hängst
er/sie/es	hängt
wir	hängen
ihr	hängt
sie/Sie	hängen

PRESENT SUBJUNCTIVE

ich	hänge
du	hängest
er/sie/es	hänge
wir	hängen
ihr	hänget
sie/Sie	hängen

PERFECT

ich	habe gehangen
du	hast gehangen
er/sie/es	hat gehangen
wir	haben gehangen
ihr	habt gehangen
sie/Sie	haben gehangen

IMPERFECT

ich	hing
du	hingst
er/sie/es	hing
wir	hingen
ihr	hingt
sie/Sie	hingen

FUTURE

ich	werde hängen
du	wirst hängen
er/sie/es	wird hängen
wir	werden hängen
ihr	werdet hängen
sie/Sie	werden hängen

CONDITIONAL

ich	würde hängen
du	würdest hängen
er/sie/es	würde hängen
wir	würden hängen
ihr	würdet hängen
sie/Sie	würden hängen

IMPERATIVE

häng(e)!/hängen wir!/hängt!/
hängen Sie!

PAST PARTICIPLE

gehangen

PRESENT PARTICIPLE

hängend

EXAMPLE PHRASES

Sie **hat** sehr an ihrem Vater **gehangen**. She was very attached to her father.
Er **hängt** an seinem Beruf. He loves his job.
Er **hat** das Bild an die Wand **gehängt**. He hung the picture on the wall.

*hängen is conjugated as a weak verb when it has a direct object.

ich = I **du** = you **er** = he/it **sie** = she/it **es** = it/he/she **wir** = we **ihr** = you **sie** = they **Sie** = you

▶ **heizen** (to heat)

weak, *formed with* haben

PRESENT

ich	heize
du	heizt
er/sie/es	heizt
wir	heizen
ihr	heizt
sie/Sie	heizen

PERFECT

ich	habe geheizt
du	hast geheizt
er/sie/es	hat geheizt
wir	haben geheizt
ihr	habt geheizt
sie/Sie	haben geheizt

FUTURE

ich	werde heizen
du	wirst heizen
er/sie/es	wird heizen
wir	werden heizen
ihr	werdet heizen
sie/Sie	werden heizen

IMPERATIVE

heiz(e)!/heizen wir!/heizt!/
heizen Sie!

PRESENT SUBJUNCTIVE

ich	heize
du	heizest
er/sie/es	heize
wir	heizen
ihr	heizet
sie/Sie	heizen

IMPERFECT

ich	heizte
du	heiztest
er/sie/es	heizte
wir	heizten
ihr	heiztet
sie/Sie	heizten

CONDITIONAL

ich	würde heizen
du	würdest heizen
er/sie/es	würde heizen
wir	würden heizen
ihr	würdet heizen
sie/Sie	würden heizen

PAST PARTICIPLE

geheizt

PRESENT PARTICIPLE

heizend

EXAMPLE PHRASES

Der Ofen **heizt** *gut.* The stove gives off a good heat.
Wir **heizen** *mit Holz.* We use wood for heating.
Ab Oktober wird **geheizt**. The heating is put on in October.

ich = I **du** = you **er** = he/it **sie** = she/it **es** = it/he/she **wir** = we **ihr** = you **sie** = they **Sie** = you

▶ helfen (to help)

strong, formed with **haben**

PRESENT

ich	helfe
du	hilfst
er/sie/es	hilft
wir	helfen
ihr	helft
sie/Sie	helfen

PRESENT SUBJUNCTIVE

ich	helfe
du	helfest
er/sie/es	helfe
wir	helfen
ihr	helfet
sie/Sie	helfen

PERFECT

ich	habe geholfen
du	hast geholfen
er/sie/es	hat geholfen
wir	haben geholfen
ihr	habt geholfen
sie/Sie	haben geholfen

IMPERFECT

ich	half
du	halfst
er/sie/es	half
wir	halfen
ihr	halft
sie/Sie	halfen

FUTURE

ich	werde helfen
du	wirst helfen
er/sie/es	wird helfen
wir	werden helfen
ihr	werdet helfen
sie/Sie	werden helfen

CONDITIONAL

ich	würde helfen
du	würdest helfen
er/sie/es	würde helfen
wir	würden helfen
ihr	würdet helfen
sie/Sie	würden helfen

IMPERATIVE

hilf!/helfen wir!/helft!/
helfen Sie!

PAST PARTICIPLE

geholfen

PRESENT PARTICIPLE

helfend

EXAMPLE PHRASES

*Er **hat** mir dabei **geholfen**.* He helped me with it.
*Diese Arznei **hilft** gegen Kopfschmerzen.* This medicine is good for headaches.
*Sein Vorschlag **half** mir wenig.* His suggestion was not much help to me.

---

ich = I **du** = you **er** = he/it **sie** = she/it **es** = it/he/she **wir** = we **ihr** = you **sie** = they **Sie** = you

▶ holen (to fetch)

weak, *formed with* **haben**

PRESENT

ich	hole
du	holst
er/sie/es	holt
wir	holen
ihr	holt
sie/Sie	holen

PRESENT SUBJUNCTIVE

ich	hole
du	holest
er/sie/es	hole
wir	holen
ihr	holet
sie/Sie	holen

PERFECT

ich	habe geholt
du	hast geholt
er/sie/es	hat geholt
wir	haben geholt
ihr	habt geholt
sie/Sie	haben geholt

IMPERFECT

ich	holte
du	holtest
er/sie/es	holte
wir	holten
ihr	holtet
sie/Sie	holten

FUTURE

ich	werde holen
du	wirst holen
er/sie/es	wird holen
wir	werden holen
ihr	werdet holen
sie/Sie	werden holen

CONDITIONAL

ich	würde holen
du	würdest holen
er/sie/es	würde holen
wir	würden holen
ihr	würdet holen
sie/Sie	würden holen

IMPERATIVE

hol(e)!/holen wir!/holt!/
holen Sie!

PAST PARTICIPLE

geholt

PRESENT PARTICIPLE

holend

EXAMPLE PHRASES

Er **holt** jeden Tag frische Milch vom Supermarkt. He fetches fresh milk from the supermarket every day.
*Soll ich ihn ans Telefon **holen**?* Shall I get him to come to the phone?
*Ich **habe** mir eine Erkältung **geholt**.* I caught a cold.

---

ich = I **du** = you **er** = he/it **sie** = she/it **es** = it/he/she **wir** = we **ihr** = you **sie** = they **Sie** = you

▶ **kennen** (to know) *(be acquainted with)* mixed, *formed with* **haben**

PRESENT

ich	kenne
du	kennst
er/sie/es	kennt
wir	kennen
ihr	kennt
sie/Sie	kennen

PRESENT SUBJUNCTIVE

ich	kenne
du	kennest
er/sie/es	kenne
wir	kennen
ihr	kennet
sie/Sie	kennen

PERFECT

ich	habe gekannt
du	hast gekannt
er/sie/es	hat gekannt
wir	haben gekannt
ihr	habt gekannt
sie/Sie	haben gekannt

IMPERFECT

ich	kannte
du	kanntest
er/sie/es	kannte
wir	kannten
ihr	kanntet
sie/Sie	kannten

FUTURE

ich	werde kennen
du	wirst kennen
er/sie/es	wird kennen
wir	werden kennen
ihr	werdet kennen
sie/Sie	werden kennen

CONDITIONAL

ich	würde kennen
du	würdest kennen
er/sie/es	würde kennen
wir	würden kennen
ihr	würdet kennen
sie/Sie	würden kennen

IMPERATIVE

kenn(e)!/kennen wir!/kennt!/
kennen Sie!

PAST PARTICIPLE

gekannt

PRESENT PARTICIPLE

kennend

EXAMPLE PHRASES

*Ich **kenne** ihn nicht.* I don't know him.
*Er **kannte** kein Erbarmen.* He knew no mercy.
***Kennst** du mich noch?* Do you remember me?

---

ich = I **du** = you **er** = he/it **sie** = she/it **es** = it/he/she **wir** = we **ihr** = you **sie** = they **Sie** = you

▶ **kommen** (to come)

strong, *formed with sein*

PRESENT

ich	komme
du	kommst
er/sie/es	kommt
wir	kommen
ihr	kommt
sie/Sie	kommen

PRESENT SUBJUNCTIVE

ich	komme
du	kommest
er/sie/es	komme
wir	kommen
ihr	kommet
sie/Sie	kommen

PERFECT

ich	bin gekommen
du	bist gekommen
er/sie/es	ist gekommen
wir	sind gekommen
ihr	seid gekommen
sie/Sie	sind gekommen

IMPERFECT

ich	kam
du	kamst
er/sie/es	kam
wir	kamen
ihr	kamt
sie/Sie	kamen

FUTURE

ich	werde kommen
du	wirst kommen
er/sie/es	wird kommen
wir	werden kommen
ihr	werdet kommen
sie/Sie	werden kommen

CONDITIONAL

ich	würde kommen
du	wurdest kommen
er/sie/es	würde kommen
wir	würden kommen
ihr	würdet kommen
sie/Sie	würden kommen

IMPERATIVE

komm(e)!/kommen wir!/
kommt!/kommen Sie!

PAST PARTICIPLE

gekommen

PRESENT PARTICIPLE

kommend

EXAMPLE PHRASES

Er **kam** die Straße entlang. He was coming along the street.
Ich **komme** zu deiner Party. I'm coming to your party.
Woher **kommst** du? Where do you come from?

ich = I **du** = you **er** = he/it **sie** = she/it **es** = it/he/she **wir** = we **ihr** = you **sie** = they **Sie** = you

▶ können (to be able to)

modal, *formed with* **haben**

PRESENT

ich	kann
du	kannst
er/sie/es	kann
wir	können
ihr	könnt
sie/Sie	können

PRESENT SUBJUNCTIVE

ich	könne
du	könnest
er/sie/es	könne
wir	können
ihr	könnet
sie/Sie	können

PERFECT

ich	habe gekonnt/können
du	hast gekonnt/können
er/sie/es	hat gekonnt/können
wir	haben gekonnt/können
ihr	habt gekonnt/können
sie/Sie	haben gekonnt/können

IMPERFECT

ich	konnte
du	konntest
er/sie/es	konnte
wir	konnten
ihr	konntet
sie/Sie	konnten

FUTURE

ich	werde können
du	wirst können
er/sie/es	wird können
wir	werden können
ihr	werdet können
sie/Sie	werden können

CONDITIONAL

ich	würde können
du	würdest können
er/sie/es	würde können
wir	würden können
ihr	würdet können
sie/Sie	würden können

PAST PARTICIPLE

gekonnt/können*

PRESENT PARTICIPLE

könnend

*This form is used when combined with another infinitive.

EXAMPLE PHRASES

Er **kann** gut schwimmen. He can swim well.
Sie **konnte** kein Wort Deutsch. She couldn't speak a word of German.
Kann ich gehen? Can I go?

ich = I **du** = you **er** = he/it **sie** = she/it **es** = it/he/she **wir** = we **ihr** = you **sie** = they **Sie** = you

▶ **lassen** (to leave; to allow)

strong, formed with **haben**

PRESENT

ich	lasse
du	lässt
er/sie/es	lässt
wir	lassen
ihr	lasst
sie/Sie	lassen

PRESENT SUBJUNCTIVE

ich	lasse
du	lassest
er/sie/es	lasse
wir	lassen
ihr	lasset
sie/Sie	lassen

PERFECT

ich	habe gelassen/lassen
du	hast gelassen/lassen
er/sie/es	hat gelassen/lassen
wir	haben gelassen/lassen
ihr	habt gelassen/lassen
sie/Sie	haben gelassen/lassen

IMPERFECT

ich	ließ
du	ließest
er/sie/es	ließ
wir	ließen
ihr	ließt
sie/Sie	ließen

FUTURE

ich	werde lassen
du	wirst lassen
er/sie/es	wird lassen
wir	werden lassen
ihr	werdet lassen
sie/Sie	werden lassen

CONDITIONAL

ich	würde lassen
du	würdest lassen
er/sie/es	würde lassen
wir	würden lassen
ihr	würdet lassen
sie/Sie	würden lassen

IMPERATIVE

lass(e)!/lassen wir!/lasst!/
lassen Sie!

*This form is used when combined
with another infinitive.*

PAST PARTICIPLE

gelassen/lassen*

PRESENT PARTICIPLE

lassend

EXAMPLE PHRASES

*Sie **ließ** uns warten.* She kept us waiting.
*Ich **lasse** den Hund nicht auf das Sofa.* I won't let the dog on the sofa.
*Sie **haben** ihn allein im Auto **gelassen**.* They left him alone in the car.

---

ich = I **du** = you **er** = he/it **sie** = she/it **es** = it/he/she **wir** = we **ihr** = you **sie** = they **Sie** = you

▶ laufen (to run)

strong, formed with **sein**

PRESENT

ich	laufe
du	läufst
er/sie/es	läuft
wir	laufen
ihr	lauft
sie/Sie	laufen

PRESENT SUBJUNCTIVE

ich	laufe
du	laufest
er/sie/es	laufe
wir	laufen
ihr	laufet
sie/Sie	laufen

PERFECT

ich	bin gelaufen
du	bist gelaufen
er/sie/es	ist gelaufen
wir	sind gelaufen
ihr	seid gelaufen
sie/Sie	sind gelaufen

IMPERFECT

ich	lief
du	liefst
er/sie/es	lief
wir	liefen
ihr	lieft
sie/Sie	liefen

FUTURE

ich	werde laufen
du	wirst laufen
er/sie/es	wird laufen
wir	werden laufen
ihr	werdet laufen
sie/Sie	werden laufen

CONDITIONAL

ich	würde laufen
du	würdest laufen
er/sie/es	würde laufen
wir	würden laufen
ihr	würdet laufen
sie/Sie	würden laufen

IMPERATIVE

lauf(e)!/laufen wir!/lauft!/
laufen Sie!

PAST PARTICIPLE

gelaufen

PRESENT PARTICIPLE

laufend

EXAMPLE PHRASES

Er **lief** so schnell er konnte. He ran as fast as he could.
Sie **läuft** ständig zur Polizei. She's always going to the police.
Das Schiff **ist** auf Grund **gelaufen**. The ship ran aground.

---

ich = I **du** = you **er** = he/it **sie** = she/it **es** = it/he/she **wir** = we **ihr** = you **sie** = they **Sie** = you

▶ leiden (to suffer)

strong, *formed with* haben

PRESENT

ich	leide
du	leidest
er/sie/es	leidet
wir	leiden
ihr	leidet
sie/Sie	leiden

PRESENT SUBJUNCTIVE

ich	leide
du	leidest
er/sie/es	leide
wir	leiden
ihr	leidet
sie/Sie	leiden

PERFECT

ich	habe gelitten
du	hast gelitten
er/sie/es	hat gelitten
wir	haben gelitten
ihr	habt gelitten
sie/Sie	haben gelitten

IMPERFECT

ich	litt
du	litt(e)st
er/sie/es	litt
wir	litten
ihr	littet
sie/Sie	litten

FUTURE

ich	werde leiden
du	wirst leiden
er/sie/es	wird leiden
wir	werden leiden
ihr	werdet leiden
sie/Sie	werden leiden

CONDITIONAL

ich	würde leiden
du	würdest leiden
er/sie/es	würde leiden
wir	würden leiden
ihr	würdet leiden
sie/Sie	würden leiden

IMPERATIVE

leid(e)!/leiden wir!/leidet!/
leiden Sie!

PAST PARTICIPLE

gelitten

PRESENT PARTICIPLE

leidend

EXAMPLE PHRASES

Sie **litt** *an Asthma.* She suffered from asthma.
Wir **haben** *unter der Hitze* **gelitten**. We suffered in the heat.
Ich kann ihn nicht **leiden**. I can't stand him.

---

ich = I **du** = you **er** = he/it **sie** = she/it **es** = it/he/she **wir** = we **ihr** = you **sie** = they **Sie** = you

▶ **lesen** (to read)

strong, *formed with* **haben**

PRESENT

ich	lese
du	liest
er/sie/es	liest
wir	lesen
ihr	lest
sie/Sie	lesen

PRESENT SUBJUNCTIVE

ich	lese
du	lesest
er/sie/es	lese
wir	lesen
ihr	leset
sie/Sie	lesen

PERFECT

ich	habe gelesen
du	hast gelesen
er/sie/es	hat gelesen
wir	haben gelesen
ihr	habt gelesen
sie/Sie	haben gelesen

IMPERFECT

ich	las
du	lasest
er/sie/es	las
wir	lasen
ihr	last
sie/Sie	lasen

FUTURE

ich	werde lesen
du	wirst lesen
er/sie/es	wird lesen
wir	werden lesen
ihr	werdet lesen
sie/Sie	werden lesen

CONDITIONAL

ich	würde lesen
du	würdest lesen
er/sie/es	würde lesen
wir	würden lesen
ihr	würdet lesen
sie/Sie	würden lesen

IMPERATIVE

lies!/lesen wir!/lest!/lesen Sie!

PAST PARTICIPLE

gelesen

PRESENT PARTICIPLE

lesend

EXAMPLE PHRASES

*Das **habe** ich in der Zeitung **gelesen**.* I read it in the newspaper.
*Es war in ihrem Gesicht zu **lesen**.* It was written all over her face.
*Dieses Buch **liest** sich gut.* This book is a good read.

---

ich = I **du** = you **er** = he/it **sie** = she/it **es** = it/he/she **wir** = we **ihr** = you **sie** = they **Sie** = you

▶ liegen (to lie)

strong, *formed with* **haben**

PRESENT

ich	liege
du	liegst
er/sie/es	liegt
wir	liegen
ihr	liegt
sie/Sie	liegen

PRESENT SUBJUNCTIVE

ich	liege
du	liegest
er/sie/es	liege
wir	liegen
ihr	lieget
sie/Sie	liegen

PERFECT

ich	habe gelegen
du	hast gelegen
er/sie/es	hat gelegen
wir	haben gelegen
ihr	habt gelegen
sie/Sie	haben gelegen

IMPERFECT

ich	lag
du	lagst
er/sie/es	lag
wir	lagen
ihr	lagt
sie/Sie	lagen

FUTURE

ich	werde liegen
du	wirst liegen
er/sie/es	wird liegen
wir	werden liegen
ihr	werdet liegen
sie/Sie	werden liegen

CONDITIONAL

ich	würde liegen
du	würdest liegen
er/sie/es	würde liegen
wir	würden liegen
ihr	würdet liegen
sie/Sie	würden liegen

IMPERATIVE

lieg(e)!/liegen wir!/liegt!/
liegen Sie!

PAST PARTICIPLE

gelegen

PRESENT PARTICIPLE

liegend

EXAMPLE PHRASES

Wir **lagen** den ganzen Tag am Strand. We lay on the beach all day.
Köln **liegt** am Rhein. Cologne is on the Rhine.
Es **hat** daran **gelegen**, dass ich krank war. It was because I was ill.

---

ich = I du = you er = he/it sie = she/it es = it/he/she wir = we ihr = you sie = they Sie = you

▶ lügen (to (tell a) lie)

strong, *formed with* haben

PRESENT

ich	lüge
du	lügst
er/sie/es	lügt
wir	lügen
ihr	lügt
sie/Sie	lügen

PRESENT SUBJUNCTIVE

ich	lüge
du	lügest
er/sie/es	lüge
wir	lügen
ihr	lüget
sie/Sie	lügen

PERFECT

ich	habe gelogen
du	hast gelogen
er/sie/es	hat gelogen
wir	haben gelogen
ihr	habt gelogen
sie/Sie	haben gelogen

IMPERFECT

ich	log
du	logst
er/sie/es	log
wir	logen
ihr	logt
sie/Sie	logen

FUTURE

ich	werde lügen
du	wirst lügen
er/sie/es	wird lügen
wir	werden lügen
ihr	werdet lügen
sie/Sie	werden lügen

CONDITIONAL

ich	würde lügen
du	würdest lügen
er/sie/es	würde lügen
wir	würden lügen
ihr	würdet lügen
sie/Sie	würden lügen

IMPERATIVE

lüg(e)!/lügen wir!/lügt!/
lügen Sie!

PAST PARTICIPLE

gelogen

PRESENT PARTICIPLE

lügend

EXAMPLE PHRASES

Er **log** ständig. He was always telling lies.
Ich **würde lügen**, wenn ich das sagen würde. I would be lying if I said that.
Das ist **gelogen**! That's a lie!

ich = I **du** = you **er** = he/it **sie** = she/it **es** = it/he/she **wir** = we **ihr** = you **sie** = they **Sie** = you

► machen (to do; to make)

weak, formed with **haben**

PRESENT

ich	mache
du	machst
er/sie/es	macht
wir	machen
ihr	macht
sie/Sie	machen

PRESENT SUBJUNCTIVE

ich	mache
du	machest
er/sie/es	mache
wir	machen
ihr	machet
sie/Sie	machen

PERFECT

Ich	habe gemacht
du	hast gemacht
er/sie/es	hat gemacht
wir	haben gemacht
ihr	habt gemacht
sie/Sie	haben gemacht

IMPERFECT

ich	machte
du	machtest
er/sie/es	machte
wir	machten
ihr	machtet
sie/Sie	machten

FUTURE

ich	werde machen
du	wirst machen
er/sie/es	wird machen
wir	werden machen
ihr	werdet machen
sie/Sie	werden machen

CONDITIONAL

ich	würde machen
du	würdest machen
er/sie/es	würde machen
wir	würden machen
ihr	würdet machen
sie/Sie	würden machen

IMPERATIVE

mach!/machen wir!/macht!/
machen Sie!

PAST PARTICIPLE

gemacht

PRESENT PARTICIPLE

machend

EXAMPLE PHRASES

Was **machst** *du?* What are you doing?
Ich **habe** *die Betten* **gemacht**. I made the beds.
Ich **werde** *es morgen* **machen**. I'll do it tomorrow.

ich = I **du** = you **er** = he/it **sie** = she/it **es** = it/he/she **wir** = we **ihr** = you **sie** = they **Sie** = you

▶ misstrauen (to mistrust) weak, inseparable, *formed with* haben

PRESENT

ich	misstraue
du	misstraust
er/sie/es	misstraut
wir	misstrauen
ihr	misstraut
sie/Sie	misstrauen

PRESENT SUBJUNCTIVE

ich	misstraue
du	misstrauest
er/sie/es	misstraue
wir	misstrauen
ihr	misstrauet
sie/Sie	misstrauen

PERFECT

ich	habe misstraut
du	hast misstraut
er/sie/es	hat misstraut
wir	haben misstraut
ihr	habt misstraut
sie/Sie	haben misstraut

IMPERFECT

ich	misstraute
du	misstrautest
er/sie/es	misstraute
wir	misstrauten
ihr	misstrautet
sie/Sie	misstrauten

FUTURE

ich	werde misstrauen
du	wirst misstrauen
er/sie/es	wird misstrauen
wir	werden misstrauen
ihr	werdet misstrauen
sie/Sie	werden misstrauen

CONDITIONAL

ich	würde misstrauen
du	würdest misstrauen
er/sie/es	würde misstrauen
wir	würden misstrauen
ihr	würdet misstrauen
sie/Sie	würden misstrauen

IMPERATIVE

misstrau(e)!/misstrauen wir!/
misstraut!/misstrauen Sie!

PAST PARTICIPLE

misstraut

PRESENT PARTICIPLE

misstrauend

EXAMPLE PHRASES

Sie **misstraute** *ihrem Gedächtnis*. She didn't trust her memory.
Ich **würde** *seinen Ratschlägen* **misstrauen**. I would not trust his advice.
Ich **habe** *ihr von Anfang an* **misstraut**. I didn't trust her from the start.

ich = I **du** = you **er** = he/it **sie** = she/it **es** = it/he/she **wir** = we **ihr** = you **sie** = they **Sie** = you

▶ mögen (to like)

modal, *formed with* **haben**

PRESENT

ich	mag
du	magst
er/sie/es	mag
wir	mögen
ihr	mögt
sie/Sie	mögen

PRESENT SUBJUNCTIVE

ich	möge
du	mögest
er/sie/es	möge
wir	mögen
ihr	möget
sie/Sie	mögen

PERFECT

ich	habe gemocht/mögen
du	hast gemocht/mögen
er/sie/es	hat gemocht/mögen
wir	haben gemocht/mögen
ihr	habt gemocht/mögen
sie/Sie	haben gemocht/mögen

IMPERFECT

ich	mochte
du	mochtest
er/sie/es	mochte
wir	mochten
ihr	mochtet
sie/Sie	mochten

FUTURE

ich	werde mögen
du	wirst mögen
er/sie/es	wird mögen
wir	werden mögen
ihr	werdet mögen
sie/Sie	werden mögen

CONDITIONAL

ich	würde mögen
du	würdest mögen
er/sie/es	würde mögen
wir	würden mögen
ihr	würdet mögen
sie/Sie	würden mögen

PAST PARTICIPLE

gemocht/mögen*

PRESENT PARTICIPLE

mögend

*This form is used when combined with another infinitive.

EXAMPLE PHRASES

Ich **mag** gern Vanilleeis. I like vanilla ice cream.
Er **mochte** sie nicht danach fragen. He didn't want to ask her about it.
Ich **habe** ihn noch nie **gemocht**. I never liked him.

ich = I **du** = you **er** = he/it **sie** = she/it **es** = it/he/she **wir** = we **ihr** = you **sie** = they **Sie** = you

▶ müssen (to have to)

modal, formed with **haben**

PRESENT

ich	muss
du	musst
er/sie/es	muss
wir	müssen
ihr	müsst
sie/Sie	müssen

PRESENT SUBJUNCTIVE

ich	müsse
du	müssest
er/sie/es	müsse
wir	müssen
ihr	müsset
sie/Sie	müssen

PERFECT

ich	habe gemusst/müssen
du	hast gemusst/müssen
er/sie/es	hat gemusst/müssen
wir	haben gemusst/müssen
ihr	habt gemusst/müssen
sie/Sie	haben gemusst/müssen

IMPERFECT

ich	musste
du	musstest
er/sie/es	musste
wir	mussten
ihr	musstet
sie/Sie	mussten

FUTURE

ich	werde müssen
du	wirst müssen
er/sie/es	wird müssen
wir	werden müssen
ihr	werdet müssen
sie/Sie	werden müssen

CONDITIONAL

ich	würde müssen
du	würdest müssen
er/sie/es	würde müssen
wir	würden müssen
ihr	würdet müssen
sie/Sie	würden müssen

PAST PARTICIPLE

gemusst/müssen*

PRESENT PARTICIPLE

müssend

*This form is used when combined with another infinitive.

EXAMPLE PHRASES

Ich **muss** *auf die Toilette.* I must go to the loo.
Wir **müssen** *jeden Abend unsere Hausaufgaben machen.* We have to do our homework every night.
Sie **hat** *abwaschen* **müssen**. She had to wash up.

ich = I **du** = you **er** = he/it **sie** = she/it **es** = it/he/she **wir** = we **ihr** = you **sie** = they **Sie** = you

▶ nehmen (to take)

strong, *formed with* haben

PRESENT

ich	nehme
du	nimmst
er/sie/es	nimmt
wir	nehmen
ihr	nehmt
sie/Sie	nehmen

PRESENT SUBJUNCTIVE

ich	nehme
du	nehmest
er/sie/es	nehme
wir	nehmen
ihr	nehmet
sie/Sie	nehmen

PERFECT

ich	habe genommen
du	hast genommen
er/sie/es	hat genommen
wir	haben genommen
ihr	habt genommen
sie/Sie	haben genommen

IMPERFECT

ich	nahm
du	nahmst
er/sie/es	nahm
wir	nahmen
ihr	nahmt
sie/Sie	nahmen

FUTURE

ich	werde nehmen
du	wirst nehmen
er/sie/es	wird nehmen
wir	werden nehmen
ihr	werdet nehmen
sie/Sie	werden nehmen

CONDITIONAL

ich	würde nehmen
du	würdest nehmen
er/sie/es	würde nehmen
wir	würden nehmen
ihr	würdet nehmen
sie/Sie	würden nehmen

IMPERATIVE

nimm!/nehmen wir!/nehmt!/
nehmen Sie!

PAST PARTICIPLE

genommen

PRESENT PARTICIPLE

nehmend

EXAMPLE PHRASES

Hast du den Bus in die Stadt **genommen**? Did you take the bus into town?
Wie viel **nimmst** du dafür? How much will you take for it?
Er **nahm** sich vom Brot. He helped himself to bread.

ich = I **du** = you **er** = he/it **sie** = she/it **es** = it/he/she **wir** = we **ihr** = you **sie** = they **Sie** = you

▶ **rechnen** (to calculate)

weak, *formed with* **haben**

PRESENT

ich	rechne
du	rechnest
er/sie/es	rechnet
wir	rechnen
ihr	rechnet
sie/Sie	rechnen

PRESENT SUBJUNCTIVE

ich	rechne
du	rechnest
er/sie/es	rechne
wir	rechnen
ihr	rechnet
sie/Sie	rechnen

PERFECT

ich	habe gerechnet
du	hast gerechnet
er/sie/es	hat gerechnet
wir	haben gerechnet
ihr	habt gerechnet
sie/Sie	haben gerechnet

IMPERFECT

ich	rechnete
du	rechnetest
er/sie/es	rechnete
wir	rechneten
ihr	rechnetet
sie/Sie	rechneten

FUTURE

ich	werde rechnen
du	wirst rechnen
er/sie/es	wird rechnen
wir	werden rechnen
ihr	werdet rechnen
sie/Sie	werden rechnen

CONDITIONAL

ich	würde rechnen
du	würdest rechnen
er/sie/es	würde rechnen
wir	würden rechnen
ihr	würdet rechnen
sie/Sie	würden rechnen

IMPERATIVE

rechne!/rechnen wir!/rechnet!/
rechnen Sie!

PAST PARTICIPLE

gerechnet

PRESENT PARTICIPLE

rechnend

EXAMPLE PHRASES

Lass mich **rechnen***, wie viel das wird.* Let me work out how much that's going to be.
Emma kann gut **rechnen***.* Emma is good at arithmetic.
Damit **habe** *ich nicht* **gerechnet***.* I wasn't expecting that.

---

ich = I **du** = you **er** = he/it **sie** = she/it **es** = it/he/she **wir** = we **ihr** = you **sie** = they **Sie** = you

▶ reden (to talk)

weak, *formed with* **haben**

PRESENT

ich	rede
du	redest
er/sie/es	redet
wir	reden
ihr	redet
sie/Sie	reden

PRESENT SUBJUNCTIVE

ich	rede
du	redest
er/sie/es	rede
wir	reden
ihr	redet
sie/Sie	reden

PERFECT

ich	habe geredet
du	hast geredet
er/sie/es	hat geredet
wir	haben geredet
ihr	habt geredet
sie/Sie	haben geredet

IMPERFECT

ich	redete
du	redetest
er/sie/es	redete
wir	redeten
ihr	redetet
sie/Sie	redeten

FUTURE

ich	werde reden
du	wirst reden
er/sie/es	wird reden
wir	werden reden
ihr	werdet reden
sie/Sie	werden reden

CONDITIONAL

ich	würde reden
du	würdest reden
er/sie/es	würde reden
wir	würden reden
ihr	würdet reden
sie/Sie	würden reden

IMPERATIVE

red(e)!/reden wir!/redet!/
reden Sie!

PAST PARTICIPLE

geredet

PRESENT PARTICIPLE

redend

EXAMPLE PHRASES

Man kann überhaupt nicht mit ihr **reden**. You can't talk to her at all.
Er **redete** *ständig von seinem Hund.* He kept talking about his dog.
Ich **werde** *mit deinem Vater* **reden**. I'll speak to your father.

---

ich = I **du** = you **er** = he/it **sie** = she/it **es** = it/he/she **wir** = we **ihr** = you **sie** = they **Sie** = you

▶ rennen (to run)

mixed, *formed with* **sein**

PRESENT

ich	renne
du	rennst
er/sie/es	rennt
wir	rennen
ihr	rennt
sie/Sie	rennen

PRESENT SUBJUNCTIVE

ich	renne
du	rennest
er/sie/es	renne
wir	rennen
ihr	rennet
sie/Sie	rennen

PERFECT

ich	bin gerannt
du	bist gerannt
er/sie/es	ist gerannt
wir	sind gerannt
ihr	seid gerannt
sie/Sie	sind gerannt

IMPERFECT

ich	rannte
du	ranntest
er/sie/es	rannte
wir	rannten
ihr	ranntet
sie/Sie	rannten

FUTURE

ich	werde rennen
du	wirst rennen
er/sie/es	wird rennen
wir	werden rennen
ihr	werdet rennen
sie/Sie	werden rennen

CONDITIONAL

ich	würde rennen
du	würdest rennen
er/sie/es	würde rennen
wir	würden rennen
ihr	würdet rennen
sie/Sie	würden rennen

IMPERATIVE

renn(e)!/rennen wir!/rennt!/
rennen Sie!

PAST PARTICIPLE

gerannt

PRESENT PARTICIPLE

rennend

EXAMPLE PHRASES

Sie **rannte** schnell weg. She ran away fast.
Er **rennt** dauernd zum Chef. He keeps running to the boss.
Ich **bin** mit dem Kopf gegen die Wand **gerannt**. I bumped my head against the wall.

ich = I **du** = you **er** = he/it **sie** = she/it **es** = it/he/she **wir** = we **ihr** = you **sie** = they **Sie** = you

▶ rufen (to shout; call)

strong, *formed with* **haben**

PRESENT

ich	rufe
du	rufst
er/sie/es	ruft
wir	rufen
ihr	ruft
sie/Sie	rufen

PRESENT SUBJUNCTIVE

ich	rufe
du	rufest
er/sie/es	rufe
wir	rufen
ihr	rufet
sie/Sie	rufen

PERFECT

ich	habe gerufen
du	hast gerufen
er/sie/es	hat gerufen
wir	haben gerufen
ihr	habt gerufen
sie/Sie	haben gerufen

IMPERFECT

ich	rief
du	riefst
er/sie/es	rief
wir	riefen
ihr	rieft
sie/Sie	riefen

FUTURE

ich	werde rufen
du	wirst rufen
er/sie/es	wird rufen
wir	werden rufen
ihr	werdet rufen
sie/Sie	werden rufen

CONDITIONAL

ich	würde rufen
du	würdest rufen
er/sie/es	würde rufen
wir	würden rufen
ihr	würdet rufen
sie/Sie	würden rufen

IMPERATIVE

ruf(e)!/rufen wir!/ruft!/
rufen Sie!

PAST PARTICIPLE

gerufen

PRESENT PARTICIPLE

rufend

EXAMPLE PHRASES

Sie **riefen** um Hilfe. They shouted for help.
Ich **habe** dir ein Taxi **gerufen**. I called you a taxi.
Er **rief** seine Schwester zu sich. He sent for his sister.

ich = I **du** = you **er** = he/it **sie** = she/it **es** = it/he/she **wir** = we **ihr** = you **sie** = they **Sie** = you

▶ scheinen (to shine; to seem)

strong, *formed with* haben

PRESENT

ich	scheine
du	scheinst
er/sie/es	scheint
wir	scheinen
ihr	scheint
sie/Sie	scheinen

PRESENT SUBJUNCTIVE

ich	scheine
du	scheinest
er/sie/es	scheine
wir	scheinen
ihr	scheinet
sie/Sie	scheinen

PERFECT

ich	habe geschienen
du	hast geschienen
er/sie/es	hat geschienen
wir	haben geschienen
ihr	habt geschienen
sie/Sie	haben geschienen

IMPERFECT

ich	schien
du	schienst
er/sie/es	schien
wir	schienen
ihr	schient
sie/Sie	schienen

FUTURE

ich	werde scheinen
du	wirst scheinen
er/sie/es	wird scheinen
wir	werden scheinen
ihr	werdet scheinen
sie/Sie	werden scheinen

CONDITIONAL

ich	würde scheinen
du	würdest scheinen
er/sie/es	würde scheinen
wir	würden scheinen
ihr	würdet scheinen
sie/Sie	würden scheinen

IMPERATIVE

schein(e)!/scheinen wir!/
scheint!/scheinen Sie!

PAST PARTICIPLE

geschienen

PRESENT PARTICIPLE

scheinend

EXAMPLE PHRASES

Die Sonne **schien**. The sun was shining.
Es **scheint**, als ob du recht hast. It appears as if you're right.
Sie **schienen** glücklich zu sein. They seemed to be happy.

▶ schlafen (to sleep)

strong, *formed with* haben

PRESENT

ich	schlafe
du	schläfst
er/sie/es	schläft
wir	schlafen
ihr	schlaft
sie/Sie	schlafen

PRESENT SUBJUNCTIVE

ich	schlafe
du	schlafest
er/sie/es	schlafe
wir	schlafen
ihr	schlafet
sie/Sie	schlafen

PERFECT

ich	habe geschlafen
du	hast geschlafen
er/sie/es	hat geschlafen
wir	haben geschlafen
ihr	habt geschlafen
sie/Sie	haben geschlafen

IMPERFECT

Ich	schlief
du	schliefst
er/sie/es	schlief
wir	schliefen
ihr	schlieft
sie/Sie	schliefen

FUTURE

ich	werde schlafen
du	wirst schlafen
er/sie/es	wird schlafen
wir	werden schlafen
ihr	werdet schlafen
sie/Sie	werden schlafen

CONDITIONAL

ich	würde schlafen
du	würdest schlafen
er/sie/es	würde schlafen
wir	würden schlafen
ihr	würdet schlafen
sie/Sie	würden schlafen

IMPERATIVE

schlaf(e)!/schlafen wir!/schlaft!/
schlafen Sie!

PAST PARTICIPLE

geschlafen

PRESENT PARTICIPLE

schlafend

EXAMPLE PHRASES

Sie **schläft** immer noch. She's still asleep.
Heute Nacht **wirst** du bestimmt gut **schlafen**. I'm sure you'll sleep well tonight.
Er **schlief** während des Unterrichts. He slept during lessons.

---

ich = I **du** = you **er** = he/it **sie** = she/it **es** = it/he/she **wir** = we **ihr** = you **sie** = they **Sie** = you

▶ schlagen (to hit)

strong, *formed with* **haben**

PRESENT

ich	schlage
du	schlägst
er/sie/es	schlägt
wir	schlagen
ihr	schlagt
sie/Sie	schlagen

PRESENT SUBJUNCTIVE

ich	schlage
du	schlagest
er/sie/es	schlage
wir	schlagen
ihr	schlaget
sie/Sie	schlagen

PERFECT

ich	habe geschlagen
du	hast geschlagen
er/sie/es	hat geschlagen
wir	haben geschlagen
ihr	habt geschlagen
sie/Sie	haben geschlagen

IMPERFECT

ich	schlug
du	schlugst
er/sie/es	schlug
wir	schlugen
ihr	schlugt
sie/Sie	schlugen

FUTURE

ich	werde schlagen
du	wirst schlagen
er/sie/es	wird schlagen
wir	werden schlagen
ihr	werdet schlagen
sie/Sie	werden schlagen

CONDITIONAL

ich	würde schlagen
du	würdest schlagen
er/sie/es	würde schlagen
wir	würden schlagen
ihr	würdet schlagen
sie/Sie	würden schlagen

IMPERATIVE

schlag(e)!/schlagen wir!/
schlagt!/schlagen Sie!

PAST PARTICIPLE

geschlagen

PRESENT PARTICIPLE

schlagend

EXAMPLE PHRASES

England **hat** *Deutschland* **geschlagen**. England beat Germany.
Ihr Herz **schlug** *schneller*. Her heart beat faster.
Die Uhr **schlägt** *drei*. The clock strikes three.

---

ich = I **du** = you **er** = he/it **sie** = she/it **es** = it/he/she **wir** = we **ihr** = you **sie** = they **Sie** = you

▶ schneiden (to cut)

strong, *formed with* haben

PRESENT

ich	schneide
du	schneidest
er/sie/es	schneidet
wir	schneiden
ihr	schneidet
sie/Sie	schneiden

PRESENT SUBJUNCTIVE

ich	schneide
du	schneidest
er/sie/es	schneide
wir	schneiden
ihr	schneidet
sie/Sie	schneiden

PERFECT

ich	habe geschnitten
du	hast geschnitten
er/sie/es	hat geschnitten
wir	haben geschnitten
ihr	habt geschnitten
sie/Sie	haben geschnitten

IMPERFECT

ich	schnitt
du	schnittst
er/sie/es	schnitt
wir	schnitten
ihr	schnittet
sie/Sie	schnitten

FUTURE

ich	werde schneiden
du	wirst schneiden
er/sie/es	wird schneiden
wir	werden schneiden
ihr	werdet schneiden
sie/Sie	werden schneiden

CONDITIONAL

ich	würde schneiden
du	würdest schneiden
er/sie/es	würde schneiden
wir	würden schneiden
ihr	würdet schneiden
sie/Sie	würden schneiden

IMPERATIVE

schneid(e)!/schneiden wir!/
schneidet!/schneiden Sie!

PAST PARTICIPLE

geschnitten

PRESENT PARTICIPLE

schneidend

EXAMPLE PHRASES

Sie schneidet ihm die Haare. She cuts his hair.
Ich habe mir in den Finger geschnitten. I've cut my finger.
Sie schnitt die Tomaten in Scheiben. She sliced the tomatoes.

ich = I **du** = you **er** = he/it **sie** = she/it **es** = it/he/she **wir** = we **ihr** = you **sie** = they **Sie** = you

▶ schreiben (to write)

strong, *formed with* **haben**

PRESENT

ich	schreibe
du	schreibst
er/sie/es	schreibt
wir	schreiben
ihr	schreibt
sie/Sie	schreiben

PRESENT SUBJUNCTIVE

ich	schreibe
du	schreibest
er/sie/es	schreibe
wir	schreiben
ihr	schreibet
sie/Sie	schreiben

PERFECT

ich	habe geschrieben
du	hast geschrieben
er/sie/es	hat geschrieben
wir	haben geschrieben
ihr	habt geschrieben
sie/Sie	haben geschrieben

IMPERFECT

ich	schrieb
du	schriebst
er/sie/es	schrieb
wir	schrieben
ihr	schriebt
sie/Sie	schrieben

FUTURE

ich	werde schreiben
du	wirst schreiben
er/sie/es	wird schreiben
wir	werden schreiben
ihr	werdet schreiben
sie/Sie	werden schreiben

CONDITIONAL

ich	würde schreiben
du	würdest schreiben
er/sie/es	würde schreiben
wir	würden schreiben
ihr	würdet schreiben
sie/Sie	würden schreiben

IMPERATIVE

schreib(e)!/schreiben wir!/
schreibt!/schreiben Sie!

PAST PARTICIPLE

geschrieben

PRESENT PARTICIPLE

schreibend

EXAMPLE PHRASES

*Er **schrieb** das Wort an die Tafel.* He wrote the word on the blackboard.
*Wie **schreibst** du deinen Namen?* How do you spell your name?
*Sie **hat** mir einen Brief **geschrieben**.* She wrote me a letter.

---

ich = I **du** = you **er** = he/it **sie** = she/it **es** = it/he/she **wir** = we **ihr** =,you **sie** = they **Sie** = you

▶ schreien (to shout)

strong, *formed with* haben

PRESENT

ich	schreie
du	schreist
er/sie/es	schreit
wir	schreien
ihr	schreit
sie/Sie	schreien

PRESENT SUBJUNCTIVE

ich	schreie
du	schreiest
er/sie/es	schreie
wir	schreien
ihr	schreiet
sie/Sie	schreien

PERFECT

ich	habe geschrien
du	hast geschrien
er/sie/es	hat geschrien
wir	haben geschrien
ihr	habt geschrien
sie/Sie	haben geschrien

IMPERFECT

ich	schrie
du	schriest
er/sie/es	schrie
wir	schrieen
ihr	schriet
sie/Sie	schrieen

FUTURE

ich	werde schreien
du	wirst schreien
er/sie/es	wird schreien
wir	werden schreien
ihr	werdet schreien
sie/Sie	werden schreien

CONDITIONAL

ich	würde schreien
du	würdest schreien
er/sie/es	würde schreien
wir	würden schreien
ihr	würdet schreien
sie/Sie	würden schreien

IMPERATIVE

schrei(e)!/schreien wir!/
schreit!/schreien Sie!

PAST PARTICIPLE

geschrie(e)n

PRESENT PARTICIPLE

schreiend

EXAMPLE PHRASES

Sie **schrie** vor Schmerzen. She screamed with pain.
Wir **haben geschrien**, er hat uns aber nicht gehört. We shouted but he didn't
  hear us.
Schreien Sie nicht so! Don't shout!

ich = I **du** = you **er** = he/it **sie** = she/it **es** = it/he/she **wir** = we **ihr** = you **sie** = they **Sie** = you

▶ schwimmen (to swim)

strong, *formed with* sein

PRESENT

ich	schwimme
du	schwimmst
er/sie/es	schwimmt
wir	schwimmen
ihr	schwimmt
sie/Sie	schwimmen

PRESENT SUBJUNCTIVE

ich	schwimme
du	schwimmest
er/sie/es	schwimme
wir	schwimmen
ihr	schwimmet
sie/Sie	schwimmen

PERFECT

ich	bin geschwommen
du	bist geschwommen
er/sie/es	ist geschwommen
wir	sind geschwommen
ihr	seid geschwommen
sie/Sie	sind geschwommen

IMPERFECT

ich	schwamm
du	schwammst
er/sie/es	schwamm
wir	schwammen
ihr	schwammt
sie/Sie	schwammen

FUTURE

ich	werde schwimmen
du	wirst schwimmen
er/sie/es	wird schwimmen
wir	werden schwimmen
ihr	werdet schwimmen
sie/Sie	werden schwimmen

CONDITIONAL

ich	würde schwimmen
du	würdest schwimmen
er/sie/es	würde schwimmen
wir	würden schwimmen
ihr	würdet schwimmen
sie/Sie	würden schwimmen

IMPERATIVE

schwimm(e)!/schwimmen wir!/
schwimmt!/schwimmen Sie!

PAST PARTICIPLE

geschwommen

PRESENT PARTICIPLE

schwimmend

EXAMPLE PHRASES

*Ich kann nicht **schwimmen**.* I can't swim.
*Er **ist** über den Fluss **geschwommen**.* He swam across the river.
*Wir **schwammen** im Geld.* We were rolling in money.

---

ich = I **du** = you **er** = he/it **sie** = she/it **es** = it/he/she **wir** = we **ihr** = you **sie** = they **Sie** = you

▶ sehen (to see)

strong, *formed with* **haben**

PRESENT

ich	sehe
du	siehst
er/sie/es	sieht
wir	sehen
ihr	seht
sie/Sie	sehen

PRESENT SUBJUNCTIVE

ich	sehe
du	sehest
er/sie/es	sehe
wir	sehen
ihr	sehet
sie/Sie	sehen

PERFECT

ich	habe gesehen
du	hast gesehen
er/sie/es	hat gesehen
wir	haben gesehen
ihr	habt gesehen
sie/Sie	haben gesehen

IMPERFECT

ich	sah
du	sahst
er/sie/es	sah
wir	sahen
ihr	saht
sie/Sie	sahen

FUTURE

ich	werde sehen
du	wirst sehen
er/sie/es	wird sehen
wir	werden sehen
ihr	werdet sehen
sie/Sie	werden sehen

CONDITIONAL

ich	würde sehen
du	würdest sehen
er/sie/es	würde sehen
wir	würden sehen
ihr	würdet sehen
sie/Sie	würden sehen

IMPERATIVE

sieh(e)!/sehen wir!/seht!/
sehen Sie!

PAST PARTICIPLE

gesehen

PRESENT PARTICIPLE

sehend

EXAMPLE PHRASES

*Mein Vater **sieht** schlecht.* My father has bad eyesight.
*Ich **habe** diesen Film noch nicht **gesehen**.* I haven't seen this film yet.
*Er **sah** auf die Uhr.* He looked at his watch.

---

ich = I **du** = you **er** = he/it **sie** = she/it **es** = it/he/she **wir** = we **ihr** = you **sie** = they **Sie** = you

▶ sein (to be)

strong, formed with **sein**

PRESENT

ich	bin
du	bist
er/sie/es	ist
wir	sind
ihr	seid
sie/Sie	sind

PRESENT SUBJUNCTIVE

ich	sei
du	sei(e)st
er/sie/es	sei
wir	seien
ihr	seiet
sie/Sie	seien

PERFECT

ich	bin gewesen
du	bist gewesen
er/sie/es	ist gewesen
wir	sind gewesen
ihr	seid gewesen
sie/Sie	sind gewesen

IMPERFECT

ich	war
du	warst
er/sie/es	war
wir	waren
ihr	wart
sie/Sie	waren

FUTURE

ich	werde sein
du	wirst sein
er/sie/es	wird sein
wir	werden sein
ihr	werdet sein
sie/Sie	werden sein

CONDITIONAL

ich	würde sein
du	würdest sein
er/sie/es	würde sein
wir	würden sein
ihr	würdet sein
sie/Sie	würden sein

IMPERATIVE

sei!/seien wir!/seid!/seien Sie!

PAST PARTICIPLE

gewesen

PRESENT PARTICIPLE

seiend

EXAMPLE PHRASES

Er **ist** *zehn Jahre alt.* He is ten years old.
Wir **waren** *gestern im Theater.* We were at the theatre yesterday.
Mir **war** *kalt.* I was cold.

---

ich = I **du** = you **er** = he/it **sie** = she/it **es** = it/he/she **wir** = we **ihr** = you **sie** = they **Sie** = you

▶ singen (to sing)

strong, *formed with* haben

PRESENT

ich	singe
du	singst
er/sie/es	singt
wir	sIngen
ihr	singt
sie/Sie	singen

PRESENT SUBJUNCTIVE

ich	singe
du	singest
er/sie/es	singe
wir	singen
ihr	singet
sie/Sie	singen

PERFECT

ich	habe gesungen
du	hast gesungen
er/sie/es	hat gesungen
wir	haben gesungen
ihr	habt gesungen
sie/Sie	haben gesungen

IMPERFECT

ich	sang
du	sangst
er/sie/es	sang
wir	sangen
ihr	sangt
sie/Sie	sangen

FUTURE

ich	werde singen
du	wirst singen
er/sie/es	wird singen
wir	werden singen
ihr	werdet singen
sie/Sie	werden singen

CONDITIONAL

ich	würde singen
du	würdest singen
er/sie/es	würde singen
wir	würden singen
ihr	würdet singen
sie/Sie	würden singen

IMPERATIVE

sing(e)!/singen wir!/singt!/
singen Sie!

PAST PARTICIPLE

gesungen

PRESENT PARTICIPLE

singend

EXAMPLE PHRASES

*Sie **sang** das Kind in den Schlaf.* She sang the child to sleep.
*Er **singt** nicht gut.* He's a bad singer.
*Ich **habe** dieses Lied früher oft **gesungen**.* I used to sing this song a lot.

---

ich = I **du** = you **er** = he/it **sie** = she/it **es** = it/he/she **wir** = we **ihr** = you **sie** = they **Sie** = you

▶ sinken (to sink)

strong, *formed with* sein

PRESENT

ich	sinke
du	sinkst
er/sie/es	sinkt
wir	sinken
ihr	sinkt
sie/Sie	sinken

PRESENT SUBJUNCTIVE

ich	sinke
du	sinkest
er/sie/es	sinke
wir	sinken
ihr	sinket
sie/Sie	sinken

PERFECT

ich	bin gesunken
du	bist gesunken
er/sie/es	ist gesunken
wir	sind gesunken
ihr	seid gesunken
sie/Sie	sind gesunken

IMPERFECT

ich	sank
du	sankst
er/sie/es	sank
wir	sanken
ihr	sankt
sie/Sie	sanken

FUTURE

ich	werde sinken
du	wirst sinken
er/sie/es	wird sinken
wir	werden sinken
ihr	werdet sinken
sie/Sie	werden sinken

CONDITIONAL

ich	würde sinken
du	würdest sinken
er/sie/es	würde sinken
wir	würden sinken
ihr	würdet sinken
sie/Sie	würden sinken

IMPERATIVE

sink(e)!/sinken wir!/sinkt!/
sinken Sie!

PAST PARTICIPLE

gesunken

PRESENT PARTICIPLE

sinkend

EXAMPLE PHRASES

Wann **ist** *die Titanic* **gesunken**? When did the Titanic sink?
Er **sank** *zu Boden*. He sank to the ground.
Die Preise für Handys **sinken**. Prices of mobile phones are falling.

---

ich = I **du** = you **er** = he/it **sie** = she/it **es** = it/he/she **wir** = we **ihr** = you **sie** = they **Sie** = you

▶ sitzen (to sit)

strong, *formed with* haben

PRESENT

ich	sitze
du	sitzt
er/sie/es	sitzt
wir	sitzen
ihr	sitzt
sie/Sie	sitzen

PRESENT SUBJUNCTIVE

ich	sitze
du	sitzest
er/sie/es	sitze
wir	sitzen
ihr	sitzet
sie/Sie	sitzen

PERFECT

ich	habe gesessen
du	hast gesessen
er/sie/es	hat gesessen
wir	haben gesessen
ihr	habt gesessen
sie/Sie	haben gesessen

IMPERFECT

ich	saß
du	saßest
er/sie/es	saß
wir	saßen
ihr	saßt
sie/Sie	saßen

FUTURE

ich	werde sitzen
du	wirst sitzen
er/sie/es	wird sitzen
wir	werden sitzen
ihr	werdet sitzen
sie/Sie	werden sitzen

CONDITIONAL

ich	würde sitzen
du	würdest sitzen
er/sie/es	würde sitzen
wir	würden sitzen
ihr	würdet sitzen
sie/Sie	würden sitzen

IMPERATIVE

sitz(e)!/sitzen wir!/sitzt!/
sitzen Sie!

PAST PARTICIPLE

gesessen

PRESENT PARTICIPLE

sitzend

EXAMPLE PHRASES

Er **saß** auf meinem Stuhl. He was sitting on my chair.
Deine Krawatte **sitzt** nicht richtig. Your tie isn't straight.
Ich **habe** zwei Jahre über dieser Arbeit **gesessen**. I've spent two years on this piece of work.

---

ich = I **du** = you **er** = he/it **sie** = she/it **es** = it/he/she **wir** = we **ihr** = you **sie** = they **Sie** = you

▶ **sollen** (to be supposed to)

modal, *formed with* haben

PRESENT

ich	soll
du	sollst
er/sie/es	soll
wir	sollen
ihr	sollt
sie/Sie	sollen

PRESENT SUBJUNCTIVE

ich	solle
du	sollest
er/sie/es	solle
wir	sollen
ihr	sollet
sie/Sie	sollen

PERFECT

ich	habe gesollt/sollen
du	hast gesollt/sollen
er/sie/es	hat gesollt/sollen
wir	haben gesollt/sollen
ihr	habt gesollt/sollen
sie/Sie	haben gesollt/sollen

IMPERFECT

ich	sollte
du	solltest
er/sie/es	sollte
wir	sollten
ihr	solltet
sie/Sie	sollten

FUTURE

ich	werde sollen
du	wirst sollen
er/sie/es	wird sollen
wir	werden sollen
ihr	werdet sollen
sie/Sie	werden sollen

CONDITIONAL

ich	würde sollen
du	würdest sollen
er/sie/es	würde sollen
wir	würden sollen
ihr	würdet sollen
sie/Sie	würden sollen

PAST PARTICIPLE

gesollt/sollen*

PRESENT PARTICIPLE

sollend

This form is used when combined with another infinitive.

EXAMPLE PHRASES

*Was **sollte** er machen?* What should he do?
*Das **sollst** du nicht.* You shouldn't do that.
*Ich **soll** um 5 Uhr dort sein.* I'm supposed to be there at 5 o'clock.

ich = I **du** = you **er** = he/it **sie** = she/it **es** = it/he/she **wir** = we **ihr** = you **sie** = they **Sie** = you

▶ sprechen (to speak)

strong, *formed with* **haben**

PRESENT

ich	spreche
du	sprichst
er/sie/es	spricht
wir	sprechen
ihr	sprecht
sie/Sie	sprechen

PRESENT SUBJUNCTIVE

ich	spreche
du	sprechest
er/sie/es	spreche
wir	sprechen
ihr	sprechet
sie/Sie	sprechen

PERFECT

ich	habe gesprochen
du	hast gesprochen
er/sie/es	hat gesprochen
wir	haben gesprochen
ihr	habt gesprochen
sie/Sie	haben gesprochen

IMPERFECT

ich	sprach
du	sprachst
er/sie/es	sprach
wir	sprachen
ihr	spracht
sie/Sie	sprachen

FUTURE

ich	werde sprechen
du	wirst sprechen
er/sie/es	wird sprechen
wir	werden sprechen
ihr	werdet sprechen
sie/Sie	werden sprechen

CONDITIONAL

ich	würde sprechen
du	würdest sprechen
er/sie/es	würde sprechen
wir	würden sprechen
ihr	würdet sprechen
sie/Sie	würden sprechen

IMPERATIVE

sprich!/sprechen wir!/sprecht!/
sprechen Sie!

PAST PARTICIPLE

gesprochen

PRESENT PARTICIPLE

sprechend

EXAMPLE PHRASES

Er **spricht** kein Italienisch. He doesn't speak Italian.
Ich **würde** dich gern privat **sprechen**. I would like to speak to you privately.
Hast du mit ihr **gesprochen**? Have you spoken to her?

Ich = I **du** = you **er** = he/it **sie** = she/it **es** = it/he/she **wir** = we **ihr** = you **sie** = they **Sie** = you

▶ springen (to jump)

strong, formed with **sein**

PRESENT

ich	springe
du	springst
er/sie/es	springt
wir	springen
ihr	springt
sie/Sie	springen

PRESENT SUBJUNCTIVE

ich	springe
du	springest
er/sie/es	springe
wir	springen
ihr	springet
sie/Sie	springen

PERFECT

ich	bin gesprungen
du	bist gesprungen
er/sie/es	ist gesprungen
wir	sind gesprungen
ihr	seid gesprungen
sie/Sie	sind gesprungen

IMPERFECT

ich	sprang
du	sprangst
er/sie/es	sprang
wir	sprangen
ihr	sprangt
sie/Sie	sprangen

FUTURE

ich	werde springen
du	wirst springen
er/sie/es	wird springen
wir	werden springen
ihr	werdet springen
sie/Sie	werden springen

CONDITIONAL

ich	würde springen
du	würdest springen
er/sie/es	würde springen
wir	würden springen
ihr	würdet springen
sie/Sie	würden springen

IMPERATIVE

spring(e)!/springen wir!/
springt!/springen Sie!

PAST PARTICIPLE

gesprungen

PRESENT PARTICIPLE

springend

EXAMPLE PHRASES

Er **sprang** *über den Zaun.* He jumped over the fence.
Der Zug **ist** *aus dem Gleis* **gesprungen**. The train came off the rails.
Ich **würde** *ihm am liebsten an die Kehle* **springen**. I could strangle him.

---

ich = I **du** = you **er** = he/it **sie** = she/it **es** = it/he/she **wir** = we **ihr** = you **sie** = they **Sie** = you

▶ **stehen** (to stand)

strong, *formed with* haben

PRESENT

ich	stehe
du	stehst
er/sie/es	steht
wir	stehen
ihr	steht
sie/Sie	stehen

PRESENT SUBJUNCTIVE

ich	stehe
du	stehest
er/sie/es	stehe
wir	stehen
ihr	stehet
sie/Sie	stehen

PERFECT

ich	habe gestanden
du	hast gestanden
er/sie/es	hat gestanden
wir	haben gestanden
ihr	habt gestanden
sie/Sie	haben gestanden

IMPERFECT

ich	stand
du	stand(e)st
er/sie/es	stand
wir	standen
ihr	standet
sie/Sie	standen

FUTURE

ich	werde stehen
du	wirst stehen
er/sie/es	wird stehen
wir	werden stehen
ihr	werdet stehen
sie/Sie	werden stehen

CONDITIONAL

ich	würde stehen
du	würdest stehen
er/sie/es	würde stehen
wir	würden stehen
ihr	würdet stehen
sie/Sie	würden stehen

IMPERATIVE

steh(e)!/stehen wir!/steht!/
stehen Sie!

PAST PARTICIPLE

gestanden

PRESENT PARTICIPLE

stehend

EXAMPLE PHRASES

Wir **standen** an der Bushaltestelle. We stood at the bus stop.
Es **hat** in der Zeitung **gestanden**. It was in the newspaper.
Dieses Kleid **würde** dir gut **stehen**. This dress would suit you.

---

ich = I **du** = you **er** = he/it **sie** = she/it **es** = it/he/she **wir** = we **ihr** = you **sie** = they **Sie** = you

▶ stehlen (to steal)

strong, *formed with* haben

PRESENT

ich	stehle
du	stiehlst
er/sie/es	stiehlt
wir	stehlen
ihr	stehlt
sie/Sie	stehlen

PRESENT SUBJUNCTIVE

ich	stehle
du	stehlest
er/sie/es	stehle
wir	stehlen
ihr	stehlet
sie/Sie	stehlen

PERFECT

ich	habe gestohlen
du	hast gestohlen
er/sie/es	hat gestohlen
wir	haben gestohlen
ihr	habt gestohlen
sie/Sie	haben gestohlen

IMPERFECT

ich	stahl
du	stahlst
er/sie/es	stahl
wir	stahlen
ihr	stahlt
sie/Sie	stahlen

FUTURE

ich	werde stehlen
du	wirst stehlen
er/sie/es	wird stehlen
wir	werden stehlen
ihr	werdet stehlen
sie/Sie	werden stehlen

CONDITIONAL

ich	würde stehlen
du	würdest stehlen
er/sie/es	würde stehlen
wir	würden stehlen
ihr	würdet stehlen
sie/Sie	würden stehlen

IMPERATIVE

stiehl!/stehlen wir!/stehlt!/
stehlen Sie!

PAST PARTICIPLE

gestohlen

PRESENT PARTICIPLE

stehlend

EXAMPLE PHRASES

Er **hat** das ganze Geld **gestohlen**. He stole all the money.
Er **stahl** sich aus dem Haus. He stole out of the house.
Du **stiehlst** uns doch nur die Zeit. You're just wasting our time.

---

ich = I du = you er = he/it sie = she/it es = it/he/she wir = we ihr = you sie = they Sie = you

▶ **steigen** (to climb)

strong, *formed with* **sein**

PRESENT

ich	steige
du	steigst
er/sie/es	steigt
wir	steigen
ihr	steigt
sie/Sie	steigen

PRESENT SUBJUNCTIVE

ich	steige
du	steigest
er/sie/es	steige
wir	steigen
ihr	steiget
sie/Sie	steigen

PERFECT

ich	bin gestiegen
du	bist gestiegen
er/sie/es	ist gestiegen
wir	sind gestiegen
ihr	seid gestiegen
sie/Sie	sind gestiegen

IMPERFECT

ich	stieg
du	stiegst
er/sie/es	stieg
wir	stiegen
ihr	stiegt
sie/Sie	stiegen

FUTURE

ich	werde steigen
du	wirst steigen
er/sie/es	wird steigen
wir	werden steigen
ihr	werdet steigen
sie/Sie	werden steigen

CONDITIONAL

ich	würde steigen
du	würdest steigen
er/sie/es	würde steigen
wir	würden steigen
ihr	würdet steigen
sie/Sie	würden steigen

IMPERATIVE

steig(e)!/steigen wir!/steigt!/
steigen Sie!

PAST PARTICIPLE

gestiegen

PRESENT PARTICIPLE

steigend

EXAMPLE PHRASES

*Die Temperatur **stieg** auf 28 Grad.* The temperature rose to 28 degrees.
*Sie **ist** auf die Leiter **gestiegen**.* She climbed up the ladder.
*Die Passagiere **stiegen** aus dem Flugzeug.* The passengers got off the plane.

---

ich = I **du** = you **er** = he/it **sie** = she/it **es** = it/he/she **wir** = we **ihr** = you **sie** = they **Sie** = you

▶ **sterben** (to die)

strong, formed with **sein**

PRESENT

ich	sterbe
du	stirbst
er/sie/es	stirbt
wir	sterben
ihr	sterbt
sie/Sie	sterben

PRESENT SUBJUNCTIVE

ich	sterbe
du	sterbest
er/sie/es	sterbe
wir	sterben
ihr	sterbet
sie/Sie	sterben

PERFECT

ich	bin gestorben
du	bist gestorben
er/sie/es	ist gestorben
wir	sind gestorben
ihr	seid gestorben
sie/Sie	sind gestorben

IMPERFECT

ich	starb
du	starbst
er/sie/es	starb
wir	starben
ihr	starbt
sie/Sie	starben

FUTURE

ich	werde sterben
du	wirst sterben
er/sie/es	wird sterben
wir	werden sterben
ihr	werdet sterben
sie/Sie	werden sterben

CONDITIONAL

ich	würde sterben
du	würdest sterben
er/sie/es	würde sterben
wir	würden sterben
ihr	würdet sterben
sie/Sie	würden sterben

IMPERATIVE

stirb!/sterben wir!/sterbt!/
sterben Sie!

PAST PARTICIPLE

gestorben

PRESENT PARTICIPLE

sterbend

EXAMPLE PHRASES

Er **starb** *eines natürlichen Todes.* He died a natural death.
Shakespeare **ist** *1616* **gestorben**. Shakespeare died in 1616.
Daran **wirst** *du nicht* **sterben**! It won't kill you!

---

ich = I **du** = you **er** = he/it **sie** = she/it **es** = it/he/she **wir** = we **ihr** = you **sie** = they **Sie** = you

▶ **studieren** (to study)   strong, *formed with* haben

PRESENT

ich	studiere
du	studierst
er/sie/es	studiert
wir	studieren
ihr	studiert
sie/Sie	studieren

PRESENT SUBJUNCTIVE

ich	studiere
du	studierest
er/sie/es	studiere
wir	studieren
ihr	studieret
sie/Sie	studieren

PERFECT

ich	habe studiert
du	hast studiert
er/sie/es	hat studiert
wir	haben studiert
ihr	habt studiert
sie/Sie	haben studiert

IMPERFECT

ich	studierte
du	studiertest
er/sie/es	studierte
wir	studierten
ihr	studiertet
sie/Sie	studierten

FUTURE

ich	werde studieren
du	wirst studieren
er/sie/es	wird studieren
wir	werden studieren
ihr	werdet studieren
sie/Sie	werden studieren

CONDITIONAL

ich	würde studieren
du	würdest studieren
er/sie/es	würde studieren
wir	würden studieren
ihr	würdet studieren
sie/Sie	würden studieren

IMPERATIVE

studiere!/studieren wir!/
studiert!/studieren Sie!

PAST PARTICIPLE

studiert

PRESENT PARTICIPLE

studierend

EXAMPLE PHRASES

Sie möchte Biologie **studieren**. She wants to study biology.
Mein Bruder **studiert** *Deutsch*. My brother is studying German.
Er **hat** *in Köln* **studiert**. He was a student at Cologne University.

ich = I **du** = you **er** = he/it **sie** = she/it **es** = it/he/she **wir** = we **ihr** = you **sie** = they **Sie** = you

---

▶ **tragen** (to wear; to carry)   strong, *formed with* haben

PRESENT

ich	trage
du	trägst
er/sie/es	trägt
wir	tragen
ihr	tragt
sie/Sie	tragen

PRESENT SUBJUNCTIVE

ich	trage
du	tragest
er/sie/es	trage
wir	tragen
ihr	traget
sie/Sie	tragen

PERFECT

ich	habe getragen
du	hast getragen
er/sie/es	hat getragen
wir	haben getragen
ihr	habt getragen
sie/Sie	haben getragen

IMPERFECT

ich	trug
du	trugst
er/sie/es	trug
wir	trugen
ihr	trugt
sie/Sie	trugen

FUTURE

ich	werde tragen
du	wirst tragen
er/sie/es	wird tragen
wir	werden tragen
ihr	werdet tragen
sie/Sie	werden tragen

CONDITIONAL

ich	würde tragen
du	wurdest tragen
er/sie/es	würde tragen
wir	würden tragen
ihr	würdet tragen
sie/Sie	würden tragen

IMPERATIVE

trag(e)!/tragen wir!/tragt!/
tragen Sie!

PAST PARTICIPLE

getragen

PRESENT PARTICIPLE

tragend

EXAMPLE PHRASES

*Ich **trug** ihren Koffer zum Bahnhof.* I carried her case to the station.
*Du **trägst** die ganze Verantwortung dafür.* You bear the full responsibility for it.
*Ich **würde** meine Haare gern länger **tragen**.* I'd like to wear my hair longer.

---

ich = I **du** = you **er** = he/it **sie** = she/it **es** = it/he/she **wir** = we **ihr** = you **sie** = they **Sie** = you

▶ **treffen** (to meet)

strong, *formed with* **haben**

PRESENT

ich	treffe
du	triffst
er/sie/es	trifft
wir	treffen
ihr	trefft
sie/Sie	treffen

PRESENT SUBJUNCTIVE

ich	treffe
du	treffest
er/sie/es	treffe
wir	treffen
ihr	treffet
sie/Sie	treffen

PERFECT

ich	habe getroffen
du	hast getroffen
er/sie/es	hat getroffen
wir	haben getroffen
ihr	habt getroffen
sie/Sie	haben getroffen

IMPERFECT

ich	traf
du	trafst
er/sie/es	traf
wir	trafen
ihr	traft
sie/Sie	trafen

FUTURE

ich	werde treffen
du	wirst treffen
er/sie/es	wird treffen
wir	werden treffen
ihr	werdet treffen
sie/Sie	werden treffen

CONDITIONAL

ich	würde treffen
du	würdest treffen
er/sie/es	würde treffen
wir	würden treffen
ihr	würdet treffen
sie/Sie	würden treffen

IMPERATIVE

triff!/treffen wir!/trefft!/
treffen Sie!

PAST PARTICIPLE

getroffen

PRESENT PARTICIPLE

treffend

EXAMPLE PHRASES

*Sie **trifft** sich zweimal pro Woche mit ihm.* She meets with him twice a week.
*Der Ball **traf** ihn am Kopf.* The ball hit him on the head.
*Du **hast** das Ziel gut **getroffen**.* You hit the target well.

ich = I **du** = you **er** = he/it **sie** = she/it **es** = it/he/she **wir** = we **ihr** = you **sie** = they **Sie** = you

▶ **treten** (to kick; to step)   strong, *formed with* **haben/sein***

PRESENT

ich	trete
du	trittst
er/sie/es	tritt
wir	treten
ihr	tretet
sie/Sie	treten

PRESENT SUBJUNCTIVE

ich	trete
du	tretest
er/sie/es	trete
wir	treten
ihr	tretet
sie/Sie	treten

PERFECT

ich	habe getreten
du	hast getreten
er/sie/es	hat getreten
wir	haben getreten
ihr	habt getreten
sie/Sie	haben getreten

IMPERFECT

ich	trat
du	trat(e)st
er/sie/es	trat
wir	traten
ihr	tratet
sie/Sie	traten

FUTURE

ich	werde treten
du	wirst treten
er/sie/es	wird treten
wir	werden treten
ihr	werdet treten
sie/Sie	werden treten

CONDITIONAL

ich	würde treten
du	würdest treten
er/sie/es	würde treten
wir	würden treten
ihr	würdet treten
sie/Sie	würden treten

IMPERATIVE

tritt!/treten wir!/tretet!/
treten Sie!

PAST PARTICIPLE

getreten

PRESENT PARTICIPLE

tretend

EXAMPLE PHRASES

Er **hat** mich **getreten**. He kicked me.
Sie **trat** auf die Bremse. She stepped on the brakes.
Pass auf, wohin du **trittst**! Watch your step!
Er **ist** mir auf den Fuß **getreten**. He stood on my foot.

*When **treten** is used with no direct object, it is formed with **sein**.

ich = I **du** = you **er** = he/it **sie** = she/it **es** = it/he/she **wir** = we **ihr** = you **sie** = they **Sie** = you

▶ trinken (to drink)

strong, *formed with* **haben**

PRESENT

ich	trinke
du	trinkst
er/sie/es	trinkt
wir	trinken
ihr	trinkt
sie/Sie	trinken

PRESENT SUBJUNCTIVE

ich	trinke
du	trinkest
er/sie/es	trinke
wir	trinken
ihr	trinket
sie/Sie	trinken

PERFECT

ich	habe getrunken
du	hast getrunken
er/sie/es	hat getrunken
wir	haben getrunken
ihr	habt getrunken
sie/Sie	haben getrunken

IMPERFECT

ich	trank
du	trankst
er/sie/es	trank
wir	tranken
ihr	trankt
sie/Sie	tranken

FUTURE

ich	werde trinken
du	wirst trinken
er/sie/es	wird trinken
wir	werden trinken
ihr	werdet trinken
sie/Sie	werden trinken

CONDITIONAL

ich	würde trinken
du	würdest trinken
er/sie/es	würde trinken
wir	würden trinken
ihr	würdet trinken
sie/Sie	würden trinken

IMPERATIVE

trink(e)!/trinken wir!/trinkt!/
trinken Sie!

PAST PARTICIPLE

getrunken

PRESENT PARTICIPLE

trinkend

EXAMPLE PHRASES

Er **trank** die ganze Flasche leer. He drank the whole bottle.
Ich **habe** zu viel **getrunken**. I've had too much to drink.
Wollen wir etwas **trinken** gehen? Shall we go for a drink?

---

ich = I **du** = you **er** = he/it **sie** = she/it **es** = it/he/she **wir** = we **ihr** = you **sie** = they **Sie** = you

▶ tun (to do)

strong, *formed with* **haben**

PRESENT

ich	tue
du	tust
er/sie/es	tut
wir	tun
ihr	tut
sie/Sie	tun

PRESENT SUBJUNCTIVE

ich	tue
du	tuest
er/sie/es	tue
wir	tuen
ihr	tuet
sie/Sie	tuen

PERFECT

ich	habe getan
du	hast getan
er/sie/es	hat getan
wir	haben getan
ihr	habt getan
sie/Sie	haben getan

IMPERFECT

ich	tat
du	tat(e)st
er/sie/es	tat
wir	taten
ihr	tatet
sie/Sie	taten

FUTURE

ich	werde tun
du	wirst tun
er/sie/es	wird tun
wir	werden tun
ihr	werdet tun
sie/Sie	werden tun

CONDITIONAL

ich	würde tun
du	würdest tun
er/sie/es	würde tun
wir	würden tun
ihr	würdet tun
sie/Sie	würden tun

IMPERATIVE

tu(e)!/tun wir!/tut!/tun Sie!

PAST PARTICIPLE

getan

PRESENT PARTICIPLE

tuend

EXAMPLE PHRASES

*Ich **werde** das auf keinen Fall **tun**.* There is no way I'll do that.
*So etwas **tut** man nicht!* That is just not done!
*Sie **tat**, als ob sie schliefe.* She pretended to be sleeping.

---

ich = I **du** = you **er** = he/it **sie** = she/it **es** = it/he/she **wir** = we **ihr** = you **sie** = they **Sie** = you

▶ sich überlegen (to consider) weak, inseparable, reflexive, *formed with* haben

PRESENT

ich	überlege mir
du	überlegst dir
er/sie/es	überlegt sich
wir	überlegen uns
ihr	überlegt euch
sie/Sie	überlegen sich

PRESENT SUBJUNCTIVE

ich	überlege mir
du	überlegest dir
er/sie/es	überlege sich
wir	überlegen uns
ihr	überleget euch
sie/Sie	überlegen sich

PERFECT

ich	habe mir überlegt
du	hast dir überlegt
er/sie/es	hat sich überlegt
wir	haben uns überlegt
ihr	habt euch überlegt
sie/Sie	haben sich überlegt

IMPERFECT

ich	überlegte mir
du	überlegtest dir
er/sie/es	überlegte sich
wir	überlegten uns
ihr	überlegtet euch
sie/Sie	überlegten sich

FUTURE

ich	werde mir überlegen
du	wirst dir überlegen
er/sie/es	wird sich überlegen
wir	werden uns überlegen
ihr	werdet euch überlegen
sie/Sie	werden sich überlegen

CONDITIONAL

ich	würde mir überlegen
du	würdest dir überlegen
er/sie/es	würde sich überlegen
wir	würden uns überlegen
ihr	würdet euch überlegen
sie/Sie	würden sich überlegen

IMPERATIVE

überleg(e)dir!/überlegen wir uns!/
überlegt euch!/überlegen Sie sich!

PAST PARTICIPLE

überlegt

PRESENT PARTICIPLE

überlegend

EXAMPLE PHRASES

Ich **habe mir** *schon* **überlegt**, *was ich machen werde.* I've already thought about what I'm going to do.
Ich muss es **mir überlegen**. I'll have to think about it.
Würden *Sie es* **sich** *noch einmal* **überlegen**? Would you reconsider?

ich = I du = you er = he/it sie = she/it es = it/he/she wir = we ihr = you sie = they Sie = you

▶ **vergessen** (to forget)   strong, inseparable, *formed with* **haben**

PRESENT

ich	vergesse
du	vergisst
er/sie/es	vergisst
wir	vergessen
ihr	vergesst
sie/Sie	vergessen

PRESENT SUBJUNCTIVE

ich	vergesse
du	vergessest
er/sie/es	vergesse
wir	vergessen
ihr	vergesset
sie/Sie	vergessen

PERFECT

ich	habe vergessen
du	hast vergessen
er/sie/es	hat vergessen
wir	haben vergessen
ihr	habt vergessen
sie/Sie	haben vergessen

IMPERFECT

ich	vergaß
du	vergaßest
er/sie/es	vergaß
wir	vergaßen
ihr	vergaßt
sie/Sie	vergaßen

FUTURE

ich	werde vergessen
du	wirst vergessen
er/sie/es	wird vergessen
wir	werden vergessen
ihr	werdet vergessen
sie/Sie	werden vergessen

CONDITIONAL

ich	würde vergessen
du	würdest vergessen
er/sie/es	würde vergessen
wir	würden vergessen
ihr	würdet vergessen
sie/Sie	würden vergessen

IMPERATIVE

vergiss!/vergessen wir!/
vergesst!/vergessen Sie!

PAST PARTICIPLE

vergessen

PRESENT PARTICIPLE

vergessend

EXAMPLE PHRASES

*Ich **habe** seinen Namen **vergessen**.* I've forgotten his name.
*Sie **vergaß**, die Blumen zu gießen.* She forgot to water the flowers.
*Sie **vergisst** ständig ihre Bücher.* She always forgets to bring her books.

ich = I **du** = you **er** = he/it **sie** = she/it **es** = it/he/she **wir** = we **ihr** = you **sie** = they **Sie** = you

▶ **verlangen** (to demand) weak, inseparable, *formed with* haben

PRESENT

ich	verlange
du	verlangst
er/sie/es	verlangt
wir	verlangen
ihr	verlangt
sie/Sie	verlangen

PRESENT SUBJUNCTIVE

ich	verlange
du	verlangest
er/sie/es	verlange
wir	verlangen
ihr	verlanget
sie/Sie	verlangen

PERFECT

ich	habe verlangt
du	hast verlangt
er/sie/es	hat verlangt
wir	haben verlangt
ihr	habt verlangt
sie/Sie	haben verlangt

IMPERFECT

ich	verlangte
du	verlangtest
er/sie/es	verlangte
wir	verlangten
ihr	verlangtet
sie/Sie	verlangten

FUTURE

ich	werde verlangen
du	wirst verlangen
er/sie/es	wird verlangen
wir	werden verlangen
ihr	werdet verlangen
sie/Sie	werden verlangen

CONDITIONAL

ich	würde verlangen
du	würdest verlangen
er/sie/es	würde verlangen
wir	würden verlangen
ihr	würdet verlangen
sie/Sie	würden verlangen

IMPERATIVE

verlang(e)!/verlangen wir!/
verlangt!/verlangen Sie!

PAST PARTICIPLE

verlangt

PRESENT PARTICIPLE

verlangend

EXAMPLE PHRASES

Unsere Lehrerin **verlangt** *wirklich sehr viel von uns.* Our teacher demands an awful lot of us.

Das kannst du nicht von mir **verlangen.** You cannot ask that of me.

Wie viel **hat** *er dafür* **verlangt**? How much did he ask for it?

ich = I **du** = you **er** = he/it **sie** = she/it **es** = it/he/she **wir** = we **ihr** = you **sie** = they **Sie** = you

▶ verlieren (to lose)

strong, inseparable, *formed with* haben

PRESENT

ich	verliere
du	verlierst
er/sie/es	verliert
wir	verlieren
ihr	verliert
sie/Sie	verlieren

PRESENT SUBJUNCTIVE

ich	verliere
du	verlierest
er/sie/es	verliere
wir	verlieren
ihr	verlieret
sie/Sie	verlieren

PERFECT

ich	habe verloren
du	hast verloren
er/sie/es	hat verloren
wir	haben verloren
ihr	habt verloren
sie/Sie	haben verloren

IMPERFECT

ich	verlor
du	verlorst
er/sie/es	verlor
wir	verloren
ihr	verlort
sie/Sie	verloren

FUTURE

ich	werde verlieren
du	wirst verlieren
er/sie/es	wird verlieren
wir	werden verlieren
ihr	werdet verlieren
sie/Sie	werden verlieren

CONDITIONAL

ich	würde verlieren
du	würdest verlieren
er/sie/es	würde verlieren
wir	würden verlieren
ihr	würdet verlieren
sie/Sie	würden verlieren

IMPERATIVE

verlier(e)!/verlieren wir!/
verliert!/verlieren Sie!

PAST PARTICIPLE

verloren

PRESENT PARTICIPLE

verlierend

EXAMPLE PHRASES

Wenn du **verlierst**, musst du mir 10 Euro zahlen. If you lose, you'll have to pay
me 10 euros.
Wir **haben** drei Spiele hintereinander **verloren**. We lost three matches in a row.
Er **verlor** kein Wort darüber. He didn't say a word about it.

---

ich = I **du** = you **er** = he/it **sie** = she/it **es** = it/he/she **wir** = we **ihr** = you **sie** = they **Sie** = you

▶ verschwinden (to disappear)

strong, inseparable,
formed with **sein**

PRESENT

ich	verschwinde
du	verschwindest
er/sie/es	verschwindet
wir	verschwinden
ihr	verschwindet
sie/Sie	verschwinden

PRESENT SUBJUNCTIVE

ich	verschwinde
du	verschwindest
er/sie/es	verschwinde
wir	verschwinden
ihr	verschwindet
sie/Sie	verschwinden

PERFECT

ich	bin verschwunden
du	bist verschwunden
er/sie/es	ist verschwunden
wir	sind verschwunden
ihr	seid verschwunden
sie/Sie	sind verschwunden

IMPERFECT

ich	verschwand
du	verschwand(e)st
er/sie/es	verschwand
wir	verschwanden
ihr	verschwandet
sie/Sie	verschwanden

FUTURE

ich	werde verschwinden
du	wirst verschwinden
er/sie/es	wird verschwinden
wir	werden verschwinden
ihr	werdet verschwinden
sie/Sie	werden verschwinden

CONDITIONAL

ich	würde verschwinden
du	würdest verschwinden
er/sie/es	würde verschwinden
wir	würden verschwinden
ihr	würdet verschwinden
sie/Sie	würden verschwinden

IMPERATIVE

verschwind(e)!/verschwinden wir!/
verschwindet!/verschwinden Sie!

PAST PARTICIPLE

verschwunden

PRESENT PARTICIPLE

verschwindend

EXAMPLE PHRASES

Sie **verschwanden** *in der Dunkelheit.* They disappeared into the darkness.
Der Zauberer ließ das Kaninchen **verschwinden**. The magician made the rabbit
disappear.
Er **ist** *seit Sonntag* **verschwunden**. He has been missing since Sunday.

ich = I **du** = you **er** = he/it **sie** = she/it **es** = it/he/she **wir** = we **ihr** = you **sie** = they **Sie** = you

▶ wachsen (to grow)

strong, *formed with* sein

PRESENT

ich	wachse
du	wächst
er/sie/es	wächst
wir	wachsen
ihr	wachst
sie/Sie	wachsen

PRESENT SUBJUNCTIVE

ich	wachse
du	wachsest
er/sie/es	wachse
wir	wachsen
ihr	wachset
sie/Sie	wachsen

PERFECT

ich	bin gewachsen
du	bist gewachsen
er/sie/es	ist gewachsen
wir	sind gewachsen
ihr	seid gewachsen
sie/Sie	sind gewachsen

IMPERFECT

ich	wuchs
du	wuchsest
er/sie/es	wuchs
wir	wuchsen
ihr	wuchst
sie/Sie	wuchsen

FUTURE

ich	werde wachsen
du	wirst wachsen
er/sie/es	wird wachsen
wir	werden wachsen
ihr	werdet wachsen
sie/Sie	werden wachsen

CONDITIONAL

ich	würde wachsen
du	würdest wachsen
er/sie/es	würde wachsen
wir	würden wachsen
ihr	würdet wachsen
sie/Sie	würden wachsen

IMPERATIVE

wachs(e)!/wachsen wir!/
wachst!/wachsen Sie!

PAST PARTICIPLE

gewachsen

PRESENT PARTICIPLE

wachsend

EXAMPLE PHRASES

*Der Baum **wächst** nicht mehr.* The tree has stopped growing.
*Er ließ sich einen Bart **wachsen**.* He grew a beard.
*Ich **bin** im letzten Jahr 10 Zentimeter **gewachsen**.* I've grown 10 centimetres in the
    past year.

---

ich = I **du** = you **er** = he/it **sie** = she/it **es** = it/he/she **wir** = we **ihr** = you **sie** = they **Sie** = you

▶ **wandern** (to roam; to go hillwalking)
weak, *formed with* **sein**

PRESENT

ich	wand(e)re
du	wanderst
er/sie/es	wandert
wir	wandern
ihr	wandert
sie/Sie	wandern

PERFECT

ich	bin gewandert
du	bist gewandert
er/sie/es	ist gewandert
wir	sind gewandert
ihr	seid gewandert
sie/Sie	sind gewandert

FUTURE

ich	werde wandern
du	wirst wandern
er/sie/es	wird wandern
wir	werden wandern
ihr	werdet wandern
sie/Sie	werden wandern

IMPERATIVE

wandre!/wandern wir!/
wandert!/wandern Sie!

PRESENT SUBJUNCTIVE

ich	wand(e)re
du	wandrest
er/sie/es	wand(e)re
wir	wandern
ihr	wandert
sie/Sie	wandern

IMPERFECT

ich	wanderte
du	wandertest
er/sie/es	wanderte
wir	wanderten
ihr	wandertet
sie/Sie	wanderten

CONDITIONAL

ich	würde wandern
du	würdest wandern
er/sie/es	würde wandern
wir	würden wandern
ihr	würdet wandern
sie/Sie	würden wandern

PAST PARTICIPLE

gewandert

PRESENT PARTICIPLE

wandernd

EXAMPLE PHRASES

Im Schwarzwald kann man gut **wandern**. The Black Forest is good for walking.
Wir **sind** am Wochenende **gewandert**. We went hiking at the weekend.
Seine Gedanken **wanderten** zurück in die Vergangenheit. His thoughts strayed back to the past.

ich = I **du** = you **er** = he/it **sie** = she/it **es** = it/he/she **wir** = we **ihr** = you **sie** = they **Sie** = you

▶ waschen (to wash)

strong, *formed with* haben

PRESENT

ich	wasche
du	wäschst
er/sie/es	wäscht
wir	waschen
ihr	wascht
sie/Sie	waschen

PRESENT SUBJUNCTIVE

ich	wasche
du	waschest
er/sie/es	wasche
wir	waschen
ihr	waschet
sie/Sie	waschen

PERFECT

ich	habe gewaschen
du	hast gewaschen
er/sie/es	hat gewaschen
wir	haben gewaschen
ihr	habt gewaschen
sie/Sie	haben gewaschen

IMPERFECT

ich	wusch
du	wuschest
er/sie/es	wusch
wir	wuschen
ihr	wuscht
sie/Sie	wuschen

FUTURE

ich	werde waschen
du	wirst waschen
er/sie/es	wird waschen
wir	werden waschen
ihr	werdet waschen
sie/Sie	werden waschen

CONDITIONAL

ich	würde waschen
du	würdest waschen
er/sie/es	würde waschen
wir	würden waschen
ihr	würdet waschen
sie/Sie	würden waschen

IMPERATIVE

wasch(e)!/waschen wir!/
wascht!/waschen Sie!

PAST PARTICIPLE

gewaschen

PRESENT PARTICIPLE

waschend

EXAMPLE PHRASES

Ich **habe** mir die Hände **gewaschen**. I washed my hands.
Er **wäschst** sich jeden Tag. He washes every day.
Die Katze **wusch** sich in der Sonne. The cat was washing itself in the sunshine.

ich = I du = you **er** = he/it **sie** = she/it **es** = it/he/she **wir** = we **ihr** = you **sie** = they **Sie** = you

▶ werben (to recruit; to advertise) strong, *formed with* haben

PRESENT

ich	werbe
du	wirbst
er/sie/es	wirbt
wir	werben
ihr	werbt
sie/Sie	werben

PRESENT SUBJUNCTIVE

ich	werbe
du	werbest
er/sie/es	werbe
wir	werben
ihr	werbet
sie/Sie	werben

PERFECT

ich	habe geworben
du	hast geworben
er/sie/es	hat geworben
wir	haben geworben
ihr	habt geworben
sie/Sie	haben geworben

IMPERFECT

ich	warb
du	warbst
er/sie/es	warb
wir	warben
ihr	warbt
sie/Sie	warben

FUTURE

ich	werde werben
du	wirst werben
er/sie/es	wird werben
wir	werden werben
ihr	werdet werben
sie/Sie	werden werben

CONDITIONAL

ich	würde werben
du	würdest werben
er/sie/es	würde werben
wir	würden werben
ihr	würdet werben
sie/Sie	würden werben

IMPERATIVE

wirb!/werben wir!/werbt!/
werben Sie!

PAST PARTICIPLE

geworben

PRESENT PARTICIPLE

werbend

EXAMPLE PHRASES

Die Partei **wirbt** *zur Zeit Mitglieder.* The party is currently recruiting members.
Unsere Firma muss um neue Kunden **werben**. Our company has to attract new customers.
Im Fernsehen **wird** *zu viel* **geworben**. There's too much advertising on TV.

---

ich = I **du** = you **er** = he/it **sie** = she/it **es** = it/he/she **wir** = we **ihr** = you **sie** = they **Sie** = you

▶ **werden** (to become)

strong, *formed with* **sein**

PRESENT

ich	werde
du	wirst
er/sie/es	wird
wir	werden
ihr	werdet
sie/Sie	werden

PRESENT SUBJUNCTIVE

ich	werde
du	werdest
er/sie/es	werde
wir	werden
ihr	werdet
sie/Sie	werden

PERFECT

ich	bin geworden
du	bist geworden
er/sie/es	ist geworden
wir	sind geworden
ihr	seid geworden
sie/Sie	sind geworden

IMPERFECT

ich	wurde
du	wurdest
er/sie/es	wurde
wir	wurden
ihr	wurdet
sie/Sie	wurden

FUTURE

ich	werde werden
du	wirst werden
er/sie/es	wird werden
wir	werden werden
ihr	werdet werden
sie/Sie	werden werden

CONDITIONAL

ich	würde werden
du	würdest werden
er/sie/es	würde werden
wir	würden werden
ihr	würdet werden
sie/Sie	würden werden

IMPERATIVE

werde!/werden wir!/werdet!/
werden Sie!

PAST PARTICIPLE

geworden

PRESENT PARTICIPLE

werdend

EXAMPLE PHRASES

Mit **wird** schlecht. I feel ill.
Ich will Lehrerin **werden**. I want to be a teacher.
Der Kuchen **ist** gut **geworden**. The cake turned out well.

---

ich = I **du** = you **er** = he/it **sie** = she/it **es** = it/he/she **wir** = we **ihr** = you **sie** = they **Sie** = you

▶ werfen (to throw)

strong, *formed with* haben

PRESENT

ich	werfe
du	wirfst
er/sie/es	wirft
wir	werfen
ihr	werft
sie/Sie	werfen

PRESENT SUBJUNCTIVE

ich	werfe
du	werfest
er/sie/es	werfe
wir	werfen
ihr	werfet
sie/Sie	werfen

PERFECT

ich	habe geworfen
du	hast geworfen
er/sie/es	hat geworfen
wir	haben geworfen
ihr	habt geworfen
sie/Sie	haben geworfen

IMPERFECT

ich	warf
du	warfst
er/sie/es	warf
wir	warfen
ihr	warft
sie/Sie	warfen

FUTURE

ich	werde werfen
du	wirst werfen
er/sie/es	wird werfen
wir	werden werfen
ihr	werdet werfen
sie/Sie	werden werfen

CONDITIONAL

ich	würde werfen
du	würdest werfen
er/sie/es	würde werfen
wir	würden werfen
ihr	würdet werfen
sie/Sie	würden werfen

IMPERATIVE

wirf!/werfen wir!/werft!/
werfen Sie!

PAST PARTICIPLE

geworfen

PRESENT PARTICIPLE

werfend

EXAMPLE PHRASES

Er **warf** den Ball über den Zaun. He threw the ball over the fence.
Sie **wirft** mit Geld um sich. She is throwing her money around.
Der Chef **hat** ihn aus der Firma **geworfen**. The boss has kicked him out of the company.

ich = I **du** = you **er** = he/it **sie** = she/it **es** = it/he/she **wir** = we **ihr** = you **sie** = they **Sie** = you

▶ wissen (to know)

mixed, formed with **haben**

PRESENT

ich	weiß
du	weißt
er/sie/es	weiß
wir	wissen
ihr	wisst
sie/Sie	wissen

PRESENT SUBJUNCTIVE

ich	wisse
du	wissest
er/sie/es	wisse
wir	wissen
ihr	wisset
sie/Sie	wissen

PERFECT

ich	habe gewusst
du	hast gewusst
er/sie/es	hat gewusst
wir	haben gewusst
ihr	habt gewusst
sie/Sie	haben gewusst

IMPERFECT

ich	wusste
du	wusstest
er/sie/es	wusste
wir	wussten
ihr	wusstet
sie/Sie	wussten

FUTURE

ich	werde wissen
du	wirst wissen
er/sie/es	wird wissen
wir	werden wissen
ihr	werdet wissen
sie/Sie	werden wissen

CONDITIONAL

ich	würde wissen
du	würdest wissen
er/sie/es	würde wissen
wir	würden wissen
ihr	würdet wissen
sie/Sie	würden wissen

IMPERATIVE

wisse!/wissen wir!/wisset!/
wissen Sie!

PAST PARTICIPLE

gewusst

PRESENT PARTICIPLE

wissend

EXAMPLE PHRASES

*Ich **weiß** nicht.* I don't know.
*Er **hat** nichts davon **gewusst**.* He didn't know anything about it.
*Sie **wussten**, wo das Kino war.* They knew where the cinema was.

---

ich = I **du** = you **er** = he/it **sie** = she/it **es** = it/he/she **wir** = we **ihr** = you **sie** = they **Sie** = you

▶ **wollen** (to want)

modal, *formed with* **haben**

PRESENT

ich	will
du	willst
er/sie/es	will
wir	wollen
ihr	wollt
sie/Sie	wollen

PRESENT SUBJUNCTIVE

ich	wolle
du	wollest
er/sie/es	wolle
wir	wollen
ihr	wollet
sie/Sie	wollen

PERFECT

ich	habe gewollt/wollen
du	hast gewollt/wollen
er/sie/es	hat gewollt/wollen
wir	haben gewollt/wollen
ihr	habt gewollt/wollen
sie/Sie	haben gewollt/wollen

IMPERFECT

ich	wollte
du	wolltest
er/sie/es	wollte
wir	wollten
ihr	wolltet
sie/Sie	wollten

FUTURE

ich	werde wollen
du	wirst wollen
er/sie/es	wird wollen
wir	werden wollen
ihr	werdet wollen
sie/Sie	werden wollen

CONDITIONAL

ich	würde wollen
du	würdest wollen
er/sie/es	würde wollen
wir	würden wollen
ihr	würdet wollen
sie/Sie	würden wollen

IMPERATIVE

wolle!/wollen wir!/wollt!/
wollen Sie!

PAST PARTICIPLE

gewollt/wollen*

PRESENT PARTICIPLE

wollend

*This form is used when combined with another infinitive.

EXAMPLE PHRASES

Er **will** nach London gehen. He wants to go to London.
Das **habe** ich nicht **gewollt**. I didn't want this to happen.
Sie **wollten** nur mehr Geld. All they wanted was more money.

ich = I **du** = you **er** = he/it **sie** = she/it **es** = it/he/she **wir** = we **ihr** = you **sie** = they **Sie** = you

▶ zerstören (to destroy)   weak, inseparable, *formed with* haben

PRESENT

ich	zerstöre
du	zerstörst
er/sie/es	zerstört
wir	zerstören
ihr	zerstört
sie/Sie	zerstören

PRESENT SUBJUNCTIVE

ich	zerstöre
du	zerstörest
er/sie/es	zerstöre
wir	zerstören
ihr	zerstöret
sie/Sie	zerstören

PERFECT

ich	habe zerstört
du	hast zerstört
er/sie/es	hat zerstört
wir	haben zerstört
ihr	habt zerstört
sie/Sie	haben zerstört

IMPERFECT

ich	zerstörte
du	zerstörtest
er/sie/es	zerstörte
wir	zerstörten
ihr	zerstörtet
sie/Sie	zerstörten

FUTURE

ich	werde zerstören
du	wirst zerstören
er/sie/es	wird zerstören
wir	werden zerstören
ihr	werdet zerstören
sie/Sie	werden zerstören

CONDITIONAL

ich	würde zerstören
du	würdest zerstören
er/sie/es	würde zerstören
wir	würden zerstören
ihr	würdet zerstören
sie/Sie	würden zerstören

IMPERATIVE

zerstör(e)!/zerstören wir!/
zerstört!/zerstören Sie!

PAST PARTICIPLE

zerstört

PRESENT PARTICIPLE

zerstörend

EXAMPLE PHRASES

Die ganzen Abgase **zerstören** *die Ozonschicht.* All the fumes are destroying the ozone layer.
Er **hat** *ihr Selbstvertrauen* **zerstört**. He has destroyed her self-confidence.
Er **zerstörte** *ihre Ehe.* He wrecked their marriage.

---

ich = I **du** = you **er** = he/it **sie** = she/it **es** = it/he/she **wir** = we **ihr** = you **sie** = they **Sie** = you

▶ ziehen (to pull)

strong, *formed with* **sein/haben***

PRESENT

ich	ziehe
du	ziehst
er/sie/es	zieht
wir	ziehen
ihr	zieht
sie/Sie	ziehen

PRESENT SUBJUNCTIVE

ich	ziehe
du	ziehest
er/sie/es	ziehe
wir	ziehen
ihr	ziehet
sie/Sie	ziehen

PERFECT

ich	bin gezogen
du	bist gezogen
er/sie/es	ist gezogen
wir	sind gezogen
ihr	seid gezogen
sie/Sie	sind gezogen

IMPERFECT

ich	zog
du	zogst
er/sie/es	zog
wir	zogen
ihr	zogt
sie/Sie	zogen

FUTURE

ich	werde ziehen
du	wirst ziehen
er/sie/es	wird ziehen
wir	werden ziehen
ihr	werdet ziehen
sie/Sie	werden ziehen

CONDITIONAL

ich	würde ziehen
du	wurdest ziehen
er/sie/es	würde ziehen
wir	würden ziehen
ihr	würdet ziehen
sie/Sie	würden ziehen

IMPERATIVE

zieh(e)!/ziehen wir!/zieht!/
ziehen Sie!

PAST PARTICIPLE

gezogen

PRESENT PARTICIPLE

ziehend

EXAMPLE PHRASES

Seine Familie **ist** *nach München* **gezogen**. His family has moved to Munich.
In diesem Zimmer **zieht** *es*. There's a draught in this room.
Sie **hat** *mich am Ärmel* **gezogen**. She pulled at my sleeve.

*When ziehen is used with a direct object, it is formed with haben.

---

ich = I **du** = you **er** = he/it **sie** = she/it **es** = it/he/she **wir** = we **ihr** = you **sie** = they **Sie** = you

▶ zwingen (to force)

strong, *formed with* haben

PRESENT

ich	zwinge
du	zwingst
er/sie/es	zwingt
wir	zwingen
ihr	zwingt
sie/Sie	zwingen

PRESENT SUBJUNCTIVE

ich	zwinge
du	zwingest
er/sie/es	zwinge
wir	zwingen
ihr	zwinget
sie/Sie	zwingen

PERFECT

ich	habe gezwungen
du	hast gezwungen
er/sie/es	hat gezwungen
wir	haben gezwungen
ihr	habt gezwungen
sie/Sie	haben gezwungen

IMPERFECT

ich	zwang
du	zwangst
er/sie/es	zwang
wir	zwangen
ihr	zwangt
sie/Sie	zwangen

FUTURE

ich	werde zwingen
du	wirst zwingen
er/sie/es	wird zwingen
wir	werden zwingen
ihr	werdet zwingen
sie/Sie	werden zwingen

CONDITIONAL

ich	würde zwingen
du	würdest zwingen
er/sie/es	würde zwingen
wir	würden zwingen
ihr	würdet zwingen
sie/Sie	würden zwingen

IMPERATIVE

zwing(e)!/zwingen wir!/
zwingt!/zwingen Sie!

PAST PARTICIPLE

gezwungen

PRESENT PARTICIPLE

zwingend

EXAMPLE PHRASES

Er **hat** ihn **gezwungen**, das zu tun. He forced him to do it.
Sie **zwangen** uns, den Vertrag zu unterschreiben. They forced us to sign the contract.
Ich kann dich nicht **zwingen**. I can't force you.

ich = I **du** = you **er** = he/it **sie** = she/it **es** = it/he/she **wir** = we **ihr** = you **sie** = they **Sie** = you

How to use the Verb Index

The verbs in bold are the model verbs which you will find in the Verb Tables. All the other verbs follow one of these patterns, so the number next to each verb indicates which pattern fits this particular verb. For example, **begleiten** (*to accompany*) follows the same pattern as **arbeiten** (*to work*), number 3 in the Verb Tables.

All the verbs are in alphabetical order. For reflexive verbs like **sich setzen** (*to sit down*) look under **setzen**, not under **sich**.

With the exception of reflexive verbs which are always formed with **haben**, most verbs have the same auxiliary (**sein** or **haben**) as their model verb. If this is different, it is shown in the Verb Index. Certain verbs can be formed with both **haben** and **sein** and there is a note about this at the relevant verb table.

Some verbs in the Verb Index have a dividing line through them to show that the verb is separable, for example, **durch|setzen**.

⇨ *For more information on **separable** and **inseparable** verbs, see page* 109.

ab|brechen	12	ab|ziehen	97	an|ordnen	54	auf|haben	33
ab|fahren	22	achten	3	an|probieren	77	auf|halten	34
ab|fliegen	26	addieren	77	an|rufen	57	auf|hängen	36
ab|tragen	5	adressieren	77	an|schalten	3	auf|heitern (*haben*)	89
ab|geben	29	ähneln +*dat*	35	an|schauen	5	auf|hören	5
ab|gewöhnen	39	amüsieren (sich *acc*)	77	an|schreien	63	auf|klären	5
ab|hängen	36	an|bauen	5	an|sehen	65	auf|lassen	43
ab|holen	5	an|bieten	9	an|sprechen	71	auf|lösen (sich *acc*)	5
ab|kürzen	37	an|brechen	12	an|starren	5	auf|machen	5
ab|laufen	44	an|brennen	13	an|stecken	5	auf|muntern (*haben*)	89
ab|lehnen	5	ändern (sich *acc*)		an|stellen	5	auf|nehmen	53
ab|lenken	5	(*haben*)	89	an|strengen (sich *acc*)	5	auf|passen	32
ab|liefern (*haben*)	89	an|deuten	3	antworten	3	auf|räumen	5
ab|machen	5	an|fahren	22	an|zeigen	5	aufrecht|erhalten	34
ab|nehmen	53	an|fangen	24	an|ziehen	97	auf|regen	5
abonnieren	77	an|fassen	32	an|zünden	55	auf|schreiben	62
ab|reisen (*sein*)	5	an|geben	29	**arbeiten**	**3**	auf|sehen	65
ab|sagen +*dat*	5	an|gehen	30	ärgern (*haben*)	89	auf|setzen	37
ab|schaffen	5	angeln	35	**atmen**	**4**	auf|stehen	73
ab|schicken	5	an|gewöhnen	39	auf|bauen	5	auf|steigen	75
ab|schneiden	61	an|haben	33	auf|bewahren	39	auf|stellen	5
ab|schreiben	62	an|halten	34	auf|bleiben	11	auf|tauchen	5
ab|schrecken	5	an|hören	5	auf|brechen	12	auf|tauen	5
ab|setzen (sich *acc*)	37	an|kommen	41	auf|essen	21	auf|teilen	5
ab|stellen	5	an|kreuzen	37	auf|fallen +*dat*	23	auf|treten	80
ab|stürzen (*sein*)	37	an|kündigen	5	auf|fangen	24	auf|wachen	5
ab|trocknen	54	an|machen	5	auf|führen	5	auf|wachsen	88
ab|waschen	90	an|melden	55	auf|geben	29	auf|wecken	5
ab|werten	3	**an|nehmen**	**2**	auf|gehen	30	auf|zählen	5